Illustrators:
Howard Chaney
Bruce Hedges

Editor:
Walter Kelly, M.A.

Editor in Chief:
Sharon Coan, M.S. Ed.

Creative Director:
Elayne Roberts

Associate Designer:
Denise Bauer

Art Coordination Assistant:
Cheri Macoubrie Wilson

Cover Art:
Sue Fullham

Imaging:
Ralph Olmedo, Jr.

Product Manager:
Phil Garcia

Publishers:
Rachelle Cracchiolo, M.S. Ed.
Mary Dupuy Smith, M.S. Ed.

Written by Ruth M. Young, M.S. Ed.

Teacher Created Materials, Inc.
6421 Industy Way
Westminster, CA 92683
©1999 Teacher Created Materials, Inc.
Made in the U. S. A.
ISBN-1-57690-380-X

Table of Contents

Table of Contents *(cont.)*

Introduction

Science Is Fun should be the motto of every classroom. Maintaining the natural curiosity young children have about the world around them is an important job for primary teachers. Infants apply their senses to learn all they can about their immediate surroundings. They can identify their mothers very early through their senses of hearing, smell, and even taste. They continue to investigate their surroundings with their senses, often getting themselves in trouble by placing things in their mouths, or touching something that is sharp or hot. After being told not to eat dirt or touch a worm, children often develop a fear of things in nature (e.g., spiders) and thus begin to lose interest in investigating. Showing them that it is all right to be curious, even encouraging this, launches lifelong learning through careful observations and application of the senses and good reasoning.

The activities in this book are designed to be engaging to students in kindergarten through third grade. They provide opportunities to investigate many exciting aspects of the world in which they live. The book is divided into the *physical*, *life*, and *earth/space* sciences to be sure all aspects of the natural world are included.

A summary of the recently issued National Science Education Standards is provided for teachers as background and guidance to encourage designing their own science lessons. The information about kindergarten through third grade children as learners should offer additional insights into how to structure the science program for these young students.

The emphasis on the fun and excitement of science through exploring is found throughout this book. Students will play with mirrors, magnets, and light to discover the magic of science. They will observe the life cycles of insects unfold and tour the local areas near school to look for live specimens in the bushes. This hopefully will encourage them to overcome their fear of things which many consider "yucky" and to appreciate tiny creatures they may not even know exist. Learning that their shadows can tell them something about the motion of Earth and sun, as well as investigating dirt and sand and observing the moon and stars, will train the children to look more closely at things they may have otherwise ignored.

This teacher's guide also includes suggestions for alternative assessment in many of the lessons. This is directly related to the learning expected from each activity and will assess the students' depth of understanding rather than simply factual knowledge alone. As you do the activities in this book, hopefully you and your students will discover that *Science Is Fun*.

4

National Science Education Standards

The National Science Education Standards* were adopted nationwide in 1996. They established standards for the science education programs for K–12 students. *Pathways to the Science Standards,** developed by the National Science Teachers Association, offers practical ideas and suggestions for teachers to apply these standards. These two documents offer information which has been well researched and, when put into practice, will result in outstanding science programs.

Science and Quality Hands-On Experience

The need to teach science through concrete hands-on experience which helps students construct their own knowledge is emphasized in these books. They point out the difference between quality hands-on experiences and those which are recipe-driven, without science content, and one-time-only activities. The role of the teacher is to help children build accurate concepts, use the science process skills, and help students learn to evaluate ideas and reject those which are incorrect.

Preconceptions and Past Experiences

Assessing students' preconceptions through techniques such as interviews, questions, drawings, predictions, and group discussion is encouraged. Developing programs which build upon past experiences will form a more sound foundation for learning. Teaching students how to ask questions of themselves will provide them with an important science tool.

Science Content and Real Experience

Science content should be taught through real experiences. Books, videos, CD-ROMs, and Internet information should be used only when they enhance understanding and extend learning. The activities within *Science Is Fun* emphasize this philosophy.

Science Content and Assessment

Assessment should directly relate to the learning of science content through hands-on experiences. This is different from testing for facts which are isolated pieces of information rather than the understanding of general concepts. Assessment can best be done through the use of open-ended questions, performance based tests, portfolios, and journals. *Science Is Fun* shows how to apply alternative assessment techniques through examples at the end of some sections or activities.

*See Resources section of this guide for further information.

National Science Education Standards *(cont.)*

It is important to understand the characteristics of the K–3 students when designing appropriate science programs for them. It is also necessary to develop scientific inquiry skills. The lessons in *Science Is Fun* incorporate these ideas.

Characteristics of the Kindergarten Through Third Grade Learner

- ❑ They are naturally interested in almost everything around them.
- ❑ They use their senses to explore.
- ❑ They learn through observing, sorting, grouping, and ordering objects.
- ❑ They find classifying by more than one attribute at a time difficult.
- ❑ They learn by trial and error.
- ❑ They find concepts such as life cycles easier if taught in a logical manner.
- ❑ They find learning more meaningful when linked to real experiences.
- ❑ They can discover the rules of nature through application of science skills.
- ❑ They are capable of taking notes, gathering and recording data, and writing a journal on a simple basis.
- ❑ They can see the connections between cause and effect and can make predictions, such as moon phases.
- ❑ They can design simple tests but not elaborate experiments.

Inquiry Skills and the Kindergarten Through Third Grade Learner

K–3 students should develop inquiry skills to enable them to . . .

- ❑ plan and carry out simple investigations.
- ❑ use simple equipment and tools to gather data from their investigations.
- ❑ communicate the results of their investigations and provide explanations for them.

The Alphabet Game

— Teacher Information —

Symmetry is defined as "a rotation or translation of a plane figure that leaves the figure unchanged although its position may be altered." Symmetry is frequently found in nature and art. This series of activities should be spread over several days to permit students to freely investigate symmetry in letters and pictures. It is not important that they understand the term *symmetry* but, rather, that they discover that some objects will have the same image (symmetry) when bisected by the mirror, while others do not. Finally, they will find that two mirrors can create a wide variety of designs. Permit them to enjoy this exploration and share what they find.

Overview: *Students will use a mirror to change letters into a variety of shapes and other letters.*

Materials

- mirror for each student (See Resources section for source of mirrors.)
- copies of the letter A for each student
- printed copies and transparency of Letters in a Mirror (page 9)
- printed copies and transparency of Changing Letters (page 10)

To the Teacher: The activity is divided into two levels. The Changing Letters activity sheet is designed for more advanced students. A list of questions is provided in the Activity section on the next page to lead the beginning students through the use of the Letters in a Mirror activity.

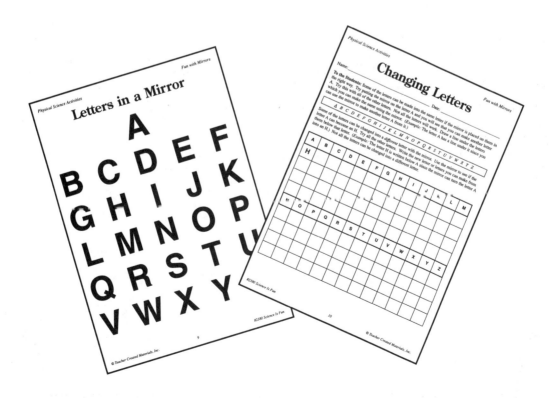

The Alphabet Game *(cont.)*

Activity

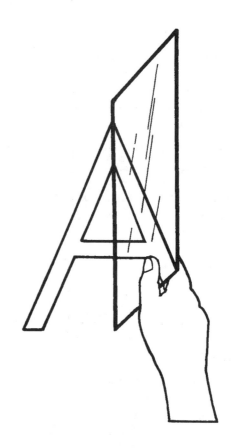

1. Distribute a mirror and a copy of Letters in a Mirror to each student. Let them use their mirrors on the letter A to see what happens when they look at its reflection with the mirror placed perpendicularly over the letter at various locations.

2. Draw a large A on the board and use a piece of cardboard to represent a mirror. Demonstrate how to position the mirror over the letter so it cuts it in half vertically. Have the students do this and ask them what they see (*another letter A is formed*). Move the cardboard (mirror) to cut the letter in half horizontally and have the students do this also. Ask them what they see (*a diamond shape*).

3. Have the students try turning their mirrors around so they will see a different view when it is held in the vertical and horizontal positions. Show them how to rotate the mirror in a perpendicular position slowly over the letter and watch the image change.

4. For the more advanced students, distribute the Changing Letters activity sheet.

5. For the beginning students, use the following instructions to help guide them through the discovery of various shapes that can be made from each letter.

   • Find the letters that can be turned into the same letter using your mirror and draw a circle around them.

   • Draw a line under the letters that could be made into different letters with the mirror.

   • Show something else you found you could do with your mirror and the letters.

   • Which letters could be changed into a number with the mirror?

Closure

Place the students in small groups and let them share their discoveries with each other.

Letters in a Mirror

A
B C D E F
G H I J K
L M N O P
Q R S T U
V W X Y Z

Changing Letters

Name:_____ Date: _____

To the Students: Some of the letters can be made into the same letter if the mirror is placed on them in the right way. Try putting the mirror on the letter A, and you will see that you can make another letter A. Try this with all of the other letters. Not all the letters will work. Draw a line under the letters which you can make the same using the mirror. (*Example:* The letter A has a line under it since you can use the mirror to make another letter A from it.)

A̲ B C D E F G H I J K L M N O P Q R S T U V W X Y Z

Some of the letters can be changed into a *different* letter with the mirror. Use the mirror to see if the letter A can become an H. Try all the other letters. Write the new letter or letters you can make from them below that letter. (*Example:* The letter H is written below A since the mirror can turn the letter A into an H.) Not all the letters can be changed into a different letter.

A	B	C	D	E	F	G	H	I	J	K	L	M
H												

N	O	P	Q	R	S	T	U	V	W	X	Y	Z

Funny Pictures

Overview: *Students will extend their discoveries with two mirrors to create new pictures.*

Materials

- mirrors
- copies and transparency of Changing Pictures with Mirrors (page 12)
- variety of colorful pictures of animals, flowers, etc., from magazines
- photograph of each student showing his or her face clearly (e.g., school photo)

Activity 1

1. Distribute a mirror and a copy of Changing Pictures with Mirrors.

2. Let students investigate how many different images they can make with each of the pictures.

3. Have students use the mirrors on photos of their own faces. Let them place the mirror on the face so it bisects it lengthwise from forehead through the nose and to the chin. They will find that their faces do not have symmetry and that they look like different persons. Be sure they rotate the mirror so they view both halves of the face and thus see another image.

4. Tell the students to place the mirror over the picture so it extends from ear to ear. Let them enjoy the funny faces which appear when they do this. Encourage them to move the mirror around the face to change it and see how many images they can see.

Activity 2

1. Distribute magazines with pictures of colorful birds, insects, and flowers.

2. Let the students place their mirrors on the pictures to change the images in various ways.

3. Pair the students and tape their two mirrors together along one edge. Have the students place their mirrors over the pictures and look between the mirrors to see multiple images. Tell them to move the mirrors closer and farther apart. Ask what they see. (The closer the mirrors are together, the more images they can see.)

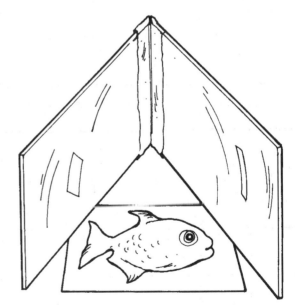

Closure

Have the students draw their own pictures and use one and then two mirrors to see the images change.

Changing Pictures with Mirrors

To the Teacher: Have students color the pictures, cut them out, and then use mirrors to see how many images can be made. They should use first one mirror and then two mirrors that are taped together.

Mixing Colors

— Teacher Information —

Some objects, such as traffic lights and neon signs, appear colored because the light that they give off contains a limited range of wavelengths. Most objects appear colored because their chemical structure absorbs certain wavelengths of light and reflects others. When white light strikes a banana, for example, it absorbs all other colors except yellow which is reflected to our eyes. The light entering the eye falls on the retina that lines the back and sides of the eyeball. Cells in the layers absorb the light and convert it to electrical signals. These travel through nerves to the brain where they are interpreted as color.

The following series of activities will enable students to experiment with colors. It is not important that students fully understand the scientific principles behind the effects they observe but, rather, that they learn to make the observations and learn how to describe them.

Overview: *Students will work with pigments or colors of dyes to discover the possible combinations which result from mixing primary colors.*

Materials

- dropper bottles of red, green, blue, and yellow food coloring (one set per group)
- 9 oz. clear plastic cups (set of 6 per group)
- red, blue, green, yellow crayons
- toothpicks
- paper towels
- black permanent marker
- What Color Do You See? data sheet (page 15)
- Color Chart data sheet (page 16)

Lesson Preparation

- Make sets of six plastic cups for each group, labeled as follows:

red + green	green + blue
blue + yellow	red + yellow
blue + red	yellow + green

Mixing Colors *(cont.)*

Lesson Preparation *(cont.)*

- Fill the cups nearly full with water

- For each group make trays of materials listed below:

  ✓ set of 6 cups of water, labeled with colors

  ✓ 6 toothpicks

  ✓ paper towel

  ✓ 1 green and 1 yellow crayon

  ✓ 2 blue and 2 red crayons

- If the activity is too complex for this class, arrange for adults or older students to work with each group as needed.

Activity

1. Show the students red, green, blue, and yellow food coloring and have them tell you the names of their colors. Explain that they are going to use the food coloring in water and observe what they see happening.

2. Divide the students into small groups and distribute a tray of materials to each group. Distribute a copy of the data sheet to each student and review it with them before they begin.

3. Divide the cups of water among the members of each group along with the food coloring and crayons which match the first color to be added to each cup.

4. Assign each member of the group to do a different color combination in his or her cup of water, and then show the results with the other members so they can complete their records.

Closure

- Have students compare the results of their experiments. (See Answer Key.)

- As a culmination of this activity, have the students complete the Color Chart data sheet.

- After they complete the chart, students will use the cups of colored water they just created and add the third color as shown in the equation. To help them understand how to do this, have each group do the first combination as you monitor their progress. They will need to add yellow to the red + green cup and green to the red + yellow cup and compare the new color before writing the answer to the equation.

Mixing Colors *(cont.)*

What Color Do You See?

Name:_____ Date: _____

Instructions

1. Put one drop of the first color into the cup.

2. Watch what happens to the coloring.

3. Use a crayon which is the same color as the drop to show how the drop spread in the water.

    I added_____coloring to the water.

4. Add a drop of the next color to the water and watch it sink and mix with the other color.

5. Use the toothpick and stir the water until the colors are mixed.

6. Add the second color and stir it into the water. Hold the cup up to the light so it will shine through the water to make it easier to see the new color. Write the two colors you mixed in the water and the new color which appeared.

    I added_____and_____and got the new color_____.

7. Look at the color equations below and find the one you have just done. In the box, write the new color which appeared when these two colors were mixed. Other members of your group have added different colors to their water. Look at the color of the water in each of their cups. Finish the chart below to tell what color appears when the two colors are mixed together.

Red + Green = [ ]   **Red + Yellow =** [ ]

Green + Blue = [ ]   **Blue + Red =** [ ]

Blue + Yellow = [ ]   **Yellow + Green =** [ ]

Mixing Colors *(cont.)*

Color Chart

Name:_____ Date: _____

Instructions: Use the What Colors Do You See? data sheet to give the names of the colors that appear when you mix two colors in water. The color mix of red + yellow has been done for you as an example of how to finish this chart.

	Red	**Green**	**Blue**	**Yellow**
Red				orange
Green				
Blue				
Yellow				

Begin with the two colors which have been mixed in the cups and mix the third color following the equations below. Write the name of the new color which appeared.

1. Red + Green + Yellow = a new color_____

2. Green + Blue + Red = a new color_____

3. Blue + Yellow + Green = a new color_____

Now, pour all the cups of colored water into a large clear container and hold it up to the light to see what color the water has become. Write the name of the color this combination of colors makes.

red + blue + green + yellow =_____

Colorful Drops

Overview: *Students will mix undiluted drops of food coloring to see the results.*

Materials

- dropper bottles of red, green, blue, and yellow food coloring (one set per group)
- waxed paper
- clear tape
- toothpicks
- paper towels
- Mixing Paints data sheet (page 18)
- Painting with Food Coloring (page 19)

Lesson Preparation

- Cut pieces of waxed paper which will fit over the upper part of the data sheet to cover the circles.

Activity

1. Review the data sheet completed during the lesson Mixing Colors.
2. Tell the students that they will be mixing food coloring today to see what colors they can create.
3. Distribute a data sheet to each student and review the instructions with them.

Closure

Have each student use the food coloring to draw a picture on the Painting with Food Coloring data sheet. They should use the combined colors made in the Mixing Colors activity, as well as drops of single colors placed on a new piece of waxed paper. They will need additional toothpicks so they can have a toothpick for every color.

Colorful Drops *(cont.)*

Mixing Paints

Name: _____ Date: _____

Instructions: Put the waxed paper over the circles and tape it in place. Read the colors written below each circle and put a drop of each of these colors in the middle of the circles. Mix them with the toothpick.

(A) Red + Green   **(B) Red + Yellow**   **(C) Green + Blue**

(D) Blue + Red   **(E) Blue + Yellow**   **(F) Yellow + Green**

Instructions: Dip the toothpick into the paint you made in the circle. Paint the box next to the color equation below. Write the name of this new color on the line beside the box.

(A) Red + Green =
The new color is

_____

(D) Blue + Red =
The new color is

_____

(B) Red + Yellow =
The new color is

_____

(E) Blue + Yellow =
The new color is

_____

(C) Green + Blue =
The new color is

_____

(F) Yellow + Green =
The new color is

_____

Colorful Drops *(cont.)*

Painting with Food Coloring

Name:_____ Date:_____

Instructions: Draw a picture in the space below and then paint it with the food coloring. Use toothpicks as brushes. Be sure to use a different toothpick for each color.

A Magic Show of Lights

Teacher Information

White light is made up of all colors except black, which is the absence of light. Light travels in waves, with each color in it having a different distance between one wave and the next called a *wavelength*. When white light passes through a prism or raindrops, the wavelengths are bent at different angles. They spread apart into all the colors of the rainbow: red, orange, yellow, green, blue, indigo, and violet (ROY G BIV).

The primary colors of light are red, green, and blue, which differ from those of pigments. The colors of any two primary colors of light form complementary colors. These are as follows:

- red + blue = purple (magenta)
- blue + green = blue-green (cyan)
- green + red = yellow
- When all three primary colors of light overlap, they form white light.

The following activities are designed to familiarize students with these concepts. The scientific principles are not stressed. It is more important for students to experience the excitement of discovery of what happens when colored lights are combined or reflected on pigments.

Overview: *Students will see a demonstration of white light changed into a rainbow of colors.*

Materials

- glass prism
- slide or filmstrip projector
- 35 mm slide frame
- aluminum foil
- single-edged razor blade
- glass of water
- mirror
- white paper
- parent letter (page 22)

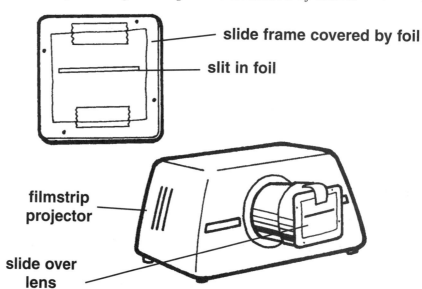

slide frame covered by foil

slit in foil

filmstrip projector

slide over lens

Lesson Preparation

- Cover the slide frame with aluminum foil and use the single-edged razor blade to cut a slit in it.
- Place the slide in the slide projector or tape it over the lens of a film strip projector.

A Magic Show of Lights *(cont.)*

Activity

1. Ask the students to tell you about rainbows they have seen. Have them tell the colors they saw in the rainbows. Explain that you are going to make a rainbow for them to see and find out what colors are in it.

2. Darken the room and then turn on the projector light. Hold the prism in front of the light coming through the slit and slowly turn it until one or two rainbows are projected. The light coming through the slit is refracted (bent) and broken into the colors of the rainbow. There may be two rainbows which appear in different directions. Try to project the rainbow on a white surface (e.g., ceiling or board) to show a clear image of the colors.

3. Have the students begin on the outside of the rainbow and call out the colors they see. List these on the board and teach them the name "ROY G BIV" to help them remember the sequence.

Closure

- Take the students outside and place the glass of water in the sunlight on a table. With a mirror, reflect the sun's light through the water and onto white paper. A rainbow should result. If it does not appear, move the mirror a bit until it does.

- Have the students look at the color sequence and say the rainbow "name" again. The sequence of this rainbow should match the name. Point out that this rainbow is just like the one which was made using the projector light and prism.

- Ask the students what color the light is that came from the projector (white). Explain that white light is really made up of all the colors they see in the rainbow. Tell them that the light from the sun is also white, and when it passes through the water or a prism, it will also create a rainbow.

- Explain that the rainbow we see in the sky when the sun is shining and there is still rain falling is created by sunlight passing through the water droplets of rain.

Extender

- Send home the parent letter which invites parents and children to experiment making rainbows.

- Let the students share their experiments and pictures with the class when they are returned to school.

Parent Letter for Making Rainbows

Date_____

Dear Parents:

Your child has seen a demonstration of how rainbows can be made by using a prism and a bright beam of light from a projector, and by using a mirror reflecting sunlight through a glass of water. Please let your child experiment with other ways to make a rainbow at home. One of the ways to do this is to use a hose and spray a fine mist of water into the air. Let sunlight pass through it. If the mist and sunlight are at just the right angle, a rainbow should be seen opposite the sun.

After the experiment, have your child fill in the information on this letter and then bring it back to school to share with the class.

Sincerely,

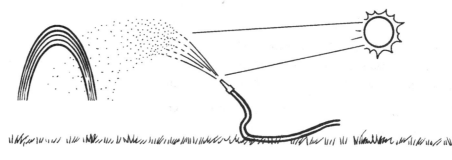

To the Child: Tell about your experiment to make a rainbow. If you were able to make one, draw a picture of what it looked like. Show the colors in the order they appeared in the rainbow.

_____

_____

Make a drawing of your rainbow experiment here.

Mixing Colored Lights

Overview: *Students will discover what happens when primary colors of light are combined to create complementary colors.*

Materials

- red, green, and blue filters (These must be pure primary colors in order to form complementary colors and white light. These filters may be purchased at Scientifics (see Resources) or a stage lighting supplier.)
- three equally bright slide and/or filmstrip projectors (Overhead projectors will not work.)
- three cardboard slide mounts
- red, blue, and green construction paper

Lesson Preparation

- Cut pieces of the three primary color filters and tape them to the slide mount frames.
- Set the three projectors on a table in front of a screen. Put a primary color slide into each projector or tape them over the lenses. Locate the projectors so they project a large image of the color which can be overlapped or spread out side by side with at least six inches between.
- Practice this activity before doing it with the students.

Activity

1. Remind the students of their experience with white light being refracted into a rainbow. Discuss briefly their experiments with pigments in which they made colors by combining them. Explain that in this lesson they will see what happens when colored lights are mixed.

2. Turn off the lights and turn on the projectors one at a time so that the colors (red, green, and blue) are side by side but not overlapping. Have the students identify the colors.

3. Overlap two of the colors at a time to produce the complementary colors, having students identify them as you do so. Write the color equations on the board.
   - *red + blue = purple (magenta)*
   - *blue + green = blue-green (cyan)*
   - *green + red = yellow*

4. Move the projectors so all three colors overlap. The light in the overlap section should be white. Write the equation on the board.

   red + blue + green = white

5. Explain that colors of light when mixed give different color combinations than those of pigment (paint).

Mixing Colored Lights *(cont.)*

Closure

- Show the students the colored construction paper and then have them identify the colors. Use a marking pen to print the name of the color in large letters on the paper. Tape the papers to the screen or the board.

- Turn out the lights and turn on one of the colored lights. Shine the colored light on the construction paper, beginning with the paper which is the same color as the light. Ask the students to tell what color they see. Repeat this, shining the colored light on the other colors. Do this for all three colored lights. Students will soon discover that the paper remains the same color only when it is shown in the same color of light.

- Put the construction paper on the screen or board so they overlap. Overlap the three colored lights to create white light and shine this on the construction paper. Ask the students to identify the colors. They will see the colors return to normal in the white light.

- Remind students that the white light is really a combination of the red, green, and blue light. Tell them that when we see things in white light, we see their color because they reflect only that color from all the colors in the white light.

Reminder: It is not important that students completely understand this scientific principle of how we see colors. This is merely an opportunity for students to investigate and experience the phenomenon of combining colored light with pigments.

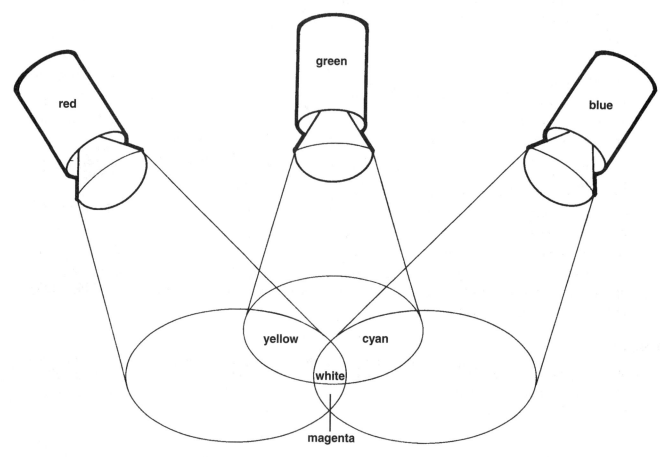

Colorful Shadows

Overview: *Students will investigate the colored shadows which can be created when using primary and complementary colors of light.*

Materials

- three equally bright filmstrip and/or slide projectors
- slide mounts covered with red, green, and blue filters
- *optional:* cassette tape recorder and march music

Lesson Preparation

- Set up the slide projectors as they were in the previous lesson, Mixing Colored Lights.

Activity

1. Review the results of combining the three primary colors of light by projecting them onto the screen. Have the students tell the primary colors first and then the complementary colors they create when combined.

2. Ask the students what color their shadows are (black). Tell them that they are going to see what their shadows look like when only the primary colors of light are shone on them. Let a student volunteer to stand between the light and the screen so he or she casts a shadow on the screen. Tell him or her to face the screen to see the color of the shadows along with the rest of the class. Begin with white light and then ask the students to predict what will happen when one of them stands in red light. Turn on the red light. (The shadow will be black.)

3. Repeat this with the other two primary colors, using different volunteers each time. (The shadows are always black.)

4. Ask the students what they think will happen if someone stands in two overlapping primary colors of light. Turn on two colors (e.g., green and blue) and have them overlap in the center. Have two student volunteers stand in the primary colors on each side to show that their shadows are black. Tell them to stretch out one arm into the center where the lights overlap. (Their arms' shadows will be green, blue, black, and cyan.)

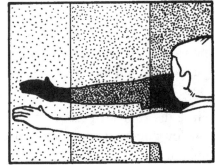

5. Ask the students to predict what the shadow will look like when someone stands in front of the white light made by adding all three primary colors. Overlap the lights until the white light appears and have a volunteer stand in the light. (There will be seven shadows—red, green, blue, cyan, yellow, magenta, and black.)

Closure

- Put on a cassette tape of march music and have the students march between the screen and the lights to see their own shadows. Have them lift their arms to wave as they march to add more motion to their shadows.

Shadow Puppet Show

Overview: *Students will use the primary and complementary colors of light to create special effects as they dramatize a favorite story.*

Materials

- projectors and filters used in previous two lessons
- tagboard or cardboard
- meat skewers or 22- or 24-gauge wire
- storybook

Lesson Preparation

- Select a favorite story for the students to dramatize. (e.g., *Rainbow Fish* by Marcus Pfister)

- Select appropriate background music for the story.

- Use the tagboard to make a puppet which represents one of the characters from the book. Holes may be used to represent eyes, nose, and mouth. Arms and legs may be made in two pieces, joined with metal brads to allow movement. Color may be added to the clothing by cutting holes to let the light through.

- Glue the skewer to the puppet so it will be supported from below. When held in the light, the puppet can cast one, four, or seven shadows, depending upon how many colored lights are used to create that light.

Activity

1. Read the story to the students or have them read it aloud. Tell them that they are going to make puppets of the characters in the story. Show them the model puppet so they can see what their puppets should look like. Discuss the various puppets to be made, including furniture, houses, tree, and other scenery which will enhance the show.

2. Have the students practice moving their puppets in front of the projected light, causing the shadows on a screen or white paper. Experiment with the right lighting to use a variety of shadow colors.

3. Assign a reader(s) to read the story aloud as the puppeteers move the puppets and scenery. If appropriate, add background music and/or sound effects (e.g., animal noises). Let the students be creative with their puppets and the story.

Closure

- Present the puppet show for parents and other classes.

- Divide the students into small groups and let them write their own stories and make the puppets to bring these stories to life.

Playing with Colors

── Teacher Information ──

Our eyes can be fooled into seeing colors which are not really there. If we stare at a colored image for about 30 seconds and then look at a white surface, we see an *afterimage*. The afterimage has the same shape as the original image but with different colors. When the original image is red, the afterimage will be green. When the image is green, the afterimage will be red. Blue areas become yellow, and yellow areas become blue. Black and white also reverse. The technical name for this amazing color-vision is *successive contrast*.

Sometimes we may see colors in areas that are only black and white. Such colors are called *phantom colors*. Phantom colors may be seen by staring at rapidly moving black-and-white patterns.

This activity is designed to demonstrate both of these phenomena. It is not important that students fully understand the physical cause of this afterimage or phantom colors. The lesson is designed to have them experience this and enjoy the special effects they observe.

Overview: *Students will experience the two phenomena of seeing an afterimage and phantom colors.*

Materials

- American flag designs (page 30)
- circle designs (page 29)
- colored pens or crayons
- timer
- wine corks
- large T-pins

Lesson Preparation

- Make copies of the flag designs for each student. Color the star area yellow and the white stripes green.
- Make copies of the circle designs on tagboard so each student will have one a pair of circles. Cut these out before distributing them.
- Attach the black and white patterned disk to the cork with the large T-pin. Push the pin into the center of the disk and then about $3/4$ inch (2 cm) into one end of the cork.

Playing with Colors *(cont.)*

Activity

1. Explain to the students that there are times when our eyes appear to play tricks on us and that you are going to show them some examples of this.

2. Distribute a copy of the flag to each student. Tell them that when you say "Go," they are to stare at the dot in the center of the flag and hold their eyes on that spot until you tell them "Stop." Explain that when they hear you say "Stop," they should immediately turn the flag over and look at the white side of the paper.

3. Tell the students to "Go" and allow 30 seconds for them to stare at the dot on the flag. Say "Stop" at the end of the 30 seconds and remind them to turn the paper over and look at the white side.

4. Ask the students to tell what they see. (The stripes should become red and white, and the star area should be blue.) Repeat this so students will be able to see the effect again.

5. Distribute the corks with the black-and-white patterned disk on them. Tell the students to hold the cork in one hand so the disk faces them, like holding a small electric fan in front of one's face. Have them spin the disk as fast as they can with their fingers. They should then watch the center of the disk, concentrating on looking for any change in color they see. (The black lines form complete circles as the disk spins. Those nearest the center become rust colored. The next set of circles appear to be green. The students may see other colors as well. They will need to practice this to adjust the speed and their vision in order to be able to see these colors.)

Closure

• Distribute the disks which have been divided into quarters and the colored felt pens or crayons to the students. Tell the students to choose two, three, or four colors and then color the quarters of the disk.

• When all disks have been colored, put them on the cork with the T-pin and have students spin them to see what colors they see. (They may see some color change or a blend of the colors as they flash by quickly.)

• Let them exchange their disks to look at those created by others in the class.

• Experiment with shapes of black and white as well as colors on blank disks cut from tagboard.

Circle Designs

Instructions: Make copies of these circles on tagboard and give each student a pair.

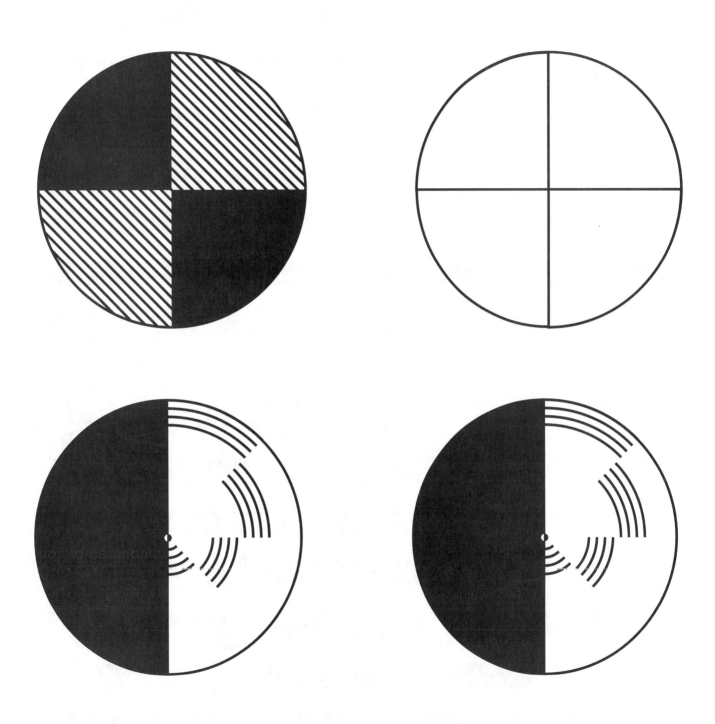

American Flag

Instructions: Make enough copies of the flag design for each student. Use a felt pen and color the star field yellow and the white stripes green.

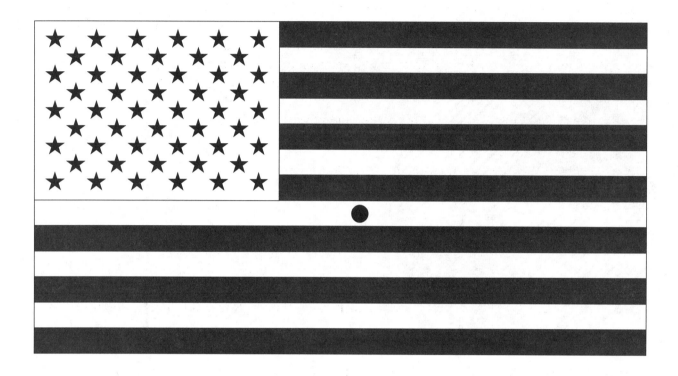

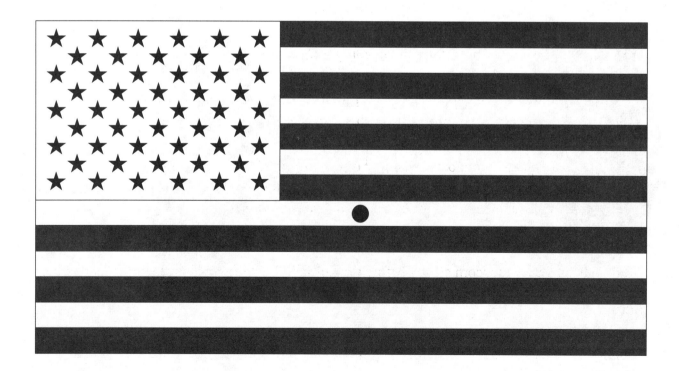

What's Cooking

— Teacher Information —

Everything is made of matter, and all matter occupies space. The amount of matter is called its *mass*. Earth's gravity gives the mass of matter *weight*. The physical properties of certain matter can be recognized by the senses—sight, smell, touch, taste, or hearing. Matter usually exists in three states—solid, liquid, and gas. Matter can undergo physical change by changing the temperature, as when ice melts into water and then evaporates into vapor, a gas. Matter is made up of chemical elements. It can change chemically, as in the case of cooking when various matter is combined to produce a cake.

The following lessons show physical properties and physical and chemical changes of matter.

Overview: *Students investigate the physical properties of popcorn.*

Materials

- popcorn maker
- Fun with Popcorn Level A and B data sheets (pages 32 and 33)

Lesson Preparation

- Begin to make popcorn so it will be well underway as the students enter the classroom.

Activity

1. As students enter the classroom they should smell but not see the popcorn being made. Have them get seated and then use the following questions to discuss the popcorn with them.
   - How do you know popcorn is being made? (*the smell and popping sound*)
   - What do you use to smell the popcorn? (*nose*)
   - How is the smell of popcorn reaching your nose? (*through the air*)
   - What do you use to hear the popcorn popping? (*ears*)
   - How is the sound of the popping reaching your ears? (*also through the air*)
2. Show them the popcorn and then ask how they can be sure it is popcorn. (*They can see it.*)
3. Ask them what they use to see the popcorn. (*eyes*)
4. List the senses on the board beside the part of the body used for that sense.
5. Have the students tell you what other senses they could use to be sure this is popcorn (*taste and feel or touch*). Add these to the list of senses and parts of the body.
6. Distribute popcorn, asking each student to take one piece, feel it, and then describe how it feels to a partner.
7. Have students chew popcorn slowly before swallowing. Let them describe the taste to a partner.

Closure

- Distribute Level A or Level B data sheet to each student according to ability. Let the students complete the data sheet to summarize the use of their senses which helped them investigate the properties of popcorn.

Fun with Popcorn

(Level A)

Name:_____ Date: _____

To the Student: You have just had a chance to learn about popcorn by using your senses. Fill in the missing words and make drawings to help you review what senses you used for each thing you did with the popcorn. One letter of each missing word is given to you to give you a hint.

1. When you first came into the room, you could ___ ___ E ___ ___ popcorn being made.

   Draw the part of your body you used for this.

2. You could also tell it was popcorn because you could ___ ___ ___ R it popping.

   Draw the part of your body you used for this.

3. The teacher showed you the popcorn so you could S ___ ___ the popcorn.

   Draw the part of the body you used for this.

4. The teacher gave you some popcorn and told you to ___ ___ ___ L it.

   Draw the part of the body you used for this.

5. Finally, the teacher let you ___ ___ S ___ ___ the popcorn.

   Draw the part of the body you used for this.

Fun with Popcorn

(Level B)

Name:_____ Date:_____

To the Student: You have just had a chance to learn about popcorn by using your senses. Fill in the missing words and make drawings to help you review what senses you used for each thing you did with the popcorn. Write what each sense told you about the popcorn.

1. When you first came into the room, you could_____popcorn being made.

   Draw the part of your body you used for this.
   Tell what this sense told you about the popcorn.

2. You could also tell it was popcorn because you could_____it making noise.

   Draw the part of your body you used for this.
   Tell what this sense told you about the popcorn.

3. The teacher showed you the popcorn so you could_____the popcorn.

   Draw the part of the body you used for this.
   Tell what this sense told you about the popcorn.

4. The teacher gave you some popcorn and told you to_____it.

   Draw the part of the body you used for this.
   Tell what this sense told you about the popcorn.

5. Finally, the teacher let you_____the popcorn.

   Draw the part of the body you used for this.
   Tell what this sense told you about the popcorn.

Identifying Matter by Sound and Feel

Teacher Information: *Investigating Physical Properties of Matter*

The physical properties of certain kinds of matter can be recognized by using the senses—sight, smell, touch, taste, or hearing. This series of activities should be spread over several days. Some can be done in learning centers, while others are for the class to do together. The activities are designed to have students develop the use of their senses while investigating the physical properties of various types of matter. These will include using the senses of smell, taste, sound, touch, and sight.

Overview: *Students will investigate the physical properties of sound that matter can make.*

Materials

- opaque, empty film canister for each student, available free at most places where film is developed
- trays (one per group)
- parent letter (page 36)
- Sound and Feel Containers List (page 37)
- What's Inside the Container? (Sound and Feel) data sheet (page 38)
- transparency of the Sound and Feel Containers List (page 37) and Sound and Feel Anwsers (page 39)

Lesson Preparation

- Send home the parent letter and a film canister for each student a few days in advance of when you conduct the activities.
- Put a number on each container, both on the lid and on the canister as they are returned. Record each student's name and container number on the Sound and Feel Containers List.
- Select 10 canisters to use and save the rest for later. Make a random list of their contents as an answer sheet.
- Students will then match the characteristics they sense when shaking the containers and copy the name of the item from the answer list beside the container's number.

Identifying Matter by Sound and Feel *(cont.)*

Activity

1. Divide the students into small groups and then distribute a copy of the data sheet What's Inside the Container? (Sound and Feel) to each group. Divide the containers into sets for each group and distribute them on a tray.

2. Have the students carefully shake the containers to see if they can guess the contents. The members of the group should come to agreement and then record their guess.

3. Rotate the containers on the trays to another group until all containers have been tested by each group. It is important to allow enough time for each group to discuss the possibilities before recording their guess.

4. Monitor the students to be sure the lids are not removed. Be certain that each member of the group is contributing to the test and discussion.

Closure

-   Have each group tell what they thought was in each container. Record their guesses on the Sound and Feel Guess List transparency.

-   Show the transparency of the list of items in the containers along with the items themselves.

-   Have the students check to see how many they could guess correctly just by hearing the sound and feeling the contents move.

-   Discuss what helped them guess these items correctly.

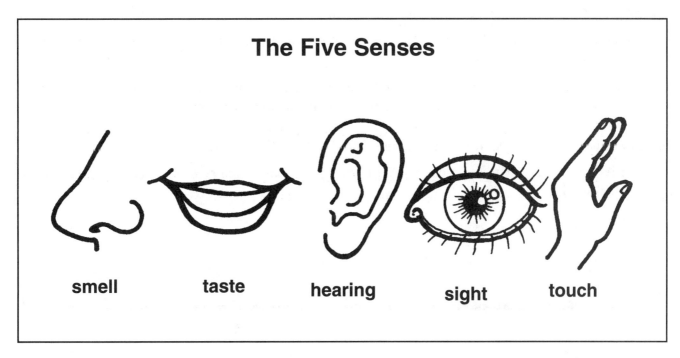

The Five Senses

smell   taste   hearing   sight   touch

Parent Letter for Sound and Feel Containers

Date_____

Dear Parents:

We are learning about the properties of matter and will be doing an activity that uses the senses of hearing and touch to identify various types of matter. Each student has been given a film canister to put some type of matter inside. Please help them find something that is appropriate to place inside the canister. Put something which makes a sound when shaken inside the canister. Be sure there is only one type of matter in each container. The canister should not be filled so full that the contents cannot make a sound when shaken gently.

Suggestions for matter which might be included in the container:

- sand
- pebble(s)
- water
- paper clip(s)

- rubber eraser
- coin(s)
- marble(s)
- cork

Students are encouraged to put something unusual in their containers.

Thank you for helping to make our activity exciting. You are welcome to join our class when we do this activity on_____.

Sincerely,

Sound and Feel Containers List

Student Names	Contents
1.	
2.	
3.	
4.	
5.	
6.	
7.	
8.	
9.	
10.	
11.	
12.	
13.	
14.	
15.	
16.	
17.	
18.	
19.	
20.	
21.	
22.	
23.	
24.	
25.	
26.	
27.	
28.	
29.	
30.	

What's Inside the Container?

(Sound and Feel)

Name:_____ Date: _____

To the Student: DO NOT OPEN THE LID. Shake the container and listen to the sound it makes. How does it feel when you shake it? Can you guess what is inside? Look at the answer list. Choose the name of the thing you think is inside the container and write it next to the container's number.

1.	
2.	
3.	
4.	
5.	
6.	
7.	
8.	
9.	
10.	

Sound and Feel Answers

To the Teacher: List the items in the canisters in random order below. This will be the answer list for students to use.

1.	
2.	
3.	
4.	
5.	
6.	
7.	
8.	
9.	
10.	

Identifying Matter by Smell

Overview: *Students will investigate the physical properties of smell of matter.*

Materials

- opaque empty film canister for each student
- masking tape
- parent letter (page 41)
- Smell Containers list (page 42)
- What's Inside the Container? (Smell) data sheet (page 43)
- transparency of (page 43)

Lesson Preparation

- Send home the parent letter and a film canister for each student a few days in advance of conducting the activities.
- Put a number on each container, both on the lid and the canister as they are returned. Record each student's name and container number on the Smell Containers list.
- Before doing the smell activity, put a hole about the diameter of a pencil in the middle of each lid with a drill or awl. Cover the hole with masking tape until the activity is to begin.
- Use only 10 containers at one time to make it easier for students to identify them.
- This lesson may be simplified by listing the contents of the containers in random order on the board. Students will then match the characteristics they sense when smelling the containers and put the container number next to the item on the list which they think is inside.

Activity

1. Divide the students into small groups and then distribute a copy of the data sheet What's Inside the Container? (Smell) to each group. Divide the containers among the groups.
2. Have the students carefully lift the tape and smell the contents of each container and then record the guess agreed upon by the group on the record sheet. They should seal the tape over the hole again.
3. Rotate the containers on the trays to another group until all containers have been tested by each group. It is important to allow enough time for each group to discuss the possibilities before recording their guess.
4. Monitor the students to be sure the lids are not removed. Be certain that each member of the group is contributing to the test and discussion.

Closure

- Have groups tell what they thought was in each container. Record their number guesses on the board beside the list of items.
- Give them the correct answers.
- Have students see how many they could guess correctly just by the smell of the contents.
- Discuss what helped them guess these items correctly.

Parent Letter for Smell Containers

Date_____

Dear Parents:

We are learning about the properties of matter and will be doing an activity that uses the sense of smell to identify various types of matter. Each student has been given a film canister to put some type of matter inside. Please help your child find something that is appropriate to place inside the canister. Put something in the container which will give off a smell. Be sure there is only one type of matter in each container.

When the canister is returned to school, a hole the size of a pencil diameter will be drilled in the lid. If the matter is liquid (e.g., vinegar), please use a cotton ball or piece of paper and put a few drops of the liquid on it. This will prevent the liquid from spilling out the hole in the lid. A piece of tape will be put over the hole to prevent evaporation.

Suggestions for matter which might be included in the container follow:

- slice of apple
- piece of banana
- water
- vanilla flavoring

- shampoo
- peppermint flavoring
- perfume
- slice of onion

Students are encouraged to put something unusual in their containers.

Thank you for helping make our activity exciting. You are welcome to join our class when we do this activity on_____.

Sincerely,

Smell Containers

Student Names	Contents
1.	
2.	
3.	
4.	
5.	
6.	
7.	
8.	
9.	
10.	
11.	
12.	
13.	
14.	
15.	
16.	
17.	
18.	
19.	
20.	
21.	
22.	
23.	
24.	
25.	
26.	
27.	
28.	
29.	
30.	

What's Inside the Container?

(Smell)

Name:_____ Date: _____

To the Student: DO NOT REMOVE the lid of your container. Lift the tape on the lid and sniff through the small hole. Can you guess what is making the smell? Find the number of the container on the list and write your guess of what is making the smell beside that number.

1.	
2.	
3.	
4.	
5.	
6.	
7.	
8.	
9.	
10.	

Identifying Matter by Taste

Overview: *Students will investigate the taste of various types of matter to be identified.*

Materials

- cotton-tipped swabs
- paper plates
- 6–8 flavorful solid and liquid foods
- copy of Taste Guess List (page 45) for each student

- 1-ounce (30 mL) cups
- toothpicks
- blindfold or sleep mask

Lesson Preparation

- Select a variety of flavors for students to taste and identify—e.g., salt crystals, sugar crystals, vinegar, and small pieces of fruit. Avoid flavors which might be disliked, such as onions.
- Place these in cups or on paper plates appropriate to the food. Pieces to be tasted should be about the size of a quarter.
- List the items being tested to make an answer key.
- Have other adults or older students assist in this activity since the taste test is given individually.
- Set up the testing site where no other student can observe. More than one site may be arranged if there are enough assistants and room so the answers will not be overheard.
- Set up a rotation for students to come to the site(s).
- The lesson may be simplified by providing a list of flavors to match as students taste the samples. To make it more challenging, add to the list flavors which will not be tested.

(**Caution:** Check to see whether any students are not permitted to eat any of the foods you are using.)

Activity

1. Explain that you are going to test students' sense of taste, seeing how many things they can identify by taste alone. Tell them they will be tested individually and should not tell anyone else what they tasted. You want them to keep this secret until all have been tested.
2. Put the name of the student being tested on a copy of the Taste Guess List. Blindfold the student who is to be tested.
3. Dip a cotton swab into the liquid and let the student place it on the tip on the tongue to test its flavor and guess what it is. Use a different swab for each flavor.
4. Pick up solid foods with a toothpick and let the child place it in his or her mouth to chew.
5. Always give the items to be tasted in the same order and permit time for students to think about the flavor before guessing. After each flavor is tasted, record the guess on the list.

Closure

- When all students have been tested, share the results of their guesses. Give them the correct tastes for each of the tests.
- Ask students what clues they used to identify flavors.
- Suggest that they try eating an evening meal with a blindfold to see how many foods they can identify by flavor and texture.

Taste Guess List

Name:_____

1.

2.

3.

4.

5.

6.

7.

8.

Identifying Matter by Touch

Overview: *Students will investigate matter through the sense of touch.*

Materials

- small coffee can
- wide packing tape
- This Is My Guess form (page 47)
- large sock with elastic ribbing
- variety of items to place in the can
- children's story which relates to this activity

Lesson Preparation

- Cut the cuff off the sock. Slip the cuff over the coffee can and tape the cut edge to the can. The cuff should be about the length of the can. The contents in the can cannot be seen, but the hand can reach in to feel it. Tape the other end of the cloth to the can.
- Collect items for the can with a variety of textures, densities, shapes, and hardnesses. Items might include such things as fruit, a glove, a marble, or scissors. Use items which students have had experience with so they can identify them by memory.
- Make a box for students to place their guesses in to identify the daily mystery object.

Activity

1. Tell students they are going to see how much they can tell about an object just by feeling it. Tell them you have put something inside a coffee can and you want them to stick a hand inside (demonstrate this) to feel the object. They should feel it to tell its shape, size, weight, and texture. When they are finished feeling it, they should pass the can to the next person. It is very important that students keep their ideas secret. Let them understand that they will first be asked to describe the object and then tell what they think it is.

2. Tell the students that you will read a story to them as they feel what is in the can. Send the can around the classroom so each student may feel the object inside as you read the story aloud. Monitor them to be sure no one gives clues to anyone else.

3. When the story ends and all have felt the object, have students work in small groups and describe the item as if they were telling someone who had not had the chance to feel it.

4. Now tell the groups to come to an agreement of what they thought was inside the can. Show several items and let the students see which fits their descriptions.

5. Explain that a new item will be placed in the can each day and students will guess what they think is inside based on how it feels. Show the forms which they will use for writing their guesses and the box in which they can place them each day.

Closure

- At the end of each day, read the guesses and show the object.
- Encourage students to bring something of their own to place inside the can.

Identifying Matter by Touch *(cont.)*

To the Teacher: Two copies of this form are provided to help you save paper.

This Is My Guess

Name:_____ Date:_____

Draw a picture to show what the thing inside the can might look like.

I think a_____is inside the can.

This Is My Guess

Name:_____ Date:_____

Draw a picture to show what the thing inside the can might look like.

I think a_____is inside the can.

From Solid to Liquid

Teacher Information: *Investigating Physical Changes of Matter*

Matter usually exists in three physical states: *solid*, *liquid*, and *gas*. A fourth state of matter, called *plasma*, exists under special conditions such as those in stars and lightning bolts. A physical change of matter does not change its chemical composition. An example of this is water. When very cold, water freezes into a solid; as it heats, it changes into a liquid and, if hot enough, begins to evaporate into the gaseous state.

The following series of activities will permit students to observe the changes in the physical states of matter, using water as an example. They should be spread out over several days.

Overview: *Students observe ice changing from a solid to a liquid.*

Materials

- 1-ounce (30 mL) cups (one per student)
- ice cubes (one per student)
- The Story of My Ice Cube data sheet (page 49)

Lesson Preparation

- Place the small cups on a tray and fill them with water.
- Place them in a freezer to form an ice cube for each student.

Activity

1. Ask the students if they have ever played with ice. Let them share their experiences.

2. Divide the students into small groups and tell them that you are going to give everyone an ice cube. Explain that you want them to play with it and tell their group members what they find out about the ice as they watch it melt.

3. Give each student an ice cube on a dish. Encourage the students to find out everything they can about their ice cubes. Permit them to touch and hold their ice cubes as well as breathe on them.

Closure

- Distribute a copy of the data sheet The Story of My Ice Cube for students to complete.
- Have the students share their ice cube stories with the members of their group.
- Save the cups of water for the next lesson in this series.

The Story of My Ice Cube

Name:_____ Date: _____

Draw four pictures to show what happened to your ice cube as you watched it melt.

1	2

3	4

Write a story telling what you saw happen to your ice cube as it melted.

From Liquid to Gas

Overview: *Students will observe water change into vapor (gas).*

Materials

- hot plate
- dark food coloring
- cups of water used in previous lesson
- heat-proof clear glass container
- large cooking thermometer used in making candy
- permanent black marker
- What Happened to the Water? data sheet (page 52)

Lesson Preparation

- Mark the glass container off in $^1/_2$ inch (1 cm) intervals with the permanent marker.
- Arrange the classroom so the students will be able to observe this demonstration. Place the hot plate on the table and arrange seating for the students around the table at a safe distance.
- Set the hot plate on its lowest setting and turn it on to preheat it.

From Liquid to Gas *(cont.)*

Activity

1. Review what the students observed as they watched their ice cubes melt in the previous activity. Ask them to tell you why their ice melted. (*The ice melted because it was too warm.*) Ask them what they think will happen if you pour the water from their melted ice cubes into the glass container and then set it on the hot plate.

2. Give each student a cup of water and let him or her pour it into the glass container. Add a drop of dark food coloring to make the water visible. Have the students notice where the water level is on the container. Use the marker and place the #1 next to the marker at the top of the water level. Number the other marks to the bottom of the container beginning with #2, etc.

3. Put the thermometer into the water and have the students look at the level of the liquid in the thermometer. Write the temperature on the board. Continue to write the temperature on the board as the water heats up and begins to boil.

4. Place the container on the hot plate and turn up the heat. Have the students observe what is happening. Leave the thermometer in the water. As they observe, ask them questions such as those below.

   • What do you see in the water? (*Bubbles will begin to form as it gets hotter.*)

   • Is the water getting warmer? How do you know? (*The thermometer liquid is rising.*)

   • Do you see anything in the container other than water? (*Steam will begin to appear.*)

5. As the water begins to boil, point out that the bubbles are bigger and that the water is in motion. Show the steam rising from the water. Have students note the water level. Ask them where they think the steam is coming from and where it is going. (*The steam is coming from the water, and it is going into the air.*)

6. Continue to record the temperature of the water (*it should level off once it begins to boil*), and point out the level of the water as it drops. Stop the demonstration before the container boils dry. Remove the container from the hot plate and place it on a pot holder on the table.

Closure

   • Ask the students what they think will happen to the rest of the water in the container. (*It will evaporate, turn to gas, and become part of the atmosphere.*)

   • Discuss what they observed, being sure they understand that the water turned to gas when it was heated.

   • Distribute the What Happened to the Water? data sheet for students to complete. Permit them to discuss this with other students as they work on the data sheet.

What Happened to the Water?

Name:_____ Date:_____

Draw four pictures to show what happened to the water as you watched it being heated.

1	**2**
3	**4**

Write a story telling what you saw happen to the water as it was heated.

From Gas to Liquid

Overview: *Students will observe two different methods for turning gas to liquid.*

Materials

- tall, clear glass
- blue food coloring
- blue ice cubes
- hot plate
- heat-proof glass container
- aluminum pie pan
- ring stand or other support to hold pie pan
- 3-inch (7.5 cm) square of dark construction paper

Lesson Preparation

- Make blue ice cubes by adding coloring to the water to make it dark blue and then freeze it.
- Add a few drops of coloring to the heat-proof glass container and fill it half full of water. Place it on the hot plate. Put the ring stand next to the hot plate and then put the pie pan on the ring stand so that it is about 3 inches (7.5 cm) above the container.

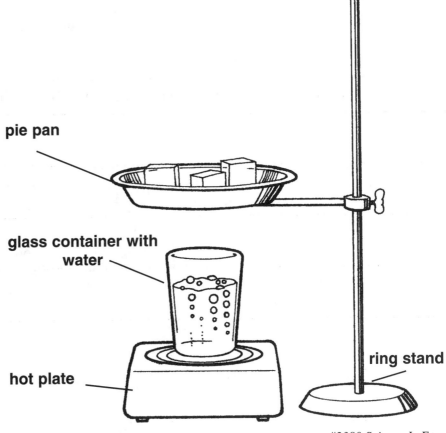

pie pan

glass container with water

hot plate

ring stand

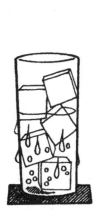

From Gas to Liquid *(cont.)*

Activity

1. Seat the students near the table. Explain that you are going to heat the water with the hot plate. Ask them what will happen when the water is heated. They should remember this from the last lesson.

2. As the water is heating, begin the other demonstration. Put a few drops of coloring in the tall glass and then fill it half full of water. Add 5–6 blue ice cubes. Have one of the students feel the outside of the glass and tell if it is wet or dry. Show the students the colored paper so they may see that it is also dry. Place the paper under the glass. The glass should be at least 3 feet (90 cm) away from the hot plate.

3. Place the blue ice cubes in the pie pan. Have the students discuss what they think will happen to the ice as the container of water below it is heated.

4. As the water begins to boil, ask questions which will help students look for details as they observe the changes. Some examples are provided below. If students do not know the answers, give them the answers so they will be able to follow the process.

   • Where is the steam coming from? (*It comes from the boiling water.*)

   • Why is the water turning to steam? (*The water is being heated and is evaporating.*)

   • What color is the steam? (*It is white or clear.*)

   • Why isn't it blue like the water? (*When water turns to gas [evaporates] anything added to that water, such as the coloring, is left behind.*)

   • What color is the water which is forming on the bottom of the pie pan. (*It is clear.*)

   • Do you think this water is leaking from the pie pan? (*No, because it is clear, not blue.*)

   • Where did it come from? (*It came from the steam hitting the cold bottom of the pan where it then condensed into a liquid again.*)

Closure

• Show the glass of blue ice water which has been sitting on the table. Have students observe that the construction paper is wet, and so is the outside of the glass. Wipe the condensation off the glass with a white tissue to show that it is not blue.

• Ask the students where this water came from. They may think it has leaked out of the glass, but tell them to look at the color of the water inside and that on the tissue so they will realize that it has not leaked. Explain that just like the steam hitting the cold pie pan, there is water vapor (gas) in the air. When the air hits a cold surface, the water vapor changes to liquid water.

Dance of the Molecules

Teacher Information

The *molecule* is one of the basic units of matter. It is the smallest particle into which a substance can be divided and still have the chemical properties of the original substance. If the substance were divided further, only atoms of the chemical elements would remain. For example, a drop of water contains billions of water molecules. If the drop could be divided into a single water molecule, it would still have all the chemical properties of water. But if the water molecule were divided, only atoms of the elements hydrogen and oxygen would remain.

Molecules are always in motion. Molecules in a solid, such as water ice, are packed closely and move very little, vibrating around a point where they balance between the other molecules. Molecules in liquid water are moving slowly but cling together loosely. Molecules in gaseous matter, such as steam, are moving so fast that they can separate and become light enough to mingle with molecules in the atmosphere.

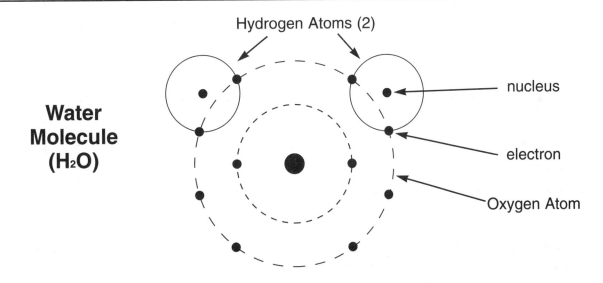

Water Molecule (H_2O)

Hydrogen Atoms (2)

nucleus

electron

Oxygen Atom

Overview: *Students will learn about the motions of water molecules in solid, liquid, and gaseous states.*

To the Teacher: This lesson is divided into two sections—a teacher demonstration and a student activity which has the students conduct the experiment demonstrated by the teacher. It is best to do these on two separate days to allow sufficient time for each of them.

Teacher Demonstration

Materials

- 3 large clear containers, at least 2-quart (2 liter) capacity
- dropper bottle of blue, red, or green food coloring
- hot, warm, and ice water
- Colors in the Water data sheet (page 57)
- crayons to match the color used in the demonstration

Dance of the Molecules *(cont.)*

Teacher Demonstration *(cont.)*

1. Prepare file cards with the labels *Hot*, *Cold*, and *Warm* to place near the containers.

2. Fill one of the large containers with tap water and let it sit long enough to reach room temperature. This will be the warm water needed for the demonstration. Place the three containers where they can be seen by all the students. Just before beginning the demonstration, fill the second container with very hot water and the third with ice water.

3. Tell the students that you are going to do a demonstration and that you want them to watch very carefully to see what happens. Explain that they should be ready to tell you what they saw after the demonstration is over.

4. Carefully put one drop of food coloring into each container. A beautiful display is created as the coloring spreads in different ways in the three jars. The coloring in the hot water will quickly disperse; in the warm water it will spread more slowly; in the cold water it will spread across the surface and then gradually sink and begin to mix with the water.

(The coloring will look somewhat like the drawings below within a minute of the drops entering the water.)

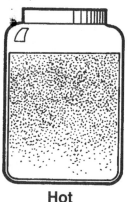   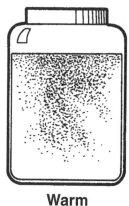   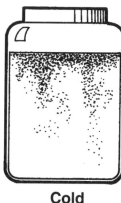

Hot   **Warm**   **Cold**

5. Discuss what the students have seen thus far, urging them to share as many details as possible. Tell them to compare the difference in the way the coloring spread in the different temperatures of water.

Closure

- As the students continue doing other activities, stop periodically to have them look at the changes in the water. Note these on the board. Be sure they know that nothing is stirring the water, yet the coloring continues to spread.

- After the coloring has spread through the hot water but is still not completely mixed in the other containers, distribute the data sheet Colors in the Water and have the students make drawings to show what the water looks like. Be sure the students are drawing the correct image for each temperature.

- Have the students share their drawings and ideas of what is happening.

(Do not give any answers at this time. This demonstration is designed to give the students an opportunity to guess what is happening based only on their observations.)

Colors in the Water

Name:_____ Date: _____

Use a crayon to show what the coloring looks like in the water.

Hot   **Warm**   **Cold**

Write what you think is making the coloring spread in the water.

_____

_____

_____

_____

_____

_____

_____

_____

Dance of the Molecules *(cont.)*

Student Activity

Materials (for eight groups of students)

- 24 clear plastic 9-ounce (270 mL) cups
- hot, warm, and ice water
- 8 small dropper bottles of food coloring (red, blue, and green)
- overhead projector
- toothpick
- 8 trays
- green, red, and blue crayons
- Dance of the Molecules data sheet (page 60)

Lesson Preparation

- Use a permanent marker to write *Hot* on a third of the cups, *Cold* on another third, and *Warm* on the last. Mark the large jars in the same manner.
- Fill a large container with water and let it reach room temperature; this will be the warm water for the activity.
- Heat water on a hot plate. This water will be mixed with tap water in the jar and cups so that it is hotter than the warm water.
- Just before doing the activity, fill the cold and warm cups with water, placing ice in the cold cups. Fill the hot cups nearly full of tap water and add the hot water. (*Caution:* Students will be testing the water temperature with their fingers, so be sure the hot water will not burn them.)
- Prepare a tray for each group with the three cups of water, dropper bottle of food coloring, and enough crayons (which match the food coloring) for each child in the group.

Activity *(Note: If this activity is too difficult for the students, do only the teacher demonstration to explain the motion of molecules.)*

1. Turn on the overhead projector and put a drop of clear water on the glass. Explain that you are going to try to make this drop of water as tiny as possible by pulling it apart with a toothpick. Using the toothpick, separate the water into the smallest drop possible.

2. Explain that even though this water drop is too small to be divided any further, it contains billions of tiny parts called *molecules*, so small they cannot even be seen clearly with the most powerful microscope. Tell students that all matter is made of molecules, even the air we breathe, the water we drink, and our own bodies. Explain the motion of molecules in the various states of matter; solid, liquid, and gas. (See Teacher Information, page 55.) Tell the students that although molecules cannot be seen, their motion can be.

3. Remind the students of the demonstration you did which used large containers of water and coloring to show the molecules in motion. Tell the students that it is now their turn to experiment with the motion of water molecules.

Dance of the Molecules *(cont.)*

Activity *(cont.)*

4. Add hot water to the cups marked *Hot*. Divide the students into small groups and distribute a tray of materials to each group. Let the students feel the water so they can see that it is cold, warm, and hot. Tell them that they are going to put a drop of food coloring into each cup of water and then watch to see what happens to the coloring. Caution them not to shake or stir the water so that they can observe the motion of the molecules.

5. Distribute the Dance of the Molecules data sheet and review it with the students. Tell them to put a crayon on their paper so they will be ready to begin making a drawing of what they see happening as soon as the drops are placed in three cups. Have them wait for you to signal when to drop the coloring into the water.

6. After all containers have coloring in them, tell the students to draw what the water looked like when the drops first entered the water.

7. About 7–10 minutes after the drops were added, have the students make another drawing of their three cups.

8. Explain that the drops of coloring plunge into the water because of the force behind them, just like a diver going into the water. The drop of coloring is also pulled down by gravity. Tell the students to look again at their cups of water and discuss any changes they see.

Closure

- Tell the students they are now going to do the Dance of the Molecules. Move the class to the playground or cafeteria.

    a. Gather the students together in a tight group to simulate molecules of water in a solid (ice). They should be squeezed tightly together and only able to jiggle slightly in place.

    b. Have them move further apart, holding hands to simulate molecules of water in a liquid.

    c. Finally, tell them to release hands and move far apart to simulate molecules of water in a vapor.

- Return to the classroom and have the students observe their cups of water. (*The coloring should be completely mixed in most of them by now.*) Look at the large jars and have the students explain what they see. Be sure they know that the molecules of hot water move faster than those in cold water. This is demonstrated by the coloring mixing faster in the hot water.

- Ask the students to answer the questions on their data sheet and then discuss these.

Dance of the Molecules *(cont.)*

Name:_____ Date:_____

Use the crayon to show what the food coloring did when it first was dropped into the cups of water.

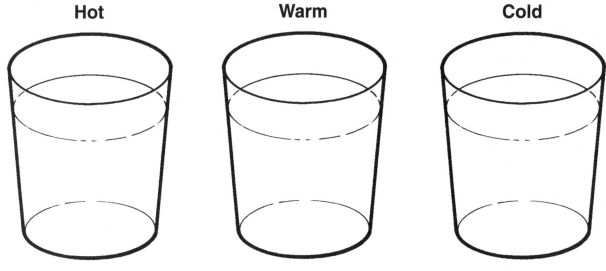

Hot   **Warm**   **Cold**

Use the crayon to show what the water looks like now that the food coloring has been in it for_____minutes.

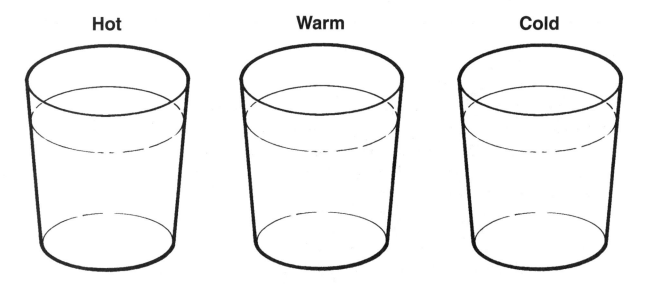

Hot   **Warm**   **Cold**

What made the coloring mix with the water? _____

_____

Why did the coloring spread at different rates in each of the cups? _____

_____

_____

Liquid + Solid = Gas

Teacher Information: *Investigating Chemical Changes of Matter*

Changes in the chemical composition of matter are called *chemical changes*. An example of this is when vinegar and baking soda are combined. The result is carbon dioxide gas. Another chemical change occurs when iron combines with oxygen in moist air to form iron oxide. This process is called *oxidation* and the result is the formation of rust.

The following activities are designed for young children to do and will enable them to observe safe chemical changes of matter.

Overview: *Students will create a chemical change by combining vinegar and baking soda. (**Caution:** To avoid students getting the mixture in their eyes, have them wear safety goggles and use only the small quantities of vinegar and baking soda suggested in this lesson.)*

Materials

- vinegar, baking soda, salt, sugar, flour
- trays
- small Styrofoam plates and plastic spoons
- 3 oz. (90 mL) paper cups
- Which One Fizzes? data sheet (page 63)
- dropper bottles or micropipets (can be ordered from Carolina Biological—Resources section)

Lesson Preparation

- Fill micropipets or dropper bottles with vinegar.
- Divide the cups into sets of four and mark them *Flour*, *Baking Soda*, *Sugar*, and *Salt*.
- Put about a teaspoon of each powder (e.g., flour) into the cups labeled with its name.
- Divide the plate into quarters with a marking pen and label the quarters with the powders' names.
- For each group of students prepare trays which will have a pipet of vinegar, set of four cups of the powders, plate, spoon, and paper towel.

Liquid + Solid = Gas *(cont.)*

Activity

Note: *If this lesson is too difficult for the level of the students, it may be done as a demonstration in small groups with the students recording their observations.*

1. Explain to students that they are going to do an experiment using four solids and one liquid. Tell them what these solids and liquid are. Caution them that when scientists do experiments they are very careful when mixing things. Also tell them that scientists watch closely to see what happens when things are mixed together.

2. Divide students into small groups, distribute the tray of materials, and familiarize the students with each item on the tray. (Have students practice first with water-filled pipets to learn to control the amount of drops.)

3. Give each student a copy of the data sheet and review it with them. Tell them that they are to rotate the responsibility of putting drops of vinegar on the white powders. Explain that you will tell them which powders to test. Have students use the spoon to place a very small amount of white powder in each quarter as you call out the powder, doing baking soda last.

4. Tell students to put a few drops of vinegar on the flour and then record what happens on their data sheet. Continue through the powders, saving baking soda for last.

Closure

• Have students share the results from their data sheets.

Extender Demonstration

To the Teacher: If appropriate for the students' level of understanding, demonstrate that the gas given off by the combination of vinegar and baking soda is carbon dioxide.

• You will need vinegar, baking soda, a wide-mouthed jar, a small clear cup, and three long matches.

• Place several teaspoons of baking soda into the jar. Light a match and hold it in the jar above the baking soda. (*The flame continues to burn.*)

• Pour tablespoon of vinegar into a small clear cup. Light a match and hold it in the cup above the vinegar. (*The flame continues to burn.*)

• Pour the vinegar over the baking soda. (*The bubbles and froth which result are a chemical change.*) When the gas bubbles appear, light another match and place it near the bubbles. (*The flame will be extinguished.*)

• Ask the students to tell what they observed, providing as much detail as they can. Tell them to think of reasons why the match went out.

• After they have the chance to discuss what they saw, explain that when the vinegar and baking soda mixed, they created a chemical change in both of them, which became a gas. This gas is carbon dioxide, which is heavier than the gas in the air, and it smothered the flame. Tell them that the flame continued to burn when placed over the baking soda and the vinegar before they were mixed since they do not give off carbon dioxide until they are mixed.

Which One Fizzes?

Name_____ Date _____

To the Students: Place a few drops of vinegar on the four powders and write what happens after you test each of them.

Powder	What Happens When Vinegar Is Added?
Flour	
Sugar	
Salt	
Baking Soda	

What Will Rust?

Overview: *Students will experiment with various types of metals to discover those which rust.*

Materials

- assorted small metal items (include steel wool)
- clear plastic cups or baby food jars
- water
- parent letter (page 65)
- Will This Rust? data sheet (page 66)
- *optional:* video camera

Lesson Preparation

- Send home the parent letter requesting a variety of metals for this activity.
- Begin this activity on a Monday since the experiment needs at least a week to yield results.

Activity

1. Ask the students if they have ever seen something which has rusted. Tell them that they are going to experiment with a variety of objects to see what will rust and what will not rust.

2. Distribute the parent letter and discuss the types of items students may bring for this experiment.

3. When students have brought their items to school, distribute a data sheet to each of them.

4. Tell the students to put their objects into the cup (jar) and then add just enough water to cover the bottom of the container. If students did not bring steel wool, prepare a jar to test it and assign a student to keep a record of it.

5. Show them how to complete the information on their data sheets, including the day, date, and time for their first drawing. Be sure they are recording as many details as possible.

6. Have students add to their records daily. You may want to make a video record of the changes daily so students can discuss the changes that occurred after the experiment is over.

Closure

- After at least five days, have the students sort the items into two groups, those which rusted and those which did not. List this information on the board. If a video record was made of the items, show it to the class. Ask students to see if they can find anything which those that rusted have in common. (*They should discover that these are all metal but that not all items rusted.*)
- Have students test the items which rusted with a magnet to see if it will pick them up. (*They will be attracted to a magnet since the metals which rusted have iron in them.*)
- After the students test the metals that rusted with their magnets, tell them the metal is iron.
- Tell students to look for signs of rusting metal at school and home and have them share their discoveries with the rest of the class.

Parent Letter for Rusting Test

Date_____

Dear Parents:

We are learning about the chemical properties of matter and will be doing experiments to discover what type of matter rusts. Your child has been requested to bring in some type of matter to test. These should be small items which will fit into a baby food jar. We plan to put water into the jar with the object and let the item sit for a week to see if it will rust. We will test items made of metal, glass, plastic, cork, and a variety of other material. Each student will keep a daily record of the changes they see in the items they are testing.

Some suggestions for the items you might send with your child follow:

- aluminum foil
- bottle caps
- coin
- steel nail
- paper clip

- steel wool
- pebble
- aluminum nail
- marble
- cork

Students are encouraged to bring something unusual to test.

Thank you for helping make our experiment interesting. You are welcome to join our class to look at the results of our experiment on_____.

Sincerely,

Will This Rust?

Name:_____ Date: _____

I am testing_____to see if it will rust.

Draw a picture of the thing you are testing every day. Color the picture as carefully as possible to show what the object and water look like. Be sure to write the day, date, and time under each drawing.

Day:_____   Day:_____   Day:_____

Date:_____   Date:_____   Date:_____

Time:_____   Time:_____   Time:_____

Day:_____   Day:_____   Day:_____

Date:_____   Date:_____   Date:_____

Time:_____   Time:_____   Time:_____

Tell what happened to the thing you were testing.

_____

_____

_____

Food + Oxygen = Oxidation

— Teacher Information —

The chemical change causing iron to rust is a process called *oxidation*. Something very similar happens in some types of food, such as white potatoes and apples. When the chemicals within these foods are exposed to the atmosphere, they combine with the oxygen—that is, they *oxidize*.

Overview: *Students will observe potatoes and apples as they oxidize.*

Materials

- white potatoes
- lemon juice in squeezable container
- Will It Change? data sheet (page 68)
- apples
- paper plates

Lesson Preparation

- Prepare two paper plates for each group, one marked "With Lemon Juice" and the other "No Lemon Juice."
- Just before the activity begins, cut slices of potatoes and apples so each group will receive two samples of each food. Keep the food in a covered container.

Activity (Adjust the level of discussion as needed.)

1. Discuss the results of the activity Will It Rust? in which the students observed various materials immersed in water. Tell them that the iron rusted because of a chemical change when it was exposed to moisture and oxygen in the air.

2. Say that some foods will also have a chemical reaction that changes them when cut open so oxygen from the air comes in contact with them. Explain that students are going to watch what happens to some food and make a record of the changes they see.

3. Divide students into small groups and give each two paper plates with a slice of potato and apple on each. Add a few drops of lemon juice to each slice on the plate marked "Lemon Juice."

4. Distribute the data sheet and discuss it with the students to be sure they know what to do.

   To the Teacher: This activity requires that drawings be made of the food when first exposed to air and again two and four hours later. A last drawing is made the next day. Set a timer for the recording intervals to remind students to observe food samples and record results.

Closure

- Have each group share the results of their observations. (*The apple and potato should have turned brown. Slices with lemon juice on them should show less discoloration.*)
- Explain that the lemon juice adds another chemical to the potato and apple that prevents the oxygen from reacting with the chemicals in the food.

Extender

- Have the students test other types of fruits and vegetables (e.g., radish, pear).

Will It Change?

Name: _____ Date: _____

To the Student: You are going to test apple and potato slices to observe what happens when they are left in the open air. Be sure that you make the drawings of your observations with lots of details to show what you see happening.

Item	What It Looks Like			
	Beginning	After 2 Hours	After 4 Hours	The Next Day
Apple				
Apple with Lemon				
Potato				
Potato with Lemon				

Tasty Chemical Changes

— Teacher Information —

Cooking is really chemical changes of matter. When various chemicals are combined, they can create pleasing flavors as well as nutritional food.

This lesson serves as a culminating activity for the study of matter.

Overview: *Students will combine a variety of matter to make pancakes.*

Materials

- ingredients for pancakes (see recipe)
- electric skillet or griddle for pancakes
- mixing bowl
- paper plates
- cotton swabs
- magnifier for each student
- Tasty Chemical Changes data sheet (page 71)
- cooking oil or spray
- measuring cups and spoons
- wire whip or electric beater
- plastic forks
- 1-ounce (30 mL) cups
- *optional:* syrup for pancakes

Lesson Preparation

- Set up cooking stations under the supervision of adults or older students. Each of these should have a skillet or griddle, spatula, cooking oil or spray, and paper plates for serving.
- Put tiny samples of the solid ingredients (sour cream, flour, baking soda, salt, cottage cheese) on paper plates for each student.
- Mix up an egg and divide it among the small cups.
- Make a large copy of the recipe to display during this lesson.

Sour Cream Cottage Cheese Pancakes

Ingredients

$^{3}/_{4}$ cup (180 mL) sour cream
2 eggs
$^{1}/_{2}$ cup (120 mL) cottage cheese

$^{1}/_{2}$ cup (120 mL) flour
$^{1}/_{2}$ teaspoon (2.5 mL) baking powder
$^{1}/_{2}$ teaspoon (2.5 mL) salt

Instructions

- Put sour cream and eggs into the bowl and mix until creamy.
- Add cottage cheese and continue to mix.
- Mix in flour, baking powder, and salt until batter is smooth.
- Let batter stand for 10 minutes. (The chemical reaction between the sour cream and baking soda will create air bubbles and make the pancakes light and fluffy.)
- Bake on lightly greased griddle or skillet.
- Yield: 12 4" pancakes. Increase recipe as needed.

Tasty Chemical Changes *(cont.)*

Activity

To the Teacher: Students may need to work in small groups with an adult or older student to record the information about the matter on their data sheets. This activity can be divided into two sessions—one day for completing the data sheet and the second for making the food.

1. Explain to the students that they are going to help mix different types of matter together to make a chemical change and create something to eat. Tell them that they are going to follow a recipe to make pancakes.

2. Have the students wash their hands, stressing it is important to have clean hands when preparing or eating food.

3. Give each student a data sheet, magnifier, and a plate with samples of the solid ingredients. Distribute the samples of the solids. Tell them to wet one finger and press it into the salt. Have them examine it with a magnifier and record what it looks like. They should rub it between their fingers to feel it. They should also smell and taste each of the samples.

4. Help them describe the salt on their data sheet.

5. Let the students continue this with each of the other solid ingredients. They can taste one of the curds of the cottage cheese. Discuss how to classify the cottage cheese as a solid, a liquid, or both.

6. Distribute cups of the egg. Let them conduct all the tests on the egg, *with the exception of tasting it.*

7. Select volunteers to take turns serving as helpers to make the batter as you mix it. Let them help measure the ingredients into the large bowl and mix it. Increase the recipe to accommodate the number of students.

8. Ask them what happened when they mixed vinegar and baking soda in the Liquid + Solid = Gas activity. (*Bubbles were formed.*) Explain that the batter needs to sit for 10 minutes while the same chemical reaction is taking place between the baking soda and sour cream. Ask them what they think the bubbles will do to the pancakes. (*They make them lighter like a sponge.*)

9. Distribute the batter into a bowl for each cooking station. Assign the students to the various stations to assist and observe the baking process.

Closure

- Let students eat their "science experiment." Have them complete their data sheets.

- Send the recipe home with students so their families may enjoy it.

Tasty Chemical Changes *(cont.)*

Name:_____ Date: _____

To the Student: Fill in the chart below to give information about the matter which will be used to make the pancakes.

Matter (Ingredients)	How It Looks, Feels, Smells, and Tastes	State of Matter (solid, liquid or gas)
salt		
flour		
baking soda		
sour cream		
cottage cheese		
eggs (Do not taste)		

Tell about the way the pancakes look, feel, smell, and taste after they are cooked.

_____

_____

_____

Draw a picture of what the pancake looked like after it was cooked.

Wind Machines

── Teacher Information ──

Machines do work for us and thus make life easier. Some tasks would be impossible to do without machines. We use machines all the time; without them our lives would be very different. This series of lessons is designed to let students experience a variety of machines. It is not important that students understand the laws of physics which govern these machines, but they should have the chance to enjoy experimenting with them.

We cannot see air, but we can feel the movement of air called wind. Wind is caused by the sun's uneven heating of the atmosphere. Warm air rises and is replaced by denser cold air, thus causing circulation. The wind has great energy to make things move and to make machines run. Windmills convert the wind's power to pump water or generate electricity. Windmills most likely originated in Iran in the A.D. 600s and were used to grind grain. Dutch windmills were widely used in the Netherlands to drain water from the land. Wind turbines are used today near Palm Springs, California, to drive generators to make electricity.

Overview: *Students will see how wind power can drive the windmill.*

Materials

- pencil with eraser
- pinwheel pattern (page 73)
- clear tape
- T-pin
- colored markers or crayon
- construction paper or cardstock

Lesson Preparation

- Copy the pinwheel pattern onto paper (*optional:* cardstock or colored construction paper).

Activity

1. Cut out the square. Decorate the pinwheel on both sides. Straight or spiral lines coming from the center to the outer edge will appear to change when the pinwheel spins. Coloring sections in different colors will create a blending of the colors as they spin.

2. Cut along the solid lines. Push the pin through the dots at the tips of each blade of the pinwheel and then into the center hole. Push the pin into the pencil eraser. Cut two thin strips of clear tape about 1 inch (2.5 cm) long. Roll the tape around the pin between both sides of the pinwheel so it will not rub against the pencil or pinhead.

3. Blow on the blades of the pinwheel and watch to see what happens. Try turning the pinwheel at different angles as you blow to notice the difference.

Closure

- Have students make pinwheels with only two blades, using the same square shape. Does the speed of the pinwheel change?
- Find pictures and information on windmills and wind turbines for students to examine.

Wind Machines *(cont.)*

Pinwheel Pattern

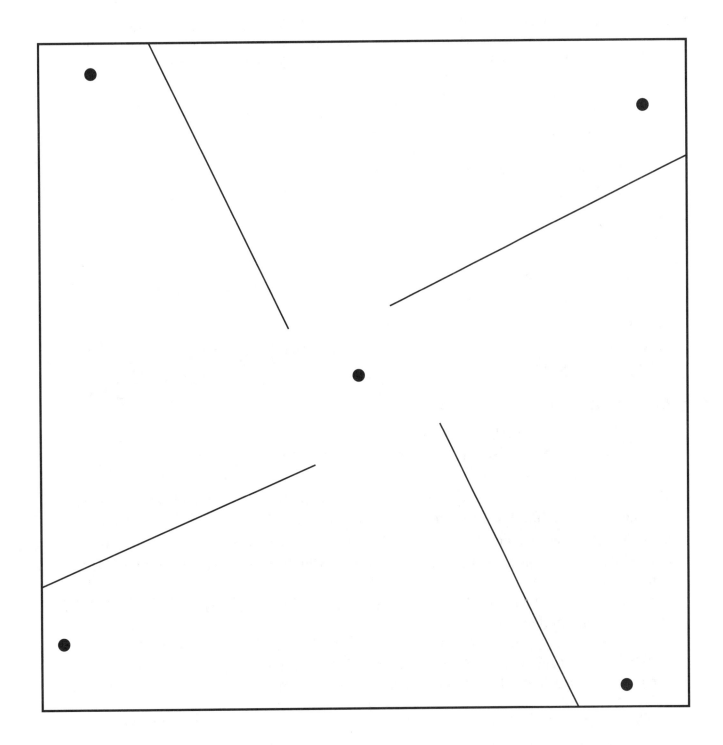

Turbines

— Teacher Information —

A *turbine* is a set of blades which are rotated by pressure from water, steam, gas, or wind. Wind rotates the turbine in jet airplane engines and helps it run. In making electricity, steam or water is sent through the turbine to change *kinetic energy* (energy of movement) into *mechanical energy* (energy in the form of mechanical power). For example, turbines are rotated by water at Niagara Falls and Hoover Dam to generate electricity (mechanical power). Waterwheels are the earliest form of turbines, dating back to the ancient Greeks about 2,000 years ago.

The *rotor* is the rotating part of a turbine. It consists of a disk or wheel mounted on an *axle*. The axle can be vertical or horizontal. The wheel has curved blades or buckets around the edges. When fluid or wind passes through the turbine, it pushes the blades, the wheel, and the axle. The axle is connected through gears to an electric generator, air compressor, or other machine.

Overview: *Students will create a model of a simple turbine and test it.*

Materials

- turbine pattern (page 75), one per student
- piece of cardstock 8.5" x 11" (21 cm x 27.5 cm)
- drinking straw
- scissors
- thin, long knitting needle

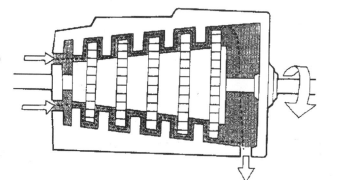

Lesson Preparation

- Copy the rotor pattern onto cardstock.
- Poke a hole in the center so it is large enough to push the straw through and hold it tightly.

Activity

1. Cut out the rotor. Place a straw through the center hole so it fits tightly.
2. Slightly bend the blades of the rotor along the dotted lines so all point in the same direction.
3. Place the knitting needle through the straw, which should fit loosely enough so that it is free to turn.
4. The straw is the axle for the rotor blades. The knitting needle is the shaft for the axle. This all forms a simple turbine.
5. This turbine model will rotate as air or water is pushed over it. One way to do this is to hold the shaft horizontal and walk in a straight line. Another way is run water from a faucet over the blades. The tagboard will get wet but should last long enough to show how a waterwheel works.

Closure

- Have the students compare the turbines to the pinwheels. Both work on the same principle.
- Use the Teacher Information to explain how turbines and rotors work.
- Find information and pictures about water mills and other types of turbines to show the students.

Turbines *(cont.)*

Directions: Cut out the rotor.

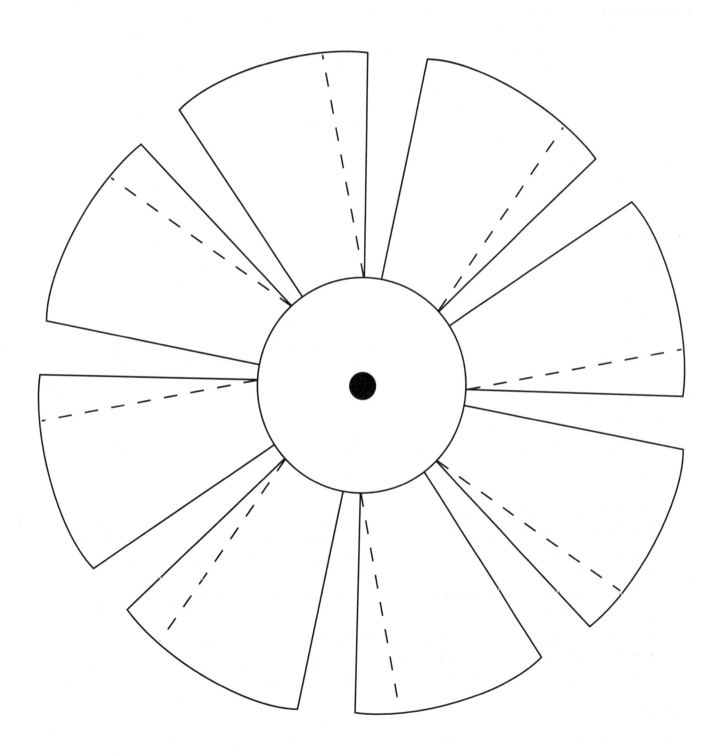

A Reaction Engine

── Teacher Information ──

The *reaction engine* takes its name from Newton's third law: For every *action* there is an equal and opposite *reaction*. In this case, the action is the water squirting out of the container. It produces a reaction force on the container, causing it to move in the opposite direction of the water. It is very much like a balloon that is rapidly losing air. When you blow up a balloon, the air pressure within is greater than the atmospheric pressure around it. When the balloon is not sealed, the air will rush out (action force). The air pushes on the balloon (reaction force), and the balloon moves in the opposite direction of the air flow.

An ancient Greek scientist, Hero of Alexandria, constructed a reaction engine using a sphere mounted on top of a water kettle. When the water was heated to a boil, steam was fed into the sphere by pipes and escaped through L-shaped tubes on opposite sides of the sphere. This allowed the gas to escape and provided the thrust to rotate the sphere.

Overview: *Students will use simple models of two reaction engines.*

Materials

- 6 plastic water bottles
- 12-inch (30 cm) long string
- masking tape
- awl or nail
- buttons or washers
- water

Lesson Preparation

- Poke a hole in the centers of the water-bottle lids with the awl or nail and thread a string through the lid. Tie a button or washer on the end of the string to prevent it from pulling out of the lid.

- Use the awl or nail to poke holes near the bottom of the six water bottles. Put a different number of holes in each bottle. There should be 1, 2, 3, 4, 5, or 6 holes, evenly spaced about 1 inch (3 cm) from the bottom. Mark the number of holes on the side of each bottle with permanent felt pen.

- Since this activity can be messy, it is best to conduct it outside.

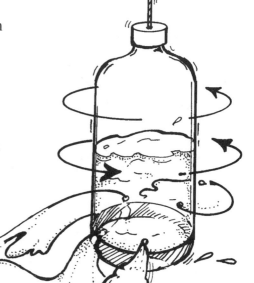

A Reaction Engine *(cont.)*

Activity

1. Put masking tape around the bottom of the bottle to cover the holes and fill the bottle. Be sure to fold over the end of the tape to make it possible to pull it off more easily.

2. Put the cap on but not too tightly so some air can flow in.

3. Hold the bottle at arm's length by the end of the string while a partner pulls off the tape.

4. Watch closely to see what happens as the water pours out.

Closure

- Line up the students with the bottles in order of the number of holes in the bottles. Have the students compare the differences in the movement of the bottles. Ask the following questions and have the students repeat the experiment before answering them. Be sure each bottle has the same amount of water in it when answering question #2.

    1. Which bottle spins fastest? (*The bottle with only one hole in it will spin fastest because it has the greatest force of water from a single hole.*)

    2. Which bottle spins the longest? (*The bottle with only one hole will spin longer since it takes more time to empty its fuel.*)

    3. What happens as the water level drops? (*The bottle slows as the water level drops, due to decreased water pressure.*)

    4. In which direction do the bottles spin? (*All bottles spin in the same direction, counterclockwise.*)

    5. What happens if the lid is on tight? (*The bottle will not spin. This is due to the lack of air pressure above the water level since the air cannot flow into the bottle at the top.*)

- Use the Teacher Information to explain how this idea was used by Hero to make a sphere spin. Explain that the steam engines used in boats and trains use this same principle to move things.

Ball Bearings

Teacher Information

Ball bearings are often used as a means to provide smooth motion between two surfaces and to cut down on friction. Because both surfaces are moving together, rolling friction is far less than the friction between two flat surfaces.

An excellent teacher reference is *The Way Things Work* (see Resources section). This delightful book can also be shared with students to help them understand ball bearings as well as many of the other simple machines used in lessons in this section.

Overview: *Students discover how ball bearings make movement.*

Materials

- two empty cans of the same size (e.g., soup, coffee) with good ridges around them
- enough marbles to cover the bottom of the cans
- rocks or sand
- items which use ball bearings (e.g., roller skates)

Activity

1. Place one can upside down and put the other can on top of it. Have the students see what happens when they try to turn the one on top. Have them fill the top can with rocks or sand to make it heavier and try this again.

2. Empty the can and this time place marbles on the bottom of the can which is inverted. Place the empty can on top and turn it. Fill the top can with rocks or sand and repeat this motion.

3. Have students compare these and explain what the difference is.

Closure

- Have students compare what happened with and without the marbles. Ask them the following questions:

   1. Which filled can was easier to turn—the one with the marbles or the one without? (*The one with marbles was easier.*)

   2. Explain why you think this happened. (*The marbles roll around and help move the heavy can on top. Without the marbles, the cans are rubbing together, and the friction between the cans makes it difficult to move them.*)

- Show the items which use ball bearings and discuss how they help the equipment work easier.

Center of Gravity

— Teacher Information —

An object acts as though all of its weight is concentrated at one point. This is known as its *center of gravity*. It is likely to be located at the part where most of the weight is. An object will tend to move until its center of gravity is at its lowest possible point.

The center of gravity on a ball is at its very center. It is balanced at any point since rolling neither raises nor lowers its center of gravity. When additional material (e.g., clay) is added to the ball, however, the center of gravity is changed, and the ball will tend to roll until the extra weight is at its lowest possible point.

Overview: *Students will experiment with various sizes of balls to change their centers of gravity.*

Materials

- balls of various sizes (from Ping-Pong ball to soccer ball)
- clay or modeling dough (larger balls will require more)
- data sheet On the Ball (page 80)

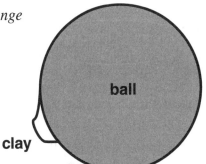

Activity

1. Divide the students into groups and give each group a ball. Let them roll the balls in straight lines on a hard surface to observe how they move.

2. Discuss how the balls behaved as they were rolled. (*They stayed in straight lines.*)

3. Give each group some of the clay or modeling dough. Explain that they are to add a lump of clay to the balls on one spot only and then roll the balls along a straight line again.

4. Discuss the changes they observed. (*The balls could not roll in a straight line.*)

5. Let the students exchange balls and try this with a different-sized ball. Compare the results. (*They will find that all balls do the same thing.*)

6. Distribute the data sheet and let the students complete the first part.

7. Ask them what they think will happen when they add different amounts of clay to their balls.

8. Let each group use their ball and clay and conduct the tests, recording their data in pictures and writing on the chart.

Closure

- Discuss what the students saw happening as they conducted tests on the balls. (*Balls will roll in a circle if a large enough amount of clay is added, a larger circle with less clay. They will wobble back-and-forth with two lumps of clay. With three . . . .*)

- Let students make drawings of what they think is happening. Most will not know how to explain this but may come up with interesting ideas to share. If explanations can be tested, have the students do so.

- Do not tell students about the center of balance just yet but go on to the next two lessons to add to their understanding of the content of center of gravity.

On the Ball

To the Student: Make drawings of what happened to your ball when you rolled it without a lump of clay and with a lump of clay on it.

Without Clay	With One Lump of Clay

Follow the directions on the chart below to test what happens to the ball when you add clay to it.

Add	Tell how the ball rolled and draw a picture of this.
one large lump	
one small lump	
two lumps of clay— one on each side of the ball	
a lump of clay in three spots	

- Why does the ball roll in a different way when you add lumps of clay to it?
- Write about this on the other side of this paper and make a drawing to go along with your explanation.

Who Will Win the Race?

── Teacher Information ──

Rolling speed is directly related to the distribution of weight around an object's center of gravity, known as its *moment of inertia*. The center of gravity in a solid sphere, disk, and hoop is the geometric center. But the weight is distributed differently in all three of these objects. The hoop has all its weight away from the center of gravity and thus has the greatest moment of inertia. The solid sphere has the smallest moment of inertia since its weight is most closely distributed around it center of gravity. The closer the mass or weight of an object is to its center of gravity, the smaller its moment of inertia and the faster it can rotate. In a race between a solid sphere, a disk, and a hoop, the sphere will always win.

Overview: *Students will test various solid spheres, disks, and hoops to find which rolls fastest.*

Materials

- solid spheres: marble, golf ball, ball bearing
- disks: jar lid, plastic plate, coaster, pizza cardboard
- hoops: large rubber washers, bicycle tire, Hula-Hoop
- Which Will Win? data sheet, page 82 (to be used with higher level students)

Lesson Preparation

- Gather as many different solid spheres, disks, and hoops as possible.
- Find an area where the objects can be tested, such as a paved, slightly inclined straight path.

Activity

1. Tell students they will test round objects to discover how they roll and which rolls the fastest.

2. Divide the students into small groups and give each a solid sphere, a hoop, and a disk.

3. Give each group a copy of the data sheet. Ask parent volunteers to help those who need it.

4. Have students complete the first part of the sheet to guess which of the objects will roll down the hill the fastest.

5. At the starting lines for the beginning of the race, explain that all three objects must be released at the same time. Let them practice this several times before the test. The greatest challenge will be keeping the hoops rolling in a straight line.

6. Let students take turns testing their three objects and recording results. Have them do the tests three times. Tell the students to answer the questions on the data sheet.

Closure

- Let students share the results of their tests. Ask them what conclusions they wrote on data sheets. (*The solid sphere wins the race, even if smaller than the other round objects.*) It is not necessary that students understand exactly what causes this.

- Have students test other objects such as cylinders (film canisters) filled and unfilled, hollow balls, and cardboard tubes.

Which Will Win?

To the Students: You are going to roll a solid sphere, hoop, and disk down a hill to see which rolls the fastest. Before testing them, put an X beside the one you think will win the race. Start rolling the sphere, hoop, and disk down the hill at the same time to see which will win. Put an X beside the one which won in the race under Trial #1. Do the test two more times and put an X beside the one which won each race.

Rolling Tests of Three Round Objects				
Objects Tested	**Which Should Win?**	**Which Does Win?**		
		Trial 1	**Trial 2**	**Trial 3**
1. solid sphere				
2. hoop				
3. disk				

Which object was the fastest in the races?_____

Which object was the next fastest in the races?_____

Tell how the objects rolled and then make a drawing to show what this looked like.

1. Solid Sphere_____

   _____

2. Hoop_____

   _____

3. Disk _____

   _____

What did you discover after doing the tests?_____

Static Cling

── Teacher Information ──

Electricity is sometimes classified as *static electricity* and *current electricity*. Both are made up of the same kind of particles. Static electricity consists of electrons or ions that do not move. Current electricity is made up of moving electrons or ions. Almost all the electricity we use is current electricity.

An object becomes electrically charged if it gains or loses electrons. For example, if a glass rod is rubbed with a piece of silk cloth, the rod loses electrons and becomes positively charged. You can create static electricity by running an inflated balloon over your hair briskly on a dry day. Your hair loses electrons and becomes positively charged. The balloon gains electrons and becomes negatively charged. The static electricity may make your hair crackle as you rub it with the balloon.

Static electricity can be investigated using a variety of materials which can be given a static charge. This is most effective during dry weather, or in a room which is being heated or air conditioned and, therefore, has less moisture in the air.

This series of lessons lets students have fun exploring static electricity.

Overview: *Students will investigate static electricity.*

Materials

- balloons
- string
- parent letter (page 84)

Activity

1. Ask the students if they have ever been shocked after walking across a rug on a dry day. Explain that this is called *static electricity*. Tell the students that they are going to investigate this type of electricity.

2. Give each student an inflated balloon tied to a string (or let them inflate their own). Demonstrate how to build a static charge by vigorously rubbing the balloon over your hair. As you pull the balloon away, some of the hair will begin to stand upright. Have the students try this with their own hair.

3. Have them rub the balloon against their hair again. Tell them to see if they can stick the balloon on the wall. (If they have created an electrical charge, it should. If not, have them rub the balloon again.)

4. After charging the balloon against their hair, let them hold it by the string and bring it near another student's balloon. (The balloons may pull together or push apart.)

Closure

- With each child, send home a deflated balloon and the letter on the next page so they can continue to investigate static electricity at home.

Parent Letter for Static Electricity Homework

Date_____

Dear Parents:

Your child has had fun investigating static electricity by using an inflated balloon today at school. Please help him or her to inflate a balloon and tie it to a string. Let him or her show you what the class has been doing with the balloon in the classroom.

They have been told to try finding what they can rub against their balloons at home to see if they can get them to stick to a wall or their clothing. You may want to help them find a variety of things to use to build a static charge, such as the carpet, upholstery, drapes, or a pet's fur.

On the lines below, your child should write about what he or she discovered with the balloon and then draw a picture of the experiment. Please have your child bring this paper back to class to share with us tomorrow.

Sincerely,

_____

_____

_____

_____

_____

_____

_____

Make a drawing of your balloon experiment here.

The Magic of Static

── Teacher Information ──

Static electricity can be investigated using a variety of materials which can be given a static charge. This is most effective during dry weather or in a room which is being heated or air conditioned and, therefore, has less moisture in the air.

Overview: *Students will have fun investigating the magic of static electricity.*

Materials

- balloons
- small wool duster or piece of wool cloth
- 8" x 10" clear plastic boxes used for pictures (available where picture frames are sold)
- paper circles from a hole punch (*optional:* confetti)
- Styrofoam packing peanuts or pieces
- bottles of water
- buckets or basins
- data sheets and instructions for each workstation (pages 86–89)

Lesson Preparation

- Set up stations for students to rotate through using the information on the data sheets. If possible, set up duplicates of each station to have fewer students at each of them.
- Test each of the stations and adjust the setup as needed to match the students' ability levels.
- Establish a rotation system which will allow at least 15 minutes at each station.
- Arrange for adult or older student volunteers to be assigned to each station to assist the students as needed, if they are not able to work alone.

Activity

1. Introduce the students to the stations. Explain the instructions which they are to follow as they work at each of them. Demonstrate how they are to use the materials at the various stations.

2. Divide the students into groups of three or four students and assign each group to begin at a different station. Allow sufficient time for each group to explore the materials at their station before moving them on to the next. This lesson should be spread over more than one day to enable the students to benefit from experimenting with the materials and sharing their ideas.

Closure

- When all students have visited each of the stations, have each group demonstrate one of the exciting new discoveries they made as they investigated static electricity.
- Invite another group of students to visit the classroom and have your students show them the discoveries they made about static electricity.

Station 1: Popping Paper

Materials

- clear plastic box
- about 40 paper circles from a hole punch

Setup

- Put the paper circles on the table top and put the clear plastic box over them.

How to Do the Test

1. Have one person hold the plastic box down over the paper circles.
2. Rub the top of the plastic box with your hand as fast as you can.

Watch to See What Happens

1. Do any circles begin to jump?_____
2. Are there any circles standing on edge?_____
3. Do any circles leap up and hang from the box?_____
4. Are there any sounds being made?_____
5. If you heard sounds, what did they sound like?_____

Try something new and then make a picture of what you discovered.

Station 2: Jumping Peanuts

Materials

- inflated balloon
- handful of Styrofoam packing peanuts
- wool duster or wool cloth

Setup

- Put a balloon, wool duster or cloth, and Styrofoam packing peanuts on the table.

How to Do the Test

1. Rub the balloon with the wool duster.
2. Hold the balloon near the peanuts.

Watch to See What Happens

1. Do the peanuts jump on the balloon?_____
2. Shake the balloon gently. Do the peanuts stick to it?_____
3. What happens if you pull or push the peanuts around on the balloon?

_____

Try something new and then make a picture of what you discovered.

Station 3: Weird Water

Materials

- inflated balloon
- wool duster or wool cloth
- bottle of water
- bucket or basin
- towels

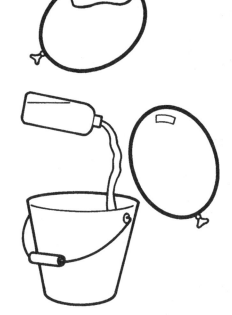

Setup

- Put all the materials on the table.

How to Do the Test

1. Rub the balloon with the wool duster.

2. Pour the water slowly into the bucket. Hold the balloon near the water.

Watch to See What Happens

1. Did the water run straight down from the bottle?_____

2. Do this same test two more times and see what happens. Be sure to refill the bottle and to rub the balloon with the duster each time. Tell what happens each time.

_____

Try something new and then make a picture of what you discovered.

Station 4: Dancing Balloons

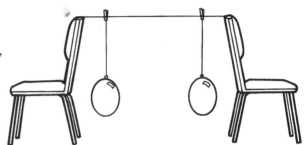

Materials

- 2 inflated balloons of different colors, each on a string
- wool duster or wool cloth
- 3 feet (90 cm) string
- 2 clamp-on clothespins
- 2 chairs

Setup

- Place the chairs close together and stretch the string taut between them. Put the clothespins on it two feet (60 cm) apart. Hang the balloons from the clothespins so they are level with each other.

How to Do the Test

1. Rub one balloon with the wool duster.

Watch to See What Happens

1. What happens after only one balloon was rubbed with the duster?

_____

2. What happens if both balloons are rubbed?

_____

3. What happens when you put your hand between the balloons?

_____

Try something new and then make a picture of what you discovered.

What Sticks to a Magnet?

Teacher Information

Magnets will stick only to items which have *iron*, *cobalt*, or *nickel* in them. Cobalt and nickel are rarely used in common metal items; therefore, most objects which stick to magnets contain iron.

Overview: *Students will test various materials to tell what can be picked up by a magnet.*

Materials

- circular magnets with a hole in the center for each student (See Resources.)
- assorted small objects of wood, paper, glass, cork, various metals (including coins)
- *optional:* samples of magnetite and metallic rocks such as galena and pyrite (See Resources.)

Lesson Preparation

- Divide the materials into eight containers, each holding samples of the same materials.

Activity

1. Ask students where they have seen magnets used. Let them share these ideas in small groups.
2. Ask what they know about magnets, listing ideas on the board.
3. Divide students into eight groups and provide them with the containers of materials.
4. Have students divide the objects into three piles. One pile should be items which they think will stick to a magnet, a second pile is for those which they think will not, and the third pile is for items which they are not sure about.
5. After students divide all items into the three piles, ask them to tell how they decided which would stick to a magnet. (*Most will say that they chose anything metal for the "yes" pile.*)
6. List the items on the board under the three headings—**Yes**, **No**, and **?**. There will be some disagreement among the groups. List those items in question under more than one heading.
7. Distribute a magnet to each student to check the objects, placing them in new piles.
8. Discuss what they discover and change the objects on the board to classify them correctly.
9. Ask students if all metal objects stick to magnets. (*Very few stick—not even the nickels. Items of gold or silver will not stick to magnets either, even though they are metal.*)

Closure

- Let the students move around the classroom to test as many objects as they can to see if they will stick to their magnets. (*Most do not.*) Do not permit them near computers for this test.
- Have them share some of the unusual items to which their magnets will stick. (If you have a ceramic sink in the classroom and the magnet sticks to it, it is cast iron coated with ceramic.)
- Tell students to find three places in their homes where magnets are in use and report this to the class the next day. Urge them to find magnets which are not very obvious.

Does One Magnet Stick to Another?

---- **Teacher Information** ----

Magnets have two poles which are designated *north* (positive) and *south* (negative). Opposite poles of two magnets will *attract*; poles which are the same will *repel* each other. Use simple terms with younger students when referring to names of the magnetic poles, as well as their reactions. Students can more easily comprehend north and south than positive and negative when talking about magnetic poles. Using *push* and *pull* to describe the repelling and attracting forces may be wise at first, since that describes what they will feel. Use the terms *repel* and *attract* when, or if, they are ready for them. It is important that they understand the concept, not the terminology.

Overview: *Students will learn about repelling and attracting forces of magnets.*

Materials

- circular magnets with holes in the center for each student (used in previous lesson)
- wooden skewers which will fit through the hole in the magnets

Activity

1. Ask students the results of homework on finding magnets in use around their homes. Then distribute a circular shaped magnet to each student.

2. Divide the students into small groups and let them "play" with the magnets. This will let them discover the magnets' properties. Allow at least 10 minutes for this. Let the students learn through their own investigations rather than giving them information.

3. After they have investigated their magnets, encourage each group to share what they discovered and demonstrate some of their findings to the class.

4. Distribute a wooden skewer to each group and have them stack their magnets on it. Ask them what they find. (*When two magnets are placed on the skewer, they will stick or push apart.*)

5. Ask each group to stack the magnets on the skewer so they all push away from the each other. Let them discover how this can be done. Have them push down on the stack of circular magnets to feel the force between them. Explain that this is called *magnetic force* and is invisible. Tell older students when the magnets push apart they are *repelling*. Write the term on the board.

6. Have students rearrange stacking so all magnets attract each other. Let them feel the force by trying to pull the magnets apart. Introduce the term *attraction* to older students.

Closure

- Ask students to pretend each hand is a magnet. Have them show you the repelling and attracting forces with their hands by pushing them apart and pulling them together.
- Have the students make drawings of two magnets to show them pushing (repelling) apart. Let them make other drawings to illustrate two magnets pulling together (attracting).

Magnetic Madness

— Teacher Information —

Poles are at the ends of bar and horseshoe magnets and on either side of rectangular or circular magnets. Magnetic poles will shift in magnets which are stored improperly. Bar magnets should be laid flat, side by side with opposite poles together. A steel "keeper" is needed to join each pair at both ends to keep the magnetic field from drifting. Keepers usually come with new bar magnets, but steel nails will work. Lay horseshoe magnets in pairs with opposite poles touching. Stack circular or rectangular magnets with opposite poles together. Marble magnets may be stored in circles in an aluminum pie pan or kept in the original plastic container.

Overview: *Students will investigate a variety of magnets.*

Materials

- variety of magnet types and sizes (e.g., horseshoe, circular, bar, and magnetic marbles)
- paper clips and 10-inch (25 cm) pieces of string

Lesson Preparation

- Place the magnets in containers to be distributed to groups of students and then exchanged. Tape to each container a list of the magnets in it. This list can be quickly checked when all are returned.

Activity

1. Review what was learned in previous lessons about the properties of magnets.
2. Divide students into groups and distribute a container of magnets to each. Let students investigate the repelling and attracting forces of all magnets. Magnetic marbles are especially exciting. (**Note:** After students work with the marbles, pry one open to show the cylindrical magnet inside the plastic sphere. This magnet is like a bar magnet with north and south poles.)
3. After students investigate their magnets, distribute 10 paper clips and a piece of string to each group. Let them use these with the magnets to investigate further.
4. Challenge students to find the strongest magnet in their collection. Ask them to lay out the magnets in order of strongest to weakest. Now, tell them to test their magnets to see if they put them in the right order. (**Note:** This can be done in a variety of ways. Students can see how many paper clips each magnet can hold or can tie a paper clip to the string and find out which magnet can attract it from the greatest distance.)

Closure

- Have each group show their strongest magnet and how they proved its strength. (They may be surprised to learn that the largest magnet in their collection may not be the strongest.)
- Send home a note to parents, requesting that they lend magnets which they may have at home to the students for this study.

Will Magnetism Pass Through Everything?

——— Teacher Information ———

Magnetism is a strong force that passes through most materials, including air, water, paper, metal, wood, skin, bone, and glass. If a magnet is placed near iron or steel, however, the metal becomes temporarily magnetized and prevents the magnetism from passing through.

Overview: *Students will experiment to see if magnetism will pass through a variety of materials and thicknesses.*

Materials

- circular magnets
- strong magnets like cow magnets (see Resources section) or ones from a speaker or engine
- clear 9-oz. (270 mL) plastic tumblers half full of water

- paper clips
- 10-inch (25.4 cm) lengths of string
- items to test: cardboard, thin paperback books, aluminum foil or pie pans, wood (ruler or desktop), metal soup cans

Activity

1. Write on the board: "Can magnetism pass through water, plastic, glass, air, paper, metal, wood, skin and bone?" (Do not suggest answers but let students design their own tests.)

2. Divide students into eight groups and distribute magnets, cups of water, paper clips, string, and the items to be tested.

3. Let students use the magnets and materials they have received to answer the question.

Possible Methods: *They can use their own hands to find if magnetism passes through skin and bone. The classroom window can be used to test glass. They can use the string tied to a paper clip and held a distance from the magnet to demonstrate the magnetic field travels through the air to attract it. Drop the paper clip into the cup of water and lower the magnet into the water. It should not touch the paper clip but be held above it to show that the magnetic force travels through the water.*

Closure

Ask the students if they found anything that could stop the magnetic field. (All items tested should let magnetism pass, except the tin can which has iron in it.)

- Let them demonstrate their tests to the rest of the class.

- If you have a powerful magnet, have a seated student place it beneath a thigh. Dangle a paper clip from a string above the thigh. The paper clip will be attracted to the magnet so that the string can be held at an angle rather than perpendicular to the leg. This will demonstrate that magnetism passes through the leg. Ask students if they can feel anything when the paper clip connects to the magnetic field. (*No, the magnetic field cannot be detected by the senses.*)

What Does the Magnetic Field Look Like?

Teacher Information

The magnetic field is invisible and has no taste, sound, or smell. It is possible to feel the magnetic field when two magnets are brought close together and repel or attract each other, but it is not possible to feel the magnetic field of a single magnet. The field is strongest at the tips of bar and horseshoe magnets.

The magnetic field can be made visible by outlining it with tiny pieces of iron called *iron filings*. The filings will form arcs between the poles on bar and horseshoe magnets or rings around the center of circular magnets. Filings will cluster and stand up, pointing in a perpendicular direction where the magnetic field is strongest. Iron filings are often mixed with the sand on school playgrounds. Sources of iron filings are eroded rocks which contain iron ore and micrometeorites, small as grains of sand, which constantly rain down through the atmosphere. Iron filings can be purchased or may be collected from the school sand.

Overview: *Students will see the magnetic fields of magnets.*

Materials

- iron filings (See Resources section.)
- variety of magnets including circular, bar, and horseshoe
- pieces of 5" x 8" (13 cm x 20 cm) thin cardboard
- small jars such as used for baby food
- old nylon pantyhose
- rubber bands
- 8 ½" x 11" (22 cm x 28 cm) piece of glass (may be from a picture frame)
- overhead projector
- aluminum pie pans

Lesson Preparation

- Make iron filing shakers by pouring about five tablespoons of iron filings into each baby-food jar. Stretch a piece of nylon stocking over the top and fasten with a rubber band.
- Practice before doing the demonstration for the students.

Demonstration

- Ask the students if they can smell, hear, taste, feel, or see the magnetic field. (*No*)
- Ask them if they have ever dropped a magnet into sand and seen tiny black pieces sticking to it.
- Tell students you are going to make the magnetic field visible for them, using these iron filings.
- Place a bar magnet on an overhead projector and cover it with a piece of glass. (**Note:** Support the glass above the magnet using lumps of clay or pencil erasers under the corners.)
- Gently shake the iron filings through the nylon mesh over the area of the magnet beneath the glass. The bar magnet and magnetic field surrounding it will be outlined with iron filings.
- Dump the filings onto a piece of paper. Place the horseshoe magnet beneath the glass. Sprinkle the filings over the horseshoe magnet to outline its magnetic field. Repeat this with a circular magnet.

What Does the Magnetic Field Look Like? *(cont.)*

Demonstration *(cont.)*

- Place two magnets (e.g., bar or circular) on the overhead stage so they will repel each other. Hold them in place with clay so they are separated. Place the glass sheet over them and sprinkle iron filings between them to outline the magnetic field. The filings will arc away from the ends of the magnets, showing the repelling force.

- Turn one of the magnets over so the magnets are now attracting. Hold them in place with clay and put the glass over them. Ask students to predict what the pattern of filings will look like between the magnets Sprinkle the iron filings over them. The filings will form arcs between the ends of the magnets, showing the attracting force.

Activity

1. Divide the students into eight groups and distribute magnets, a jar of iron filings, a piece of cardboard, aluminum pie pan, and a piece of newsprint to each group.

2. Tell the students to place their magnets in the pie pan, using just one magnet at first. They should put the cardboard over the magnet. One student should sprinkle iron filings over the cardboard and see the magnetic field outline which results.

3. Caution the students to keep the iron filings away from the magnet. Have them always dump the filings onto a piece of paper placed far away from the magnets.

4. Let students investigate different magnetic field patterns, using various magnets in repelling and attracting positions.

Closure

- Have students use the equipment and the overhead projector to demonstrate some of the interesting patterns they discovered.

bar magnet

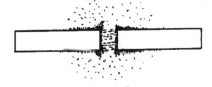

attracting

horseshoe magnet

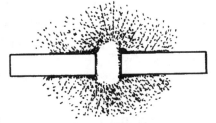

repelling

Making a Picture of the Magnetic Field

Teacher Information

Paper impregnated with a chemical which makes it sensitive to sunlight can be used to make prints of the patterns created when iron filings outline magnetic fields. This paper is safe and easy to use and creates a permanent record of the magnetic fields outlined by iron filings. This lesson must be done on a windless, sunny day. The students will create designs in the classroom and carry them out into the sunlight so the sun can bleach the paper, leaving the print of the iron-filing shadows.

Overview: *Students will make permanent pictures of various magnetic fields.*

Materials

- sun-sensitive paper (available from Delta Education in Resources section)
- assorted magnets, aluminum pie pan, and cardboard used in previous lesson
- iron filings in jars
- dishpan filled with water
- pieces of newspaper

Lesson Preparation

- Make sun prints of varieties of magnetic field patterns as models for the students:

  1. Place the magnet(s) in the aluminum pie pan, covering them with the cardboard and adding a piece of sun-sensitive paper, blue side up, over the cardboard.

  2. Sprinkle the iron over the blue side of the sun-sensitive paper to create a clear pattern. If necessary, dump off the filings and try again until a clear pattern appears.

  3. Once the pattern is ready, carefully carry the setup, including the magnet(s), outside and place it in full sunlight. Let the pattern sit in sunlight until the paper around the iron filings has faded nearly white. This may take 5–7 minutes on a sunny day if the sun is high.

  4. Carry the setup inside and dump the iron filings off the paper. Place the paper into the pan of water which will fix the pattern, creating a white image of the area covered by filings.

  5. Once the white image appears, remove the paper from the water and place it on newspaper. Place another newspaper over the prints and weigh them down with books to keep the paper flat as it dries. After about 20 minutes, the books may be removed and the paper left to finish drying.

  6. Frames can be made using black paper larger than the sun-sensitive paper by at least 1" (2.5 cm) on all sides. Place cardboard the size of the sun-sensitive paper in the center of the black paper. Fold the paper around the cardboard edges and pinch the four corners of the paper so they stand up to form a frame. Glue the magnetic field print inside the frame.

- Create a frame for the magnetic field pattern.

Making a Picture of the Magnetic Field *(cont.)*

Activity

1. Tell students that they will be making a print of the magnetic field patterns using a special paper that will fade in the sunlight except where the iron filings cover the paper. Show them the samples of the magnetic field patterns you made so they get an idea of what this will look like when they finish.

2. Divide students into small groups and distribute the materials used in the last lesson. Let them re-create some of their magnetic field patterns with the iron filings as a review of the process. After they have practiced making several patterns, let each group create one they will use for their print.

3. Distribute a piece of sun-sensitive paper to each student. Have them turn it blue side down and write their names on the back. They should keep the paper with the blue side down to avoid bleaching it from the light entering the classroom. One person from each group should set up the magnetic field pattern, this time placing the sun-sensitive paper on top of the cardboard. They need to be sure the blue side is up and that they sprinkle the iron filings over the sun-sensitive paper. The pattern will look exactly like the one they make with the filings.

4. Once the magnetic pattern is finished, students should carry pie pans with magnet(s), cardboards, and sun-sensitive paper outside to expose it to the sun. This is a critical time since once the sun shines on the paper it will begin to fade it. The paper should therefore stay as still as possible so filings are not moved. The pie pan should be laid in the sun, perhaps on a table to avoid having to lean and possibly shake the filings. Students should remain with the paper until it fades to white.

5. Students should return to the classroom as each paper fades sufficiently, dump off the iron filings, and then leave it in water until colors are set. The paper should be laid between layers of newspapers and pressed flat with a book.

Closure

- The finished product can be mounted on a frame of construction paper.

- Mount the pictures on a bulletin board and let students compare them. Have them identify the pictures which show repelling and attracting magnetic fields.

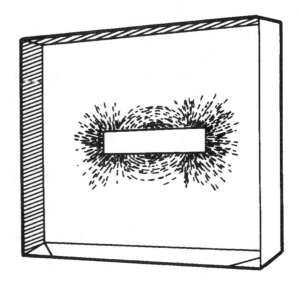

What Happens When You Suspend a Magnet?

Teacher Information

There are actually two north and two south poles on Earth. As Earth spins on its axis, one spot called the North Pole appears to point to the same point in the sky—the North Star or Polaris. The second "north pole" is located nearby at approximately 80 degrees north latitude and 105 degrees longitude in northern Canada. This is the location of the north magnetic pole. Earth's magnetic field acts as if there is a bar magnet inside it, with the north magnetic pole near the north geographic pole, and a south magnetic pole near the south geographic pole. The force is so strong it will pull on a freely suspended magnet which is not near any sources of iron. The suspended magnet's north pole points to the north magnetic pole and the south pole points to the south magnetic pole. This seems to contradict the rule of opposite poles attracting, so in this case the north pole of the magnet is referred to as the north-seeking pole.

Overview: *Students will learn about Earth's magnetic field.*

Materials

- strong bar magnet or cow magnet (See Resources section.)
- string
- globe showing locations of the north and south magnetic poles
- circular magnets
- small white self-adhesive dots (*optional: small pieces of masking tape*)

Lesson Preparation

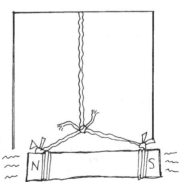

- Make a harness from the string for the magnet as shown.
- Suspend it from the classroom ceiling away from metal items.
- Balance the magnet in its harness so it is parallel to the floor.
- Let it swing freely; it should come to rest in a north-south direction.
- Test the magnet by tapping it and watching it swing. It should gradually come to rest in the same north-south direction.
- Place a piece of masking tape on each side of the magnet end pointing north, the "north-seeking" end of the magnet. You have just constructed a compass; the magnet is the compass needle.

Demonstration

- Show students the suspended magnet and have them notice the direction it is pointing at rest. They should see the tape at one end and use this as a reference point. Do not tell them this is the north end of the magnet.
- Tap the magnet gently to set it spinning and tell the students they need to watch it until it stops.
- As the spinning slows, point out that it appears that some invisible force is tugging it to stop.
- When the magnet comes to a complete stop, show that it is pointing the same direction as it was before. Ask students if they can explain why this is happening. Most will not be able to explain the reason, but some may guess it is pointing north-south.

What Happens When You Suspend a Magnet? *(cont.)*

Activity

1. Divide the students into groups and give each a circular magnet and a string about 10" (25 cm) long. Have them tie the string through the hole of their circular magnet.

2. Take the students outside to an area where there are trees low enough for them to reach the branches. Be sure the magnets are not within four feet of each other and that there is no wind blowing.

3. Hang the bar magnet from one of the branches also, away from the other magnets.

4. Demonstrate with the bar magnet how the students should gently twist their magnet around about five times to wind the string and then let it go so the magnet can swing freely.

5. Have them watch their magnets until they stop. Let them compare the positions of all the magnets (they should all be pointing in the same general direction). Have them look at the bar magnet and see what direction it is pointing. It should be lined up with their circular magnets.

6. Give each group a self-adhesive dot (or masking tape) and have them apply it to the side of the circle which is facing north, the same direction the north-seeking pole on the bar magnet is pointing.

7. Let them twist the magnets around on the strings again and watch to see if they stop in the same position. They have just identified the north-seeking pole on their magnets.

Closure

- Return to the classroom and show the students the globe and the location of the magnetic poles on the globe. Tell them about Earth's magnetic field and explain that it is so strong that it is able to pull their magnets in the north-south direction.

- Explain that if they could put a huge piece of glass over the Earth and sprinkle iron filings on it, they would see the pattern of the bar magnet they used in the last lesson. The iron filings would form a huge arc from the north magnetic pole to the south magnetic pole. This magnetic field completely encircles Earth, and the zones of charged particles spread along the lines of that field are known as *Van Allen belts*, named for the scientist who suggested their existence.

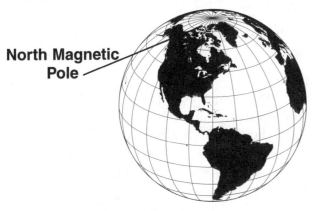

North Magnetic Pole

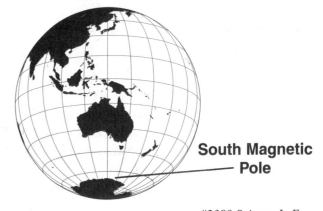

South Magnetic Pole

How Can You Make a Compass?

Teacher Information

A natural magnetic rock was discovered long ago in the Greek province of Magnesia. The rock was named *magnetite* for the place in which it was found. Later, someone discovered that magnetite could be used to magnetize iron needles. Sailors would place the magnetized needle on a chip of wood so it would float on water. It always pointed north-south, and thus could be used to guide their ships.

Overview: *Students will make a simple compass.*

Materials

- circular magnets (one per student)
- steel straight pins (one per student)
- small chips of a Styrofoam cup
- aluminum pie plates partially filled with water
- pinch of iron filings on small pieces of paper
- overhead projector
- bar magnet suspended from the ceiling
- *optional:* compass (available from Delta Education or nature stores)

Activity

1. Tell students that nonmagnetized material which is attracted to a magnet can be temporarily magnetized, using a magnet. Show the students that the straight pin you are about to magnetize is not a magnet by dipping it into a pinch of iron filings on an overhead projector. (If it is not magnetized, the iron filings should not stick to it. A few particles of the filings may adhere even to a nonmagnetized pin, but more will do so after it is magnetized.)

2. Demonstrate how the pin can be magnetized by pressing one straight pin against the projector glass, holding it firmly at the head end. Using the flat side of a circular magnet, stroke the pin from the head end to the point, lifting the magnet when you reach the point of the pin. Return to the head of the pin and stroke it again, pushing the magnet firmly against the pin as you do so. Continue stroking the magnet firmly and quickly *in one direction only*, counting about 50 strokes.

3. Show the students that the pin is now magnetized by dipping it into the iron filings again. It should pick up a cluster of the iron filings.

4. Distribute a pin and magnet to each student and have them magnetize their pins in the same manner as you demonstrated.

5. Give each group a pinch of iron filings on a paper so they can test their pins' magnetism by dipping them into the iron filings. If not many filings stick, have them continue stroking their pins with the magnet for about 25 strokes.

6. Let them test their pins to see if they repel or attract another magnetized pin. This can be done by laying a magnetized pin on the table and touching the point or head of another magnetized pin to the point or head of the pin on the table. (The first pin should attract or repel the other pin, depending upon the location of the poles of each pin. Some pins may have north at the head of the pin, while others may have north at the pointed end. This is determined by the side of the magnet being used during the magnetizing process.)

How Can You Make a Compass? *(cont.)*

Activity *(cont.)*

7. Have students reverse *one* of the pins and repeat the experiment; if they repelled before, they should now attract and vice versa.

8. Distribute a chip of Styrofoam to each student and help them gently push their pins through it so the head and point of each pin are exposed and the pin is parallel to the surfaces of the Styrofoam. This becomes the compass needle.

9. Provide each group with a pie pan of water. Have students place one compass needle in the center of the pan of water and watch how it moves. After it has come to rest, compare it with the bar magnet hanging from the ceiling. The pin should be pointing in the same direction.

10. Have the students gently push each compass needle around; it should return to the same direction. If it floats to the side of the pan, gently return it to the center. If it does not line up north-south, the magnetism is weak and the pin needs to be rubbed head-to-point another 50 strokes. Let students test their compass needles one at a time in the pan of water. (If two or more pins are placed in the pan at the same time, they will attract to each other rather than to Earth's magnetic field.)

Closure

- Show the students an actual compass, if available, and have them compare the direction its needle is pointing with the direction of the bar magnet hanging from the ceiling and the direction of the floating compass needles.

- Show them the magnetite which was used in the first activity in this series and show that it is a natural magnet by dipping it into iron filings. Explain that magnetite was used by early sailors to create magnetic needles and simple compasses much as the students have done.

- Distribute lined paper, pencils, rulers, crayons, and drawing paper to each student. Tell students to imagine they have suddenly become magnetic. Have them write about how this would change their lives. Tell them to make drawings to go along with their stories and label the parts of their drawing.

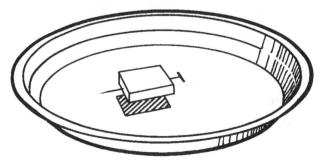

What Shape Is a Bubble?

— Teacher Information —

Students can learn a great deal about shapes, color, and physics through these activities by blowing bubbles. The following lessons are intended to have students learn these concepts while enjoying blowing bubbles in a variety of ways. It is not important that they understand the scientific principles behind what they experience but, rather, that they learn to make observations and experiment with the materials in a creative manner.

Overview: *Students will blow bubbles through various shapes of bubble wands.*

Materials

- 20 or 22 gauge wire
- wire cutters
- aluminum pie pans
- dishwashing detergent (Dawn is one of the best.)
- large empty paint bucket
- large empty coffee can
- parent letter (page 104)

Lesson Preparation

- Prepare a bubble solution of 16 parts of water to 1 part of liquid detergent. Use the large coffee can to measure the water and pour it into the paint bucket. Add the detergent last. Pour the solution back into the bucket after each lesson to reuse it.
- Cut 12-inch (30 cm) lengths of wire. Form these into bubble blowers of different geometric shapes. These may include triangles, squares, rectangles, and odd shapes—but not circles.
- Fill the pie pans approximately ¾ full of bubble solution.
- Conduct this lesson outside since it will be messy.

Activity

1. Ask students if they have ever blown bubbles. Ask them about the shapes of the bubbles and the bubble blowers.
2. Tell them that they are going to blow bubbles but that they will use differently shaped bubble blowers. Distribute a bubble blower to each student. Have them predict what shape their bubble will be. (*Most will think the shape of the bubble will match the shape of the blower. Do not correct them at this time.*)
3. Divide the students in small groups and distribute a container of bubble solution to each group. Let each student dip a bubble blower into the solution and practice blowing bubbles through it. This may be done by blowing on the film of bubble solution or pulling it through the air.
4. Have them observe the shapes of their bubbles. (*They will all be spherical.*)

What Shape Is a Bubble? *(cont.)*

Closure

- Remind students of what they learned in the Mixing Colored Lights activity (page 23). Have the students look at the color of their bubbles. *(They will see the complementary colors of light. This is due to the refracted light on the surface of the bubbles mixing the primary colors of light.)*

- Pour some bubble solution into the clear container. Add food coloring to the solution. Ask students to predict what color bubbles they will see. Dip the bubble blower into the solution and blow several bubbles for them to see. *(They will be the same color as before the coloring was added. This is because the film of solution on the bubble blower contains very little of the food coloring.)*

- Send home the parent letter to have students provide a variety of bubble blowers for the next lesson.

Parent Letter for Bubble Blowers

Date_____

Dear Parents:

Your child has had fun learning about shapes by blowing bubbles. We used bubble blowers made from wire bent into various geometric shapes. The students learned that no matter what shape of bubble blower they used, the bubbles were always spherical. Ask your child to tell you about this experience.

Each student has been asked to bring a bubble blower for our next class, which is on_____. Some suggestions for bubble blowers follow:

- soup, coffee, juice, or other cans with both ends removed
- plastic berry baskets
- short length of PVC pipe

The recipe for the bubble solution we used is very simple. You may want to make some to use with your child.

You will need these things:

- liquid dishwashing detergent, such as Dawn
- water
- measuring container
- storage container for the solution

Solution: 16 parts of water to 1 part of detergent. You may make any quantity. For example, $\frac{1}{2}$ cup of detergent added to 8 cups of water will yield about 8 $\frac{1}{2}$ cups of solution. If you want more solution, use a larger measuring container such as a coffee can. The solution may be stored and reused for a long time.

Instructions: Measure 16 parts of water into the storage container. Add one part of detergent and slowly stir it into the water. Avoid making bubbles as you stir. Pour some of the solution into a cup and use a homemade bubble blower to make bubbles.

We will be experimenting with heaping bubbles, as well as using string and straws to make huge bubbles. You are welcome to join us in the fun of learning about bubbles. Our next session will be_____.

Cordially,

I'm Forever Blowing Bubbles

Overview: *Students will see the types of bubbles they can make using a variety of bubble blowers.*

Materials

- bubble blowers students bring from home
- plastic drinking straws
- bubble solution
- containers for bubble solution (e.g., pie pans, dishpans, plastic shoeboxes)

Lesson Preparation

- Gather some possible bubble blowers for students to use to supplement those they bring from home. These may include drinking straws individually or with 4–5 grouped, using a rubber band to hold them together.
- Pour the bubble solution into the containers.

Activity

1. Divide the students into small groups and provide each with a container of bubble solution.

2. Let the students experiment with their own bubble makers, as well as exchanging with other students and using some you made for them.

3. Encourage students to try various methods of making bubbles by blowing or pulling the bubble blower through the air.

Closure

- Have students demonstrate some of the things they discovered about blowing bubbles.

- Ask the students to share their experiences they may have had while blowing bubbles at home.

Bubble Buildings

Overview: *Students will construct buildings from bubbles.*

Materials

- cups of bubble solution
- plastic drinking straws
- Styrofoam plate

Lesson Preparation

Pour a cup of bubble solution for each student.

Activity

1. Discuss the activities the students have done thus far in making bubbles.

2. Distribute a cup of bubble solution and a straw to each student. Have students blow bubbles using their drinking straws. In order to do so, they dip their straws into the solution, remove them, and slowly blow through the other end of the straw.

3. Give each student a Styrofoam plate. The students should use their straws to blow bubbles onto the plate so they pile up. This will form an interesting igloo-shaped building.

4. Have the students compare the shapes the bubbles make as they attach to each other. They will see that the same geometric shape forms where they join.

5. Tell them to see if they can blow a bubble inside a bubble. (*This can be done by inserting a straw into a bubble and blowing gently to form another bubble.*)

6. Encourage them to experiment with this activity to see how large their buildings can become.

Closure

- Have the students sketch their buildings, showing the geometric shapes they see.

Big, Bigger, Biggest Bubbles

Overview: *Students will make large bubbles.*

Materials

- bubble solution
- large containers such as dishpans
- *optional:* wading pool and Hula-Hoop
- drinking straws
- cotton string

Lesson Preparation

- Arrange for adult or older students to assist with this activity.

- Make bubble blowers for each student, using two drinking straws and cotton string. Cut an 18-inch (46 cm) length of string and thread it through two straws. Tie the string in a knot. Stretch the string and straws into a rectangular shape by holding the straws in each hand.

- Practice making bubbles with this device. Pour enough bubble solution into a dishpan to fill to a depth of about two inches (5 cm).

1. Hold one of the straws in each hand and bring your hands together. Dip the string, straws, and your hands into the solution to thoroughly wet them. Pull the string and straws out, keeping your hands together.

2. Back away, slowly opening your hands and stretching the string and straws into a rectangle with a film of bubble solution in the center.

3. Pull air into the film with a swooping motion of your hands. The air will stretch the film into the shape of a wind sock. Bring the hands together quickly to capture the air inside the film and release the bubble. The bubble will attempt to form a sphere, but if is too large, it will be in a sausage shape.

Big, Bigger, Biggest Bubbles *(cont.)*

Lesson Preparation *(cont.)*

- Have patience. This does take some practice before one is able to make the large bubble.

- Make preparations to conduct this activity outside or cover the floor with newspaper.

Activity

1. Demonstrate how to make the large bubbles. Do this several times so students are able to see how to hold their hands as they make the bubbles.

2. Distribute a bubble blower to each student and assign them to one of the dishpans of solution. Assign adult and/or older student helpers to the bubble stations.

3. Challenge the students to work together to see who can make their bubbles last the longest, fly the highest, or become the largest size.

Closure

- Have the students make drawings about their bubble-blowing experiences and take them home to share with their families.

Square Bubbles

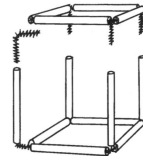

Overview: *Using special bubble blowers, students will be able to make bubbles which are not spherical.*

Materials

- bubble solution
- pipe cleaners
- glue gun
- dishpans
- drinking straws

Lesson Preparation

- Cut the drinking straws into three-inch (7.5 cm) lengths and the pipe cleaners into two-inch (5 cm) lengths.
- Create cubes, pyramids, and other geometric solid shapes using the short straws and pipe cleaners. Instructions on making a cube are as follows:

    1. You will need 12 short straws and 16 short pipe cleaners.

    2. Form a square with four straws, inserting a short pipe cleaner bent at a 90° angle into each straw. Make another square like this.

    3. Join the two squares together to form a cube. Use straws and pipe cleaners between the corners of each square.

    4. Use the glue gun to seal the pipe cleaners into the ends of the straws to strengthen the cube.

- Form pyramids and other geometric solids in this same way.
- Experiment with the shapes by submerging them in bubble solution. The film will cling to the shape and form walls. It will begin to draw into the center. In the case of the cube, the film will draw together to form a square. Use a straw dipped in bubble solution and blow a bubble onto the square. It will expand to form a cube-shaped bubble.
- Pour bubble solution into dishpans and set up centers for the students to work with a variety of the solid geometric shapes.

Activity

1. Ask the students what shape bubbles they have been making thus far (*spherical*). Tell them that you are going to show them how to make other shapes of bubbles. Demonstrate the shapes which can be made using the geometric solids made from straws.

2. Assign the students to the stations set up with the solution and geometric shapes. Have them work in pairs to use the shapes and create interesting bubbles. Issue straws to them so they can blow into the center of each of the shapes after film is on each surface.

Closure

- Have the students draw the various geometric shapes they used to create bubbles. Tell them to show what the shapes of the bubbles were that formed inside these geometric shapes
- If appropriate for this lesson, let them have pipe cleaners and straws to create their own geometric shapes to use with the bubble solution.

Fun with Insects Introduction

Insects are found all over the world, even in Antarctica. They have been on Earth at least 400 million years and appear to be in no danger of disappearing in the future. There are more insects and more kinds of insects than all other animals on Earth which are visible to the naked eye. Insects have been called man's worst enemy, but this is not true. It is important to respect their role in the balance of nature and know that most life on Earth could not exist without them. Insects are an important food source for many animals, they are pollinators of many commercial plants, they are garbage collectors, and they are silk weavers. They are gems of natural beauty and a constant source of interest.

Insects have an outside skeleton (*exoskeleton*), six legs, and three body parts. Compare the physical features of the insect to crabs and lobsters, and you can see that they are related. Insects also may have one or two pairs of wings attached to the middle section of the body (*thorax*). They usually have two sets of jaws, two kinds of eyes (simple and compound), and one pair of antennae. There are exceptions to these physical features, however. Some insects have a thorax and abdomen which seem to run together. Immature stages (*larvae*) of many insects look like jointed worms with six real legs and perhaps some extra false ones.

Another confusion comes about due to animals which look like insects. These include spiders and scorpions, but they have too few body parts (two) and too many legs (eight). Crustaceans (e.g., crabs, lobsters, and shrimp) also look like insects but may have five pairs of legs and two pairs of antennae. Sowbugs and pillbugs are land crustaceans. Centipedes and millipedes have many segments to their bodies with one pair of legs (in the case of centipedes) or two pairs (in the case of millipedes) attached to each segment.

Insect Examples

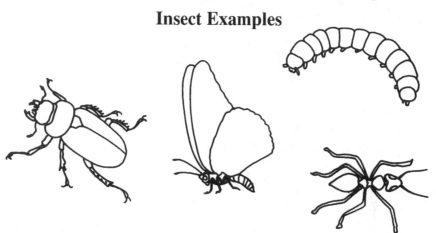

The study of insects begins with a hunt on the school grounds and a pretest to separate insects from noninsects. As students continue the activities in this section, they will learn about insects by raising mealworms, ants, butterflies, and silkworms in the classroom. As a culminating activity, students will create imaginary insects for their own insect zoo.

We're Going on an Insect Hunt

Overview: *Students will gather specimens of insects and noninsects.*

Materials

- 3" x 5" (8 cm x 13 cm) unlined file cards
- 1" cube plastic bug boxes with a magnifying lid (See Delta Education in Resources.)
- snack-sized zip-lock bag
- parent letter for insects (page 112)
- overhead projector with transparencies of insect and noninsect

Lesson Preparation

- Take a walk around the grounds near the school, searching for insects and noninsects. Look in hidden places such as on plants, under fallen leaves, and along tree bark.
- Map a route for the students to take as they search for specimens during this activity.

Activity

1. Distribute a file card to each student and ask each one to draw an insect on it. Tell students to make their pictures as large as the card. Let them know that you want them to show as many details of the insect as they can, including the shapes of the body parts and legs.

2. Have the students show their drawings to others and point out the details, such as legs.

3. Tell the students that they are going on an insect hunt around the school ground. Take them to the search area and distribute a magnifying box to each student. Explain that they are to find only one insect to place in the box and then bring it to a central location you establish. You may wish to use a signal to call them back together after a set time.

4. When the students have each found an insect, gather them together and look at what they have found. Let the students exchange magnifying boxes to look closely at their insects. If any have placed noninsects in their boxes, do not correct them at this time.

Closure

- Return to the classroom and select examples of the insects to see enlarged on the overhead projector. Place an insect in a zip-lock bag on the projector stage. Have students point out its physical features (e.g., number of legs, body parts, and shape). (*Note:* The heat from the projector will affect the insect, so it should not be subjected to the light for long periods.)
- Have the students draw their insects on the other side of the card they used at the beginning of the class period. Collect these cards to use as assessment at the end of this lesson series.

Homework

Send home a copy of the parent letter with a small zip-lock bag stapled to it.

Parent Letter for Insects

Date_____

Dear Parents:

We are studying insects in science. Today we began our study by having each student make a drawing of an insect. Then we all took a walk around the school grounds, with each student collecting an animal he or she thought was an insect. We looked at these with magnifying lenses and the overhead projector to make them larger and easier to see their details. The students then drew the insects they had collected.

The next step in our study is for each student to capture an insect in his or her yard and bring it to school tomorrow. After we have examined these insects, they will be released in the school yard.

You will find a small zip-lock bag attached to this note. Please help your child capture an insect to put inside the plastic bag and bring it back to school tomorrow for our science class. Since we are just beginning our study of insects, your child may choose an animal which looks like an insect but is not really a true insect. It is important that children discover the differences for themselves, so please do not tell them if their choice is not an insect.

Tomorrow, we will look at the specimens the children bring to class. We will also compare the specimens with the drawings children have made of the insects they found on our insect hunt today.

Be sure to ask your child about the experience today and ask him or her to draw a picture below of the insect collected today.

Today's Insect

Thank you for helping your child find an interesting insect to bring to school.

Cordially,

Is This an Insect?

Overview: *Students will learn to distinguish insects from noninsects.*

Materials

- transparency and copies of the data sheet Is This an Insect? (page 114)
- insects students bring from home
- 3" x 5" (8 cm x 13 cm) unlined file cards and magnifying boxes
- overhead projector with transparencies of Outside Parts of Insects and Inside Parts of Insects (pages 115–118)

Lesson Preparation

- Gather examples of noninsects (e.g., spider, pill bug, millipede) to use with the students.
- Collect insect specimens students bring and place them in magnifying boxes. Put them where they can be viewed by students before beginning the class.

Activity

1. Distribute file cards and insects in magnifying boxes. Have students draw their own specimens. Give them the pictures made yesterday to look for differences and likenesses.
2. Show students' specimens in zip-lock bags on the overhead projector.
3. Distribute copies of Is This an Insect? and have students circle the letters of those they think are insects. Show the transparency and have students vote on which ones they think are insects. Circle the letters for those they choose.
4. Use the transparency of Parts of Insects and explain. Place examples of insects in a zip-lock bag (one at a time) to show on the overhead. Let students see if they can find six legs and three body parts. Use several examples of noninsects to show differences from insects.

Closure

- Show the data sheet transparency again and ask students to vote again on which are insects. Ask them to point out details which help find real insects. Tell them the names of the insects and noninsects on this sheet.

Insects	*Noninsects*
B. silverfish	G. grasshopper	A. scorpion
C. ant	I. butterfly	F. tarantula (spider)
D. stag beetle	K. cockroach	H. centipede
E. earwig	L. butterfly larva	J. millipede

- Place live examples of insects and noninsects on the overhead projector. Have students write which ones they think are insects. Collect the papers, review the specimens, and let students vote aloud. If there is disagreement, have them explain what made them decide how to vote. Tell them the correct answers.

Is This an Insect? *(cont.)*

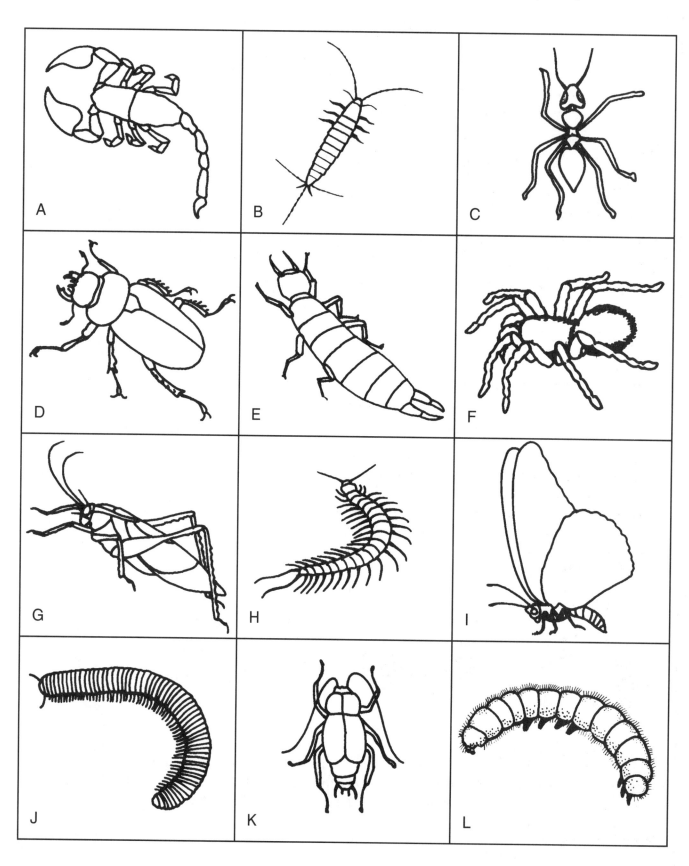

Outside Parts of Insects

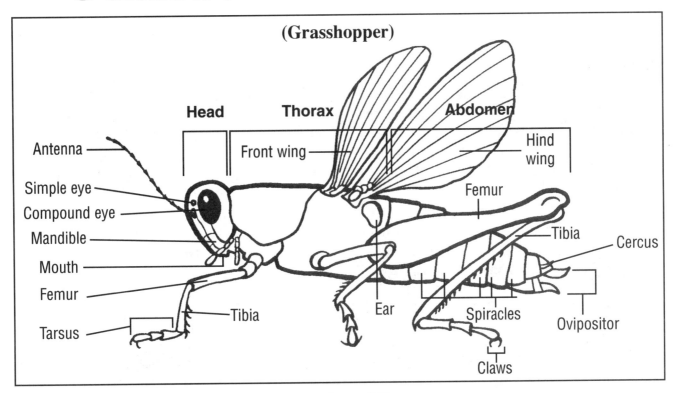

(Grasshopper)

Explanation of Terms

Skeleton: The insect's skeleton is outside of its body and is called an *exoskeleton*. It is like a suit of armor that protects the soft internal parts. It is divided into three parts—*head*, *thorax*, and *abdomen*. The muscles are attached to the inside wall of this exoskeleton.

The insect's three body parts are described below:

A. Head: There are five or six segments to an insect's head, but they are too tightly packed together to be seen separately. The head is made up of the *mouthparts*, *eyes*, and *antennae*.

Mouthparts: The mouth opening in the head varies according to what the insect eats.

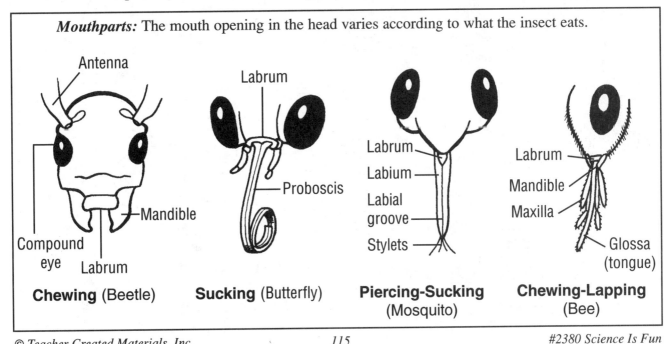

Chewing (Beetle)　　**Sucking** (Butterfly)　　**Piercing-Sucking** (Mosquito)　　**Chewing-Lapping** (Bee)

Outside Parts of Insects *(cont.)*

Explanation of Terms *(cont.)*

A. Head: *(cont.)*

Eyes: Most adult insects have two large bulging compound eyes on either side of their heads. These are made up of separate lenses, sometimes thousands of them. Each lens sees a piece of the image, and these pieces combine to form a mosaic. This is not a very clear image, but because of the shape of the eyes, the insect can see up, down, ahead, and back at the same time. This type of eye is especially good for seeing motion. Many insects also have smaller, single-lens eyes. These can see only light and dark, not an image. Insects have different color ranges than humans, mostly seeing only green, blue, and ultraviolet.

Antennae: Almost all insects have two antennae between their eyes. These are used mostly to smell and to feel. Some insects also use these to taste and to hear. The antennae are segmented and flexible, appearing in various shapes.

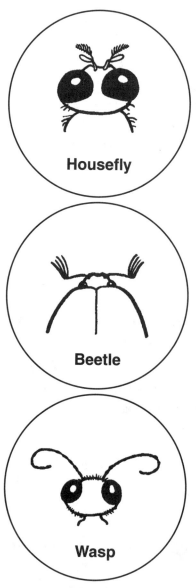

Outside Parts of Insects *(cont.)*

Explanation of Terms *(cont.)*

B. Thorax: The wings and legs are attached to this middle section of the body, which consists of three tightly fused segments. Most adult insects have wings. A single pair of wings is attached to the middle segments. If there are two pairs of wings, they are attached to the middle and last segments of the thorax.

The six legs are attached in pairs to each segment of the abdomen. The legs each have five main sections with movable joints between them. Legs are often adapted for swimming, digging, or jumping. Honeybees have pollen-collecting baskets on their hind legs. The front legs of butterflies are small, hairy, and often have special organs for finding food. Feet may have hooks and sticky pads (e.g., flies and bees) to help them hold to slippery surfaces or walk upside down.

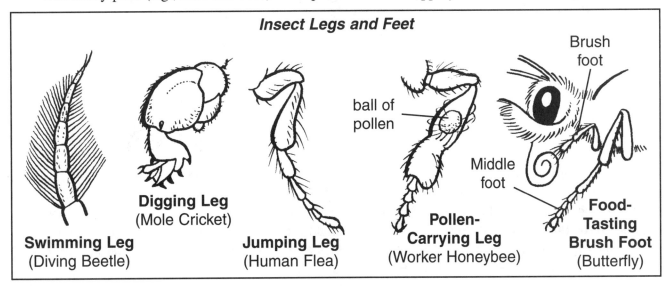

Insect Legs and Feet

Swimming Leg (Diving Beetle)   **Digging Leg** (Mole Cricket)   **Jumping Leg** (Human Flea)   ball of pollen   **Pollen-Carrying Leg** (Worker Honeybee)   Brush foot   Middle foot   **Food-Tasting Brush Foot** (Butterfly)

C. Abdomen: This last section of the body contains the organs for digesting food, reproducing, and getting rid of waste products. The abdomen consists of 10–11 segments connected by flexible membranes. The segments can slide into one another like a telescope when the abdomen is empty or expand when it is full.

Some insects have a pair of feelers (*cerci*) on the last segment of the abdomen. The cerci on earwigs and some other insects form a pair of tongs which are used for self-defense or for capturing prey.

Many female insects have an egg-laying tool called the *ovipositor* in the last segments of the abdomen. It can be used to insert eggs into such things as soil, plants, or the bodies of other animals. Ovipositors of insects like bees and wasps have been adapted into a stinger.

Inside Parts of Insects

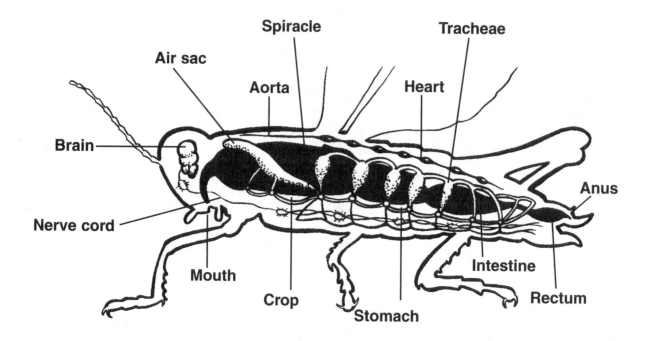

Digestive System: The digestive system of insects consists basically of a long tube that extends from the mouth to the anus. Food is chewed or sucked up by the mouthparts and then moves along the tube to the *crop* where it is stored and partly digested. The food later passes into the *gizzard*, which has muscular walls that contract and grind the food into small bits. Next, the food passes into the stomach where most digestion takes place. Nourishing parts of the food are absorbed into the blood, and wastes move into the intestine. Liquid and solid wastes are expelled through the anus.

Respiratory System: An insect breathes by means of tiny holes called *spiracles* along the sides of its body. Each hole leads into a large tube called a *trachea*. The large tubes divide into small tubes which also divide into still smaller tubes that branch out to all the cells of the body. This system of tubes carries oxygen to the cells and takes away carbon dioxide.

Circulatory System: An insect's blood does not flow through veins and arteries like ours. It fills the whole cavity of the insect's body and bathes all the organs and muscles. The blood circulates in a long tube just under the exoskeleton of the back. The pumping part of the tube, the *heart*, is in the abdomen. The front part of the tube extends into the head and is called the *aorta*. As the heart contracts, the blood is forced along the tube and out through the aorta. The blood first bathes the brain and then flows to other parts of the body. It then reenters the tube through the *ostia* along the sides of the tube. An insect's blood is greenish, yellowish, or colorless.

Nervous System: This consists of a brain in the head and two nerve cords that lie side by side along the floor of the thorax and abdomen. The brain receives information from the eyes and antennae and controls the insect's body activities as a whole. Another nerve center in the head is connected to the brain and controls the insect's mouthparts.

Mealworms

—— Teacher Information ——

Mealworms are not worms but the larval stage of a dark, flightless beetle. They are very clean, dry, and harmless to handle. It is easy to maintain mealworms in the classroom. They provide an excellent source for the study of the life cycle of an insect. They begin life inside a tiny egg, hatching as a larva within seven to ten days. The time spent in the larval stage varies. The larvae grow rapidly when the temperature is moderate and food is plentiful. They usually grow to about 25 mm in length and then become white pupae. The pupa is not rigid and will wiggle if touched, perhaps as a defense mechanism from predators. Legs and wings can be seen forming on the pupa through its thin skin, especially as it nears maturity. When the pupa begins to turn dark, it will soon become an adult. The adult begins laying eggs within two or three weeks after emerging from the pupal stage.

Mealworms are used as fishing bait and food for a variety of pets, including lizards. It is best to purchase the jumbo size larvae so students can see more details. The larger-sized mealworms are usually available at bait stores. They are kept in the refrigerator to slow their growth while in the store but should be kept at room temperature in the classroom.

These activities are designed to be conducted over many weeks, enabling students to observe and record the mealworms' physical changes during all stages of their lives.

Overview: *Students will investigate the characteristics and life cycle of mealworms.*

Materials (for each student)

- jumbo-sized mealworms (available at pet stores or bait shops)
- blank 3" x 5" (8 cm x 13 cm) file cards
- two different colors of small sticky notes
- magnifier
- metric ruler

Mealworm Care: Since mealworms can eat through cardboard, use a plastic box to house them. Mealworms will eat dry grain such as oatmeal or bran, which may be used as both food and home for the larvae. Place 25–50 mealworms into the box and fill it with the grain to a depth of about 2.5" (6 cm). There is no need to put a lid on the box until beetles appear. You may want to place a piece of cheese cloth over the plastic box. Some moisture may be provided by putting a moist paper towel on top of the meal. The mealworms will nibble at the paper, which is not harmful to them. Replace the paper towel periodically and keep it moist. If the meal becomes moldy, too much moisture is being added.

Mealworms *(cont.)*

Activity 1

- Introduce the mealworm to the students so they will see that it is harmless and fragile, needing to be handled with care. You may want to place the mealworm in a small cup until the students feel at ease with handling it.

- Distribute a mealworm to each student and let each watch it for a while to observe how it moves. Monitor this study so none of the mealworms wanders off or falls off the tables. Encourage students who are reluctant to handle the larva to give it a name, making it a pet and less likely to arouse fear.

- After students have become familiar with their mealworms, issue each of them a magnifier and help them look closely at the physical characteristics of their larvae. They should notice that a larva has three pairs of legs with claw-like feet in front and four pairs toward the rear (false legs) with suction-cup feet. A single motionless leg is located at the very end of the larva. It has two short antennae, which help to identify the head. The eyes are not visible. The larva's body is divided into about 13 segments to enable it to be flexible, like our fingers.

- Lead a discussion of the observations students have made and then allow more time for observing the larvae. Encourage them to look closely for details of body parts and how larvae use their feet as they move.

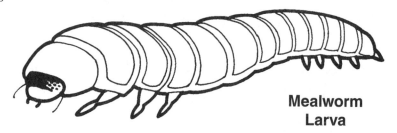

Mealworm Larva

Activity 2

- Distribute mealworms and magnifiers to the students and let them observe the larvae again. Discuss what they have discovered about the mealworms thus far.

- Give each student a file card and have each draw his or her mealworms. (*Optional:* Draw the outline of the mealworm body and make copies on file cards for each student to fill in the details of features such as legs, segments, and antenna.) Be sure they write their names on the cards.

- Explain that these drawings are to be scientific, so no faces or shoes should appear. Monitor the students' progress and encourage them to use their magnifiers to look for details. You may want to display the drawings until they are needed for the next activity.

- Have students count the number of segments they see on their larvae. They may use the magnifiers to be sure their count is as accurate as possible. Give each student a self-adhesive note. Have each one write his or her name on it as well as the number of segments counted.

- Ask for the number of segments students counted. Write the number of segments reported below a horizontal line drawn on large paper. Have students put their sticky notes in a vertical row above the number, without overlapping them. Draw a vertical line to the left side of the notes, beginning at the horizontal line. Divide this line with numbered marks to indicate the number of self-adhesive sticky notes. The data on the notes will form a bar graph.

Mealworms *(cont.)*

Activity 2 *(cont.)*

- Help students determine the average number of segments by looking at the graph. If any count is more than two segments above or below the average, have those students recount their larva's segments with the assistance of another student.

Activity 3

- Distribute the mealworms and the drawings made in Activity 1. It is not necessary for students to have the same mealworms as they had in the previous activity.

- Give students metric rulers. Tell them they are to measure the length of their mealworms. Let the students use their problem-solving skills to determine how this can be done. Have them record the length on the file card by drawing a line the length they measured and writing the length to the nearest millimeter.

- Distribute a sticky note to each student and on it have each record his or her name as well as the length of the mealworm. Create a bar graph with the resulting data on another piece of large paper. Discuss the various lengths of mealworms. Have students remeasure any which are doubtful. Let them determine the average size of their mealworms.

Activity 4

- Let each student have his or her own mealworm to observe for the next two or three weeks. Each mealworm can be placed in a small plastic container with a lid. Poke holes in the lid to permit an air flow.

- Have students maintain a record on file cards, including dates, measurements, and careful drawings. Be sure they add color when they draw the beetle.

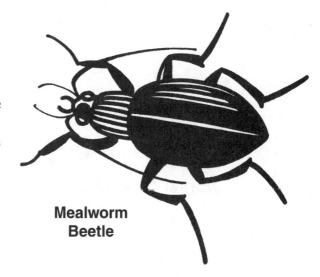

Mealworm Beetle

- Tell students to use their data to calculate the time elapsed between the mealworm as a larva and when it becomes a pupa, as well as the time elapsing from pupal stage to adult. This data can be graphed to determine the average time in each cycle for the students' mealworms.

Closure

- Display the graphs and student drawings.

- When the study ends, let the students make a booklet of their file cards, adding a cover of their own design.

Note: Since mealworms serve as pet food, a student with a lizard, land turtle, or other pet may be able to get permission from home to take the mealworm culture at the end of this study.

Ants

Teacher Information

There are over 2,500 species of ants, all social animals which live and work together in colonies. They are the most familiar of insects and have often been compared to human societies. Each ant in a colony has specific duties. A single *queen* ant reproduces all of the colony's members. She may live as long as 20 years. The *male* ant is responsible for mating with the queen. This occurs outside the colony when the queen and males develop wings. After mating, the males die and the queen tears off her wings and returns to her nest as an additional queen or begins her own nest. The *soldier* ants are responsible for protecting the members of the colony. The *worker* ants are all female and are responsible for the maintenance of the colony. Their jobs may range from husking seeds and carrying out dirt to digging new tunnels and feeding the larvae. An ant colony consists of many (sometimes millions) of ants working cooperatively to form a single society.

Carpenter Ants in a Colony

queen

male

worker (normal size)

soldier

122

Ants in the Wild

Overview: *Students observe and collect data about ants in the wild.*

Materials

- 3" x 5" (8 cm x 13 cm) file cards
- *optional:* magnifier for each student
- Observing Ants in the Wild data sheet (page 124)

Lesson Preparation

- Find a source of wild ants near school for students to observe. Watch how they behave and try the various experiments which will be conducted with the students in this lesson.
- During observations of the ants, you may consider having students use a piece of newspaper to sit on. This will help those somewhat frightened by insects to feel more secure than just sitting on the ground.
- Consider taking photographs of all students observing ants during this study. The photos can be included in the book they will be making of their data sheets.

Activity

1. Distribute a file card to each student and have each draw an ant from memory. It should be as large as the file card to show details. Tell students they will study ants for many weeks, beginning by watching ants near school to see how they behave.
2. Take the students to an area near school to observe ants in the wild. Have them watch ants moving, asking them to describe the movement. (*Usually ants move in a line, following a scent trail laid down by the earlier ants.*)
3. Conduct some simple experiments with the ants so students can see how they react.
   - Draw a line through the line of ants so students can see how the ants react. (*The ants will become disoriented for a while but then find their way again.*) Let them watch to see how the ants reestablish the new trail. Ask students to think what method the ants might have used to find their path again.
   - Place an obstacle (e.g., pebble) in the line of ants so students can watch and discuss their reaction. (*They may go around it or climb over it.*) See if they can guess why the ants behave in the manner they do.
   - Put food (pieces of meat, candy, seeds, sugar cereal) in the ants' path and observe how they react. If they carry off the food, point out how much larger the pieces are than the ants. Have students notice that ants use their mouths to hold the food.
   - Let the students think of ways to study the ants and carry out their experiments.
4. Follow the ants' trail to find where it begins and ends.

Closure

- Return to the classroom and group the students. Distribute the data sheets to the students and have them write illustrated stories about their observations of ants in the wild.
- Collect the drawings to keep for an ant book students will assemble at the end of their study.

Observing Ants in the Wild

To the Student: Draw pictures about six different things you learned as you watched the ants in the wild. Write a sentence about the picture in each of the boxes below your picture.

1	2
3	4
5	6

Ant Farming

Overview: *Students will make observations of ants being placed in a commercial habitat.*

Materials

- one or two commercial ant farms (See resources.)
- magnifiers for each student
- Ants in an Ant Farm data sheet (page 126)
- *optional:* video camera

Lesson Preparation

- Order the ant farm(s) early enough to allow time to send in the coupon for the live specimens. Assemble the ant farm(s) but do not add the ants. Label the sides of the ant habitats A and B for observations.

- You may want to record the assembling of the ant farm(s) on video, as well as the ants' first reaction to being inside it. This can be the introduction of a video record which is made throughout the raising of the ants.

Activity

1. Remind the students of their observations of ants in the wild. Explain that the ants live under the ground, and it is impossible to watch them there. Let them know that you are going to prepare a special home for some ants that will let them observe what their homes look like.

2. Gather the students near the ant farm(s) and let them observe as you put the material into the habitat(s). Follow the directions to introduce the ants into the ant farm(s). Let students observe what the ants do as they enter their new home. Encourage them to look for details.

3. Distribute the Ants in an Ant Farm data sheet to each of them. Tell the students to draw the details of what they observed as the ants' nest was being prepared and how the ants reacted when they were released into it.

Closure

- Have the students share their drawings with others in the class.
- Collect the drawings for the students' ant book.

Ants in an Ant Farm

To the Student: Draw pictures about six different things you saw happen as you watched the farm being filled and what the ants did when they were put into their new home. Write a sentence about the picture in each of the boxes below.

1

_____
_____

2

_____
_____

3

_____
_____

4

_____
_____

5

_____
_____

6

_____
_____

Ants Up Close

Overview: *Students will make observations of ants in captivity.*

Materials

- ant farm(s) prepared in previous lesson
- colored pens or colored pencils
- *optional:* video camera and tripod
- Ant Farm Observations data sheet (page 128)
- magnifiers

Lesson Preparation

- Set the ant farm(s) at work station(s) in the room, away from direct sunlight.
- Design a schedule for small groups of students to observe the ant farms daily for at least 10 minutes.
- Decide on the color to be used each day for showing the new tunnel additions.
- A video camera may be used to make a scientific record of the changes in the ant farm(s). The recording can be done as time-lapse photography. This will require that a few seconds of video be taken each day of the same side of one ant farm and from the same location. The zoom lens can be used to take closeups of the ants at work. Mark the placement of the ant farm on the table and the location of the camera so they will be the same during the daily recordings. When played back, the view of the ants working will be speeded up to show this in a few minutes rather than many days. Students can then make more detailed observations, just as scientists do.

Activity

1. Discuss what the students saw as the ant farm(s) was assembled in the previous lesson. If available, show the video made during that lesson.

2. Distribute a data sheet to each student and explain how they will work in groups to observe the ants each day. Review the information on the data sheet so they will see that they are to make pencil drawings on their data sheets of the tunnels the ants made and then color them with the color you designate for that day. They will use a new color to continue the recording the next day, beginning where the tunnel left off the previous day. In this way, the new additions to the tunnel will be obvious.

3. Have the students continue to make daily records of the ant farm for at least two weeks.

Closure

- After the ants have formed many tunnels, cover one side of the habitat with black paper. Let students continue to record the uncovered side for about a week and then remove the paper.
- Have students compare the differences between sides. (*They should see many more tunnels on the side which was covered.*) Tell them to discuss why they think this happened. (*Ants live underground where it is dark. When the ant farm is covered, it was much more like their natural habitat.*)

Ant Farm Observations

Name:_____ Date: _____

To the Student: Observe the ant farm for at least two weeks, making drawings to show the changes you see. Add the changes in the tunnels to the last drawings in pencil and then trace over them with colored pen or pencil. Use a different color each day and record that day's color on the key by coloring the circle beside the date. If there is no change, record the data and write "no change" in the color column. Record both sides of the ant farm each day.

Key

Date   Color

Ant Farm Side A

A

Key

Date   Color

Ant Farm Side B

B

Make notes of interesting things you see happen. Be sure to include the dates of these observations. If you need more space for your notes, use another piece of lined paper.

Ant Book

Overview: *Students will create a book from their ant data sheets.*

Materials

- ant data sheets and drawings from previous lessons
- large construction paper or file folders
- crayons or colored pens
- transparency and copies of Body Parts of an Ant (page 130)

Activity

1. Let the students discuss some of the things they have learned about ants in this study. If available, show the video record of the ant. Discuss it as it is being viewed to point out the details of body structure and ant behavior.

2. Show the transparency of Body Parts of an Ant and discuss its details, as appropriate for this class.

3. Tell the students that they are going to create a science book from all the data sheets they have been doing during this study. Explain that this is just what real scientists do with their records.

4. Distribute large construction paper or file folders and crayons or pens. Tell the students to design a cover for their book which will show what they have learned about ants. Encourage them to be creative.

Closure

- Let students draw a picture on the inside of their book cover to show what they may have looked like to the ants they were studying. Remind them that the ants, like most insects, only see things which are close to them. Thus, they would see details of their faces only. Provide mirrors for the students to look at themselves as they do their drawings or have them draw each other.

- Have the students place their file card drawings and data sheets inside their covers. Distribute a copy of the Body Parts of an Ant for them to include in their book. If photographs of the students were taken during this study, distribute them to be enclosed in their book.

Body Parts of an Ant

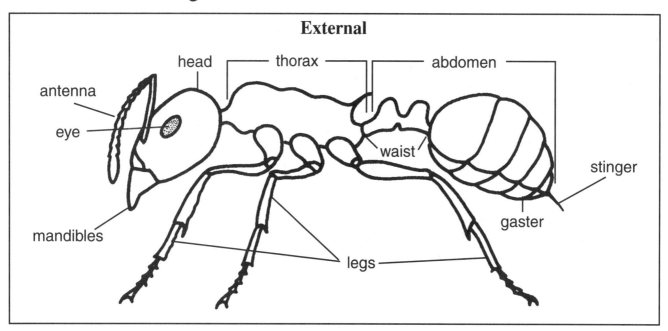

An ant is an insect and therefore has three main body parts—(1) the *head*, (2) the *thorax*, and (3) the *abdomen*. The main features of the head are the *eyes*, *antennae*, and *mandibles* (jaws). Three pairs of legs are attached to the thorax. The narrow front part of the abdomen is called the *waist*. Some ants have a *stinger* at the tip of the abdomen.

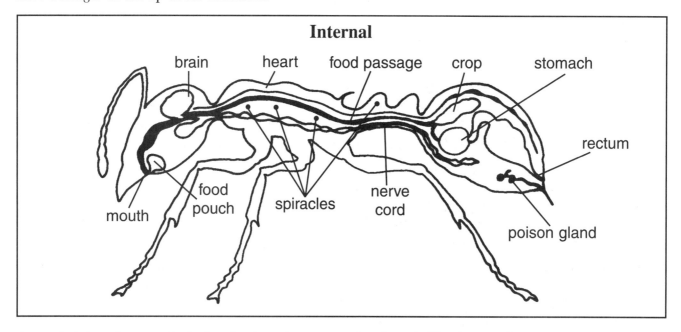

An ant's internal organs include a *brain* and *nerve cord* and a tubelike *heart*. The ant breathes through *spiracles*, which are tiny openings along the sides of its body. Its digestive system includes a food pouch that squeezes the liquid out of food. The liquid moves through a food passage to the *crop*, a storage pouch, and then to the *stomach*, where digestion occurs. Wastes pass through the *rectum* and out of the body. Only ants with stingers have the poison glands at the top of the abdomen.

Butterflies

Teacher Information

Butterflies are found nearly everywhere in the world. One of the most common of these is the painted lady butterfly, which will be used in this study. In the wild these butterflies are not harmful to commercial crops since they eat the mallow (malva) or hollyhock leaves, which are weeds.

The larva hatches from a tiny, pale green egg and then begins to feed. As the larva grows, it sheds its tight skin (a process called *molting*) and leaves it in a black furry ball. About 10 days after hatching, the larva hangs upside down and prepares to become a *pupa*. After 24 hours, the caterpillar's skin splits, and the thin brown *chrysalis* which has formed under the skin encases the pupa and will harden in about four hours. Butterfly pupae are enclosed in a chrysalis, not a cocoon. The pupae of most moths are encased in a *cocoon* made of silken thread produced by the moth larva and woven around its body.

The adult butterfly emerges in 7 to 10 days and expands its wings with fluid pumped from its abdomen. The wings take about an hour to harden before the butterfly can take flight. Some red fluid may be expelled, a waste material accumulated during the pupal stage.

Painted lady butterflies are easy to raise. The larvae and food are available commercially (see Resource section). Small plastic vials with lids are supplied, one for each larva. The food, in the form of a paste, is sent with the larva and is divided among the vials. The larvae are placed inside, and then the vials are capped. The containers are kept in a well-lighted area where the temperature is 75°–80° F (24°–27° C). Each larva will form its chrysalis on the lid of its vial as it enters the pupa stage. The pupa is then transferred into an enclosure where the adult will eventually emerge.

When the adult butterfly first emerges, its long tubelike mouth (*proboscis*) is in two parts. The butterfly extends the pieces of the proboscis several times until the parts are joined lengthwise into one hollow tube. It curls up outside the head when not in use. The butterfly will drink nectar through this strawlike mouth in the wild. In captivity, it can drink juice from pieces of fruit such as orange or watermelon. These may be placed on the bottom of the butterfly enclosure and replaced every two days.

Butterflies will mate after emerging, and the females may begin to lay eggs within five to seven days after they emerge. The eggs will hatch in three to five days. It is best to free the butterflies within three days of their emerging so the eggs can be laid in the wild. Release the butterfly on a sunny day in an area where there are plants, preferably weeds.

The release is a great event, and all students should participate. If they sit or stand very still as the butterflies are released, they may be treated to having a butterfly land on them. It is as if the butterflies are bidding their "parents" farewell before flying off to make their own way in the world. Students may see the butterflies in the area for several days after the release.

Recording Larvae Growth

Teacher Information

This activity and the next will require approximately five to nine days from the day the painted lady larvae arrive.

Materials

- 30 live painted lady butterfly larvae (Purchase from Insect Lore; see Resources section.)
- vials with lids and food (included with butterfly larvae)
- two paper towels
- copies of Painted Lady Butterfly Larvae Record (page 133)
- metric ruler
- magnifier

Lesson Preparation

- Use the lid from one of the vials to draw 30 circles on the paper towel. Cut the circles out to be placed inside the lid. Use a pencil and label each paper circle (1–30).
- Distribute nutrient into the vials and carefully transfer one larva into each. Put the paper circle (number should be visible through the vial) and then lid over the tops of containers.
- If there are no holes in the lids, use a pin to poke about five holes in each.
- Use a permanent felt pen and label each lid with the same number as the paper inside the lid.

Activity

1. Ask the students how many have seen butterflies. Let them describe these to the class. Tell the students that they are going to raise painted lady butterflies from the larva stage.
2. Distribute a magnifier and larva to each student. Caution them to keep vial lids closed to avoid letting germs enter. Explain that they should not shake or drop the container or the larva will become frightened. Tell them to examine the larva with their magnifiers and discuss the details with a partner. (*Some may see green balls on the food; these are feces from the larva.*)
3. Distribute a record sheet to each student and have each put his or her name and vial number on it. Show them how to write today's date below the first vial.
4. Help them measure the larva through the container, gently turning it on its side if necessary.
5. Have students draw their larva, using a magnifier to view the details of legs, feet, and head. The drawings should be life-size and show the larva's location inside the vial.

Closure

- Students will keep daily records of their larva until it becomes a pupa.
- Have them compare the growth of their larva with those of other students in the class. Let them calculate and record the difference between each day's growth.
- Save all records students make to enclose in a butterfly book at the end of this study.
- *Optional:* Make a time-lapse video of one larva's growth to adulthood so students can replay it at the end of the study.
- *Optional:* Take photographs of the students and their butterflies at different stages to include in their butterfly book.

Painted Lady Butterfly Larvae Record

Name:_____ Vial #_____

To the Student: Measure and record your butterfly larva each day without removing the lid of the vial.

Date: _____

Length: _____mm

Date: _____

Length: _____mm

Growth: _____mm

Date: _____

Length: _____mm

Growth: _____mm

Date: _____

Length: _____mm

Growth: _____mm

Date: _____

Length: _____mm

Growth: _____mm

Date: _____

Length: _____mm

Growth: _____mm

Date: _____

Length: _____mm

Growth: _____mm

Date: _____

Length: _____mm

Growth: _____mm

Date: _____

Length: _____mm

Growth: _____mm

Getting to Know Your Larva

Student Name: _____ Vial #_____

To the Student: Use your magnifier to see the details of your painted lady larva and complete the information below.

1. Look at the bristles which are called setae *(sē tē)* on the caterpillar (larva).

   • What color are they? _____

   • Are there little setae coming out of the bigger ones? _____

   • Draw a large picture of one seta in the circle.

2. Why do you think the larva has setae? _____

   _____

3. Look at the legs of your larva. How many does it have? _____

4. Are the legs exactly alike? _____

Draw the legs on the right places on the larva outline below.

Painted Lady Butterfly Larva

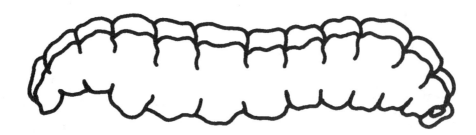

5. Draw the mouthparts of the larva below. Use your magnifier to make this picture large enough to show the details.

Larva Mouthparts

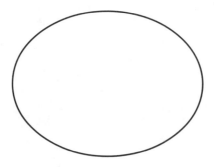

How Does Your Larva Grow?

Overview: *Student will graph and analyze the growth data of the painted lady larvae.*

Materials

- Painted Lady Butterfly Larvae Record (from previous activity)
- transparency and copies of Graphing Larva Growth (page 136)

Lesson Preparation

Wait until the larvae have all become pupa to do this activity.

Activity

1. Discuss what students have learned about the larvae up until this point. Be sure they know that the black "fuzzy" balls are not feces but the skin which is shed by the larvae as they become too big for it. It is important for students to notice that not all larvae become pupa at the same time, even though they were all the same age when first being measured. Just like other animals, including humans, growth varies with each individual.

2. Let students examine the pupa and make a final drawing of it on their record sheet.

3. Distribute a copy of Graphing Larvae Growth to each student and go over the instructions. Use the transparency to show how to place dates on the graph. Show them how to plot the first data from record sheets, showing the larva length in millimeters when they began measuring. Let them add the rest of the data and then show them how to connect the data points as a line graph.

4. Compare the differences in the lengths of the various larvae. Like the students, even though the larvae are all about the same age, their sizes are different.

Closure

- Help students complete the graph summary by filling in the missing information. This can be done by following the line between the data points on either side of the missing data and seeing where it crosses the line for the missing date(s). As in the example, data for the 11th and 12th were not plotted. The line joining the data for the 10th and 13th shows the length on these dates was approximately 12.5 and 12.7 mm, respectively.

- Explain how they can tell when their larva grew most rapidly. (*The graph line will rise rapidly.*) In the example shown here, the fastest growth was between the 10th and 12th.

- See if all the larvae had their fastest growth at the same time. (*This is not very likely to happen.*)

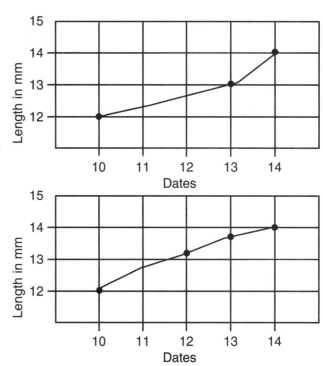

Graphing Larva Growth

Name:_____ Vial #_____

To the Student: Make a graph using the data you collected on the Painted Lady Butterfly Larva Record. Write the dates for this study along the bottom of the graph, including weekends and holidays. Plot the data on the graph. Connect the dots when all data has been entered.

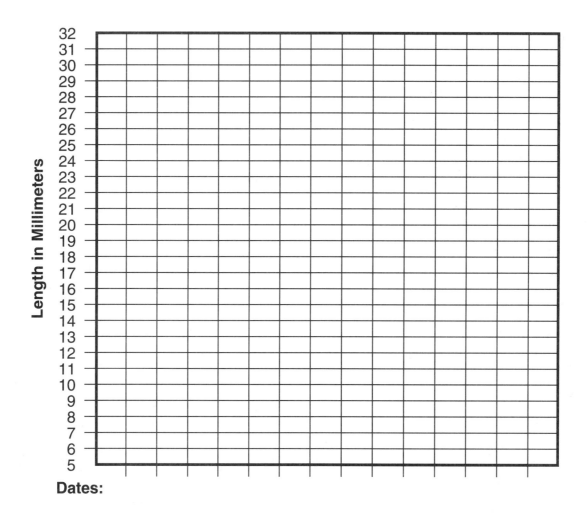

Dates:

Graph Summary

List the dates when you did not measure the larva. Use your graph to find this missing data and record it.

Date	Larva Size from Graph
_____	_____ mm
_____	_____ mm
_____	_____ mm

Use the graph to find between which dates your larva grew most rapidly: _____ and _____

Chrysalis to Butterfly

── Teacher Information ──

Once the larva has formed a chrysalis, it should be carefully transferred to a butterfly enclosure. Students will draw their chrysalides and keep a record of them throughout the period of their development. Hopefully, they will witness the emergence of at least one of the butterflies.

Overview: *Students will watch the transformation of pupa to adult butterfly.*

Materials

- two pairs of 12-inch (30 cm) embroidery hoops (available at most stores which carry yarn)
- 1.5 yards (1.4 m) netting 45" (114 cm) wide from a fabric store
- 12-inch diameter circle of cardboard (laminated to make it reusable)
- Chrysalis to Butterfly record (page 139)
- The Butterfly's Story (page 141)

Lesson Preparation

Follow the instructions below to make butterfly enclosures. It will be best if several are made to spread the pupae out and make it easier for students to continue their study. Each butterfly enclosure will look like a tube of net gathered at the top and bottom and held open at each end by the embroidery hoops.

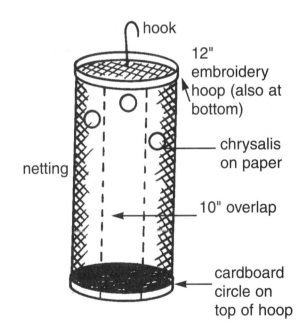

- Work on a large table with an assistant to help you. Lay the netting flat on the table and fold it lengthwise so it forms a 10-inch (25 cm) overlap.
- Tie heavy string or yarn around the netting about 6 inches (15 cm) from each end to form the tube.
- Insert the inner hoop from one pair of hoops inside the net tube as close to the top as possible.
- Place the outer hoop over this one on the outside of the net tube to secure the hoop to the net.
- Place the other hoop at the bottom of the tube.
- Use a large paper clip to make the hook and suspend the tube from the ceiling.
- Have someone else hold the net tube up while you adjust the hoops so the tube hangs straight.
- Place the cardboard circle inside the net tube at the bottom where it can rest on the hoop.
- Remove the chrysalis (pupa) from the vial, being careful not to dislodge it from the paper. Pin the paper to the inside of the net tube, keeping the chrysalis facing away from the net. Use toothpicks to keep the overlap area closed to prevent the butterflies from escaping.

Chrysalis to Butterfly *(cont.)*

Activity

1. Let the students find their butterfly chrysalis by the number on the paper to which it is attached. (If a pupa has become dislodged from the paper, just lay it on the bottom of the tube on top of the paper so the number can identify it. It should be able to emerge.)

2. Tell the students that the larva is undergoing a great many changes during this stage of its life. Distribute a copy of the Chrysalis to Butterfly record and explain that they should draw the chrysalis in the box. Tell them to draw what they think the larva will become when it emerges beside the drawing of the chrysalis.

3. Help students complete their pictures using colors that match those of the chrysalides.

4. Over the next few days, have students watch their pupae carefully to look for colors of wings showing through. See if they can find which end is the head and alert them to look for legs. The chrysalides should not be removed or handled during this time.

5. The butterfly should begin to emerge about 7–10 days after it becomes a pupa. (*Note:* The butterfly "emerges" from the chrysalis; it does not "hatch" as it does from the egg.)

Closure

- Read the painted lady butterfly information (page 131) regarding what to look for during emergence and be ready to share this with the students as the pupae begin to darken. This will prepare the students to make careful observations of those which emerge during class time.

- When a butterfly begins to emerge, have all the students gather to watch the process. They should watch as the butterfly pumps fluid into its wings and extends and curls its tongue to glue the two halves together. If red fluid is excreted, remind them that this is normal. The butterfly is getting rid of wastes that formed while it was a pupa.

- Place cut fruit (e.g., watermelon or oranges) on the bottom of the enclosure. The butterflies will gather there, and students can observe them use their long tubelike mouths to drink the juice. They can survive for several days inside the butterfly enclosure but should be released when all pupae have emerged. Follow the teacher information (page 131) for more details on how the butterflies may be released.

- After the butterflies are released, distribute a copy of The Butterfly's Story to each student.

Chrysalis to Butterfly *(cont.)*

Student Name: _____ Vial #_____

To the Student: Use a magnifier to look carefully at your chrysalis. Make a large drawing of the chrysalis below. Draw the antennae, eyes, wings, legs, and abdomen, which you can see through the skin of the chrysalis. Be sure to label these parts on your drawing.

Painted Lady Chrysalis

- Carefully color the chrysalis as close to its real colors as possible.

- When the chrysalis is about seven days old, it will turn dark. What do you suppose this means?

  _____

- When the chrysalis turns dark, look for the wings and see if you can detect the colors of the wings through the thin shell. What colors do you see? _____

- What is the date you first began your observations of the larva? _____

- When did the chrysalis become a butterfly? _____

- From the larva stage, how many days did it take the larva to become a butterfly? _____

- Draw a picture of your beautiful butterfly below.

My Painted Lady Butterfly

The Butterfly's Story

Overview: *Students will culminate their study of butterflies by writing the life story of a butterfly and making a butterfly book using their data sheets.*

Materials

- butterfly record sheets made in previous lessons
- large construction paper
- copies of The Butterfly's Story worksheet (page 141)
- colored pens or crayons
- *optional:* colored tissue

Activity

1. Review all that students have learned about butterflies as they observed the painted lady butterflies. If available, show the time-lapse video record of this.

2. Tell the students that they are going to make a butterfly book that will be like a scientist's notebook since it will have all the records they made of their butterflies.

3. Distribute a copy of The Butterfly's Story and review the instructions with the students. Tell them this will be the last page they place in their butterfly book. Encourage them to use their data sheets as they write the story and complete the life cycle chart.

Closure

- Distribute construction paper to the students and have them create a cover for their butterfly book. They could make a butterfly on the cover using torn pieces of brightly colored tissue paper.

- Have students make their butterfly book enclosing their data sheets and The Butterfly's Story, as well as any photographs taken of butterflies during their study.

The Butterfly's Story *(cont.)*

Student Name: _____

To the Student: Pretend you are a butterfly talking to a butterfly larva. Tell the larva how it will change as it grows up. Make drawings inside the circles of what the larva will look like as it changes.

Hello, little larva. Someday you will be a beautiful butterfly just like me. Let me tell you how you are going to change into a butterfly.

First, you will _____

_____

_____.

You will look like this:

Since you get too big for your skin, you will

_____.

The old skin looks like this:

You will look like this:

Finally, you will hang _____.

You will look like this:

Now it is time for you to _____

_____.

You will look like this:

At last you will _____

and become a _____.

Silkworms

— Teacher Information —

Raising silkworms (*sericulture*) is one of man's oldest occupations, beginning in China nearly 5,000 years ago. The silk spun by a silkworm in making its cocoon is woven into the most beautiful fabric in the world, at one time used only for royalty in China. Possession of silkworms was a closely guarded secret by the Chinese for several thousand years. Not until the 11th century did European traders manage to steal a few eggs and carry them to Europe to begin silkworm rearing. Sericulture spread rapidly throughout Europe and Asia during the following centuries.

Silkworm eggs are available commercially. It is important to order the eggs in the spring when mulberry trees begin to produce leaves, for these are the silkworm's only source of food. The tiny eggs may be placed in the bottom of a small cardboard box. Before hatching, the eggs will turn darker around the edges. When the tiny worms hatch, they will be about the size of a comma. They should be picked up with a small paintbrush and placed on a clean, fresh young mulberry leaf.

During the first week, fresh leaves should be placed on top of old ones which contain the larvae. After the first week, the larvae will be large enough to eat the leaves before they dry out, and you will need only to lay clean fresh leaves over them. Sometime during each day remove old or bare leaves from the rearing box. Silkworms have become so domesticated through thousands of years that they depend completely on humans to care for them. To clean the leaves, rinse and drain them before using. Leaves may be stored in the refrigerator in a plastic bag.

The larvae molt about four times as they outgrow their skins. After 25–30 days the silkworms will stop eating. Soon after this, they begin to rear their heads and move them back and forth above the rest of the body. The larvae become slightly smaller and may have a slight color change. The silkworm begins to look for a quiet corner to form its cocoon. It builds the wall of the cocoon by making rows and rows of two continuous strands of silk. It produces the silk in two special glands and sends it out a tube called a *spinneret*, located near its lower lip. The silk comes out a liquid but quickly dries in the air. After the cocoon is done, the silkworm sheds its skin, and the pupa wiggles free, encased inside the cocoon. Within the pupa, the new silk moth begins to form.

The moth escapes from the cocoon by producing a fluid from the mouth that dissolves a hole through the silk. When the hole is big enough, the moth slips through. This usually takes place early in the morning. The moth will fill its tiny wings with fluid. These are far too small for it to fly away. Mating begins almost immediately and may last about a day. Egg laying begins as soon as pairs separate. These are laid in neat rows upon any surface. Egg laying may continue for about a week, most eggs being laid on the first three days. Females may lay about 500 yellow eggs, which later turn grey. The eggs must be refrigerated (not frozen) until the next spring before they will hatch. When the leaves return in the spring, the cycle can begin again.

Silkworm Larvae

Overview: *Students will raise silkworm larvae and record growth.*

Materials

- 25 silkworm eggs (See Carolina Biological in Resources section.)
- mulberry leaves (required as food)
- silk cloth (e.g., scarf) and polyester cloth
- cardboard boxes (Gift boxes will do.)
- Silkworm Growth Record data sheet (page 145)
- magnifier and metric ruler for each student
- transparency of Life Cycle of the Silkworm Moth (page 144)
- snack sized zip-lock bag
- *optional:* microscope
- *optional:* video camera

Lesson Preparation

- Order silkworm eggs to arrive when mulberry leaves are available.
- Usually eggs arrive glued to paper, just as they were laid. Snip off a tiny piece of the paper with 1–3 eggs attached and place it in a zip-lock bag.
- After the larvae hatch, divide them into several small, shallow cardboard boxes.

Activity

1. Let students feel the silk and polyester cloth. Explain that the polyester cloth is made from petroleum. Tell them that the silk is made by the caterpillar (*larva*) of a special moth. Let them know that they are going to raise the larvae of the silk moth so they can see this fabric being spun.

2. Divide students into small groups and provide each with a magnifier and a bag with silkworm eggs. Let students see the eggs through a microscope if available. Tell them the bag will keep the eggs clean and safe and should therefore not be opened.

3. Give each student a copy of the Silkworm Growth Record and help them complete their first drawing of the egg. The records should be collected after each class and returned to the students after the eggs hatch so students can add more information.

4. Show the Life Cycle of the Silkworm Moth so students can see about how long it will take to witness the entire cycle.

5. After eggs hatch and the larvae are divided into separate boxes, divide students into small groups and assign each to watch a different box. Have students use the magnifiers (and microscope) to make their records. Help students measure the tiny silkworm and record its length. You may need to make more copies of the record sheet for students since the larvae take so long to grow.

Closure

- When silkworms are large enough to pick up, place them on pieces of mulberry leaf. Give one to each student to watch it as it eats the leaf. Have them make drawings of their silkworms eating and write descriptions of what they see, hear, and feel. Save this and the other record sheet(s) for their silkworm book.

- If possible, make a video record of the growth of the silkworms in time-lapse, about 30 seconds of video each time to show the larva's growth and complete life cycle.

Life Cycle of the Silkworm Moth

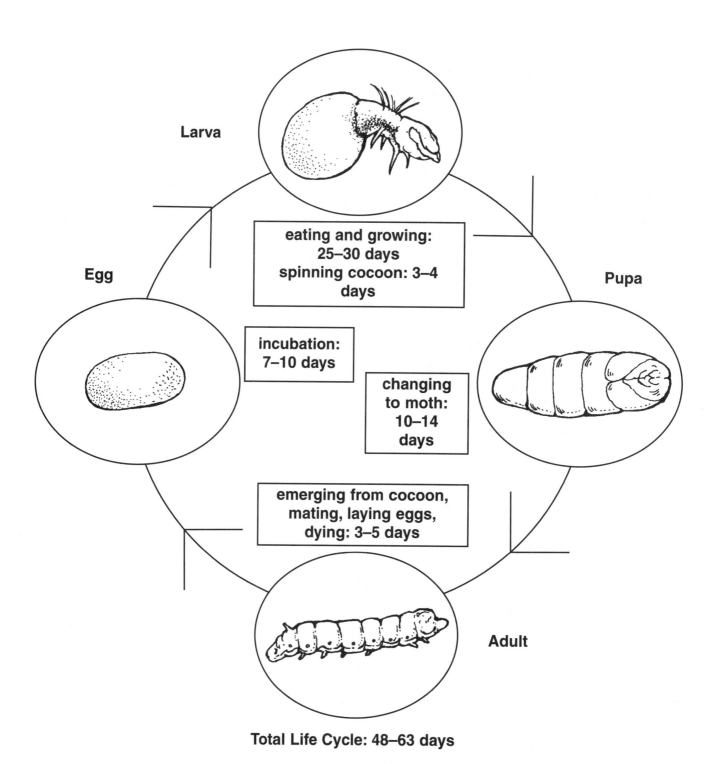

Larva

eating and growing:
25–30 days
spinning cocoon: 3–4
days

Pupa

Egg

incubation:
7–10 days

changing
to moth:
10–14
days

emerging from cocoon,
mating, laying eggs,
dying: 3–5 days

Adult

Total Life Cycle: 48–63 days

Silkworm Growth Record

Name:_____ Date Study Began: _____

To the Student: Keep a record of the silkworm so you can find out how it grows and changes.

Show what a silkworm egg looks like through a magnifier.

After the egg hatches, use a magnifier to help you see the tiny larva. Measure
it and record the date and size on the chart. Finally, make a drawing of the silkworm.

Date	Size	Picture	Date	Size	Picture

On the back of this paper, tell some of the things you have learned about your silkworm during this
study.

Larva to Pupa

Overview: *Students will observe the pupa stage of the silkworm moth and unwind the silk from several cocoons.*

Materials

- silkworm larvae (entering or at pupa stage)
- egg cartons
- copies of the Silkworm Growth Record from previous lesson
- Life Cycle of the Silkworm Moth data sheet (page 148)
- hot water
- empty spools
- mugs or cups

Lesson Preparation

- Transfer the pupae to the egg cartons as they are forming their cocoon or after they are formed. The remaining larvae may continue to be fed and kept in their boxes. Place the cocoons in separate egg boxes so they will continue to be observed by the same groups of students.

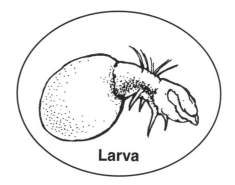

Larva

- When some of the larvae have entered the pupa stage and their cocoons are completed, select one from each group plus one more. These will be killed so the silk can be taken from the cocoon. If the adult moth emerges, the silk thread is broken and will not unwind as one thread. The extra cocoon will be opened to show students the pupa inside, which is different from the larva. To kill the pupa, bake the cocoons in an oven at about 200° for 30 minutes.

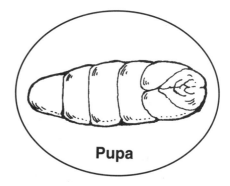

Pupa

- To prepare the cocoons for unwinding, place them in boiling water and boil them for about five minutes, turning them over and over with a fork. The silk will begin to loosen, and some tangled threads will appear around each of the cocoons. Remove them with a fork and place each in a cup of hot water. Find the end of the strand with your fingers by dipping the cocoon up and down in the water until you find a single strand of silk that pulls away easily. Put the end of that strand over the empty spool and begin to unwind it onto the spool. One large cocoon may have half a mile of unbroken thread. The dead pupa will be found after all the thread is unwound.

Larva to Pupa *(cont.)*

Activity

1. Review the Silkworm Growth Records with the students to summarize what they have learned to this point about the silkworm larvae. Have students add new information to the record.

2. Distribute a copy of the Life Cycle of the Silkworm Moth data sheet and have students complete the data which have been gathered thus far.

3. Compare their data with that on the same chart used at the beginning of this study. Discuss the differences in the length of time their silkworms went through their stages and those shown on the other chart. Have the various groups compare their data as well.

4. After the cocoons are about five days old, select those to be used for gathering the silk threads and one to be opened to show the pupa inside. Follow the instructions in the Lesson Preparation section to start the process of unwinding the cocoon.

5. Assign stations for students to work in and wind the silk on to the spool of thread. Keep the water in the cup to help the cocoon remain soft. It should be replaced with clean, warm water periodically. This process may take some time, for a large cocoon may have as much as ½ mile (.8 km) of silk in it.

6. Use cuticle scissors to cut open the extra cocoon and let the students see its contents. Find the last skin shed by the larva within the cocoon. Discuss how the pupa is different from the larva. Let students use magnifiers to examine the pupa and see if they can find the legs and segmented body. When the silk is unwound from the cocoons, have them examine those pupae as well.

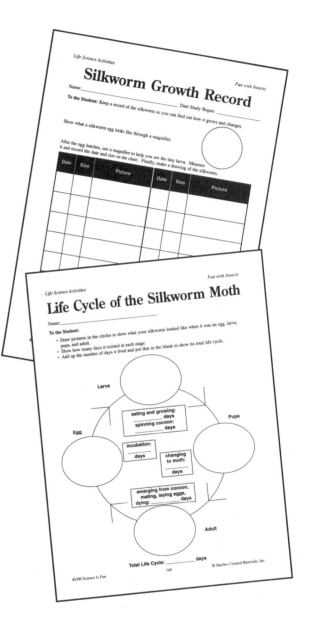

Closure

- Have the students add the drawing of the pupa to their Life Cycle charts and Silkworm Growth Records.

- After one cocoon is completely unwound, help the students measure its length. Rewind it on another spool or as it is measured.

Life Cycle of the Silkworm Moth

Name:_____

To the Student:

- Draw pictures in the circles to show what your silkworm looked like when it was an egg, larva, pupa, and adult.
- Show how many days it existed in each stage.
- Add up the number of days it lived and put that in the blank to show its total life cycle.

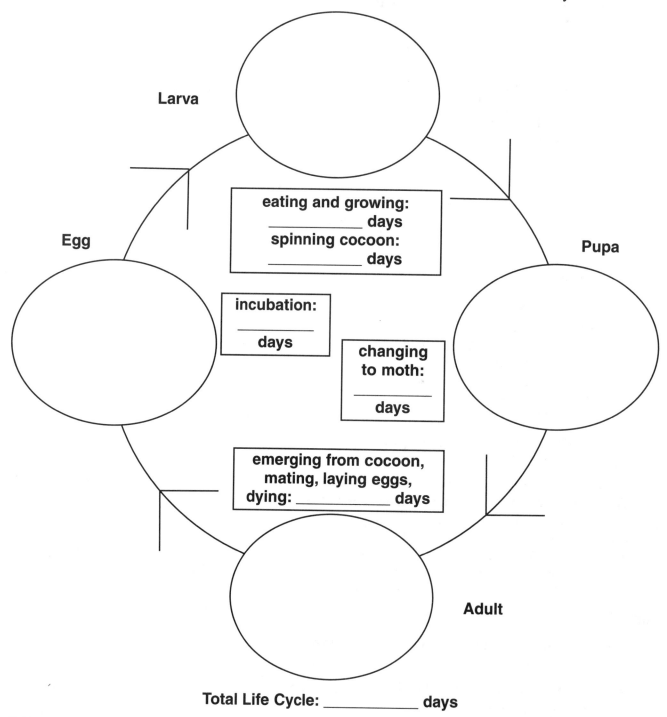

Larva

Egg

Pupa

eating and growing:
_____ days
spinning cocoon:
_____ days

incubation:
_____
days

changing to moth:
_____
days

emerging from cocoon, mating, laying eggs, dying: _____ **days**

Adult

Total Life Cycle: _____ **days**

Pupa to Adult

Overview: *Students will observe the silkworm become an adult moth.*

Materials

- silkworm cocoons
- recording charts
- magnifiers

Lesson Preparation

- Begin this lesson when the adult silkworm moths begin to emerge from the cocoons.
- Continue to add to the videotape, if one is being made of the life cycle of the silkworm.

Activity

1. Have the students gather around to observe as one or more moths begin to emerge. Help students look for details as they observe the moths emerge, as well as over the next few days. Examples of what to look for are given below.

   - moths exuding a liquid which dissolves a hole in the cocoon through which they emerge
   - fluid being pumped into the wings (This may take about 15 minutes.)
   - physical features such as legs, antennae, eyes, and body
   - movement of the moths
   - moths mating and laying eggs

2. Discuss the differences between the adult moth and the larva. Explain that the silkworm moth cannot fly since its wings are too small. Tell them that long ago it had larger wings but they have been bred to have smaller wings by those who raised them over many years. This keeps the moths from flying away and makes it easier to collect their eggs.

3. Have students make detailed drawings of the adults on the Life Cycle charts and Silkworm Growth Record. Measure the adults so they may add this information to their charts.

4. Explain that the moths will not eat—in fact, they have no teeth or biting parts in their mouths. They will only live long enough to mate and for the female to lay eggs; then they die.

Closure

- Have the students complete their Silkworm Journals by placing their drawings and charts inside a construction paper cover on which they make drawings of what they observed.
- Tell the students to write a summary of what they learned about these remarkable insects.
- Provide each student with some of the silk from the cocoon to tape into their journals.

Imaginary Insect Zoo

── Teacher Information ──

Students have learned about a wide variety of insects in this Fun with Insects section. This culminating activity will be fun as well as serving as an assessment.

Overview: *Students will make imaginary insects which have the essential characteristics of an insect, such as six legs and three body parts.*

Materials

- variety of items for construction of insects (e.g., pipe cleaners, egg cartons, cellophane)
- scissors
- glue gun
- white glue
- pictures of a variety of colorful and unusual insects
- copies of parent letter (page 151)
- copies of data sheet This Is My Insect (page 152)

Lesson Preparation

- Send letters to the parents requesting their assistance in gathering materials to use in creating fanciful insects.
- Assemble a variety of materials students can use in their construction, such as cardboard, crepe paper, paint, paper clips, and other school supplies.
- Set up a hot-glue area (operated by an adult) if students need creations glued this way.
- Place colorful and unusual insect pictures on a bulletin board. Put books of insects nearby.

Activity

1. As a post test, give the pretest Is This an Insect? that was used at the beginning of the study of insects. Have students discuss the results of the test and encourage them to tell how they can distinguish an insect from a noninsect.
2. Explain that students are going to make an insect zoo from imaginary insects that they create. Distribute the parent letter to each student and read and discuss it so they know what to collect for their insect constructions.
3. Show students the pictures of insects on the bulletin board and in books you have provided. Let them examine these to get some ideas about the materials they might need to make an insect.
4. After collecting materials, place them in a central area, permitting students to share the materials if they wish to do so. Review what makes an insect different from a noninsect.
5. Let students work on their imaginary insects. Allow sufficient time, perhaps several days.

Closure

- Distribute copies of the data sheet This Is My Insect to students and let them complete it to tell about their creation.
- Set aside an area for the insect zoo and arrange the students' insect models in it. Put each child's description with his or her model. Have students make invitations for other classes and parents, inviting them to visit the zoo.

Parent Letter for Insect Materials

Date_____

Dear Parents:

Your child has learned much about insects as our class looked at a wide variety of insects brought from areas around our houses and school grounds. We have also raised mealworms, ants, butterflies, and silkworms. Now, we are ready to create our own unique zoo of imaginary insects. We need your help in gathering the materials students can use to create their imaginary insects. Some of these are listed below:

- aluminum foil
- pipe cleaners
- thin wire
- feathers
- colored cellophane
- small buttons
- toilet tissue rolls
- egg cartons

We have looked at pictures of many different types of insects to give the students ideas. Talk with your child, asking what may be needed to make his or her insect. If you can spare extra items beyond those your child will use, they will be gratefully accepted for other students to use.

The class will begin to create the insects on_____. Please send the materials to school with your child before this date. Our Imaginary Insect Zoo should be ready for you to visit within a week after we begin construction. You will receive a notice announcing its grand opening and inviting you to visit.

Thank you for your help in enriching our study of insects.

Cordially,

This Is My Insect

Name: _____ Date: _____

My insect's name is _____ .

It eats _____ .

Tell how your insect can . . .

- **smell:** _____

- **hear:** _____

- **see:** _____

- **taste:** _____

- **eat:** _____

- **move around:** _____

- **protect itself:** _____

Make a drawing to show your insect's life cycle.

Fun with Plants Introduction

Plants grow in almost every part of the world—mountaintops, oceans, deserts, and polar regions. Plants have amazing abilities to adapt to many different environments, much as insects have done. Without plants, there would be no life on Earth. They provide the air we breathe and the food humans and other animals eat. Plants also supply us with many useful products such as lumber and cotton fibers.

Scientists believe there are more than 350,000 species of plants. Their size varies from barely visible plants that grow on the forest floor to the largest living life forms on Earth, giant sequoia trees of California. Some are more than 290 feet (88 m) high and over 30 feet (9 m) wide. Plants are also the oldest living things on Earth. One bristlecone pine tree in California started growing 4,000 to 5,000 years ago.

Plants develop from a tiny form called an *embryo*, which is usually contained within a seed. Seeds vary in size; the tobacco seed is so small that more than 2,500 grow in a pod less than ³/₄ inch (19 mm) long. The largest seed is the coconut, which may weigh up to 20 pounds (9 kg). The seed provides food for the embryo plant until it can push its leaves above ground and begin to manufacture its own food. This is done from air, sunlight, and water by a process known as *photosynthesis*. Roots bring nourishment to the plant by absorbing dissolved minerals from the soil and water. Seeds require warmth, moisture, and oxygen to grow. The stages of a sprouting seed, called *germination*, are shown below.

Seed Germination

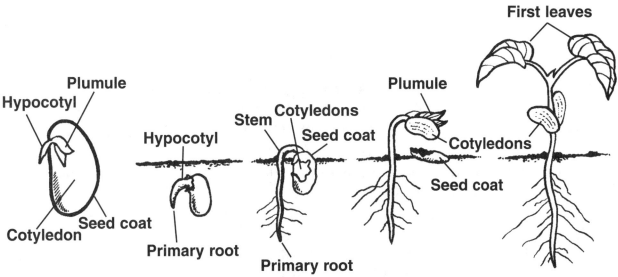

| Cross section of a seed shows the embyro in a seed coat. | The seed splits and the hypocotyl forms the primary root. | As the root grows down, the stem breaks through the soil. | The cotyledons free the plumule, and the seed coat drops off. | As the stem grows upward, the plumule forms the first leaves. |

The activities in this section are designed to provide students with opportunities to observe a wide variety of plants. This will begin with a search for seeds at school and home. Students will gather data as they observe seeds germinating and do simple research on growing plants in different environments. Other methods of growing plants from parent plants (*cloning*) will be experienced using yams, carrots, begonia leaves, and pineapple. Seeds and flowers will be dissected to discover their parts. Finally, students will create a model of a flower and a plant.

Is This a Seed?

Overview: *Students will sort a variety of materials to learn how to identify seeds.*

Materials

- variety of seeds (including seeds from fruits such as avocado, orange, and apple) These may be purchased in packets at a nursery. They will be used in the next activity as well.
- small objects which may look like seeds (e.g., BBs, Styrofoam pellets, marbles)
- paper plates
- blank file cards

Lesson Preparation

- Mix the materials to be used in sorting for seeds (listed above).
- Divide this among paper plates for groups of students to sort.

Activity

1. Give each student a blank file card and have each draw a seed on it. Do not give them any help since this is a pretest. Have them share their drawings and tell what they think a seed looks like. Collect the cards to use in a later class.

2. Explain that students are going to do an activity to see if they can tell seeds from things which are not seeds. Divide the students into small groups and distribute a plate of the mixture to each group. Give each group a copy of the sorting sheet Is This a Seed? Discuss the sorting sheet with them so they see that there are three choices for the things they will sort. Tell them to take turns putting each item from the paper plate into the box in which they think it belongs.

3. As students sort the items, encourage them to discuss objects with the group members if they are unsure of where each belongs. Tell them to put any item in the "?" box if the group cannot agree on classifying it as a seed or nonseed.

4. When all sorting has been done, have the groups move to another group's area and, without moving any of the items, see if they agree. Discuss the results of the sorting to find which items were in the "?" box and which items were placed in different categories by the groups. (Do not give the answers; this same activity will be repeated at the end of the study.)

Closure

- Take students on a "seed hunt" around the school grounds. Collect these, if permitted, and then bring them into the classroom to begin a display of seeds. Include nonseed items which the students may have thought were seeds. Set aside a table area where students can display the seeds and nonseeds they collected.
- Send home the parent letter requesting that seeds be sent to school to help in this study. Add these to the seed display table. Put some strange seeds (e.g., a coconut) in the display.

Is This a Seed? *(cont.)*

Instructions: Look at each object on the plate and put it in one of the boxes below. If you are not sure if it is seed or nonseed, put it in the "?" box.

Seeds

Nonseeds

?

Parent Letter for Seeds

Date_____

Dear Parents:

We have begun our study of plants by sorting a variety of materials to find seeds. Our class also went for a walk around the school grounds to search for seeds. The boys and girls are still learning the differences between seeds and nonseeds. Each of them has been asked to look around the house and outside in the yard to find examples of what they think might be seeds to bring to class. Please help them in this assignment but do not tell them if an item is a true seed or not. They might look for seeds in some of the following places:

- cereal

- bushes

- soil

- spices used in cooking

- flowers

- trees

The students have been asked to bring these seeds to school during this week. We have a special area dedicated to our collection of seeds and nonseeds. These will be sorted later after we have learned more about seeds.

As always, you are welcome to come visit our classroom and see this display.

Thank you for your help with our study of seeds.

Cordially,

Can You Match This?

Overview: *Students will match seeds with those from seed packets.*

Materials

- 30 different packets of seeds with pictures of the plants they will become (Select examples of large and small seeds. You should have more seeds than there are students.)
- white glue
- blank file cards
- cards with seed pictures drawn by students in the first lesson.
- *optional:* whole coconut

Lesson Preparation

- Glue an example of the seed from each packet near the picture of the plant on the package.
- Number the file cards 1–30 and glue an example of each seed to them. Keep a record of the seed glued to each card.
- Spread seed packets around the room in reach of students.

Activity

1. Give each student a blank file card and have each draw a picture of a seed. Give them the pictures they drew in the first lesson and have them compare their pictures. Collect the cards and save them for future use.
2. With the students, review the seed collection on the display table. Divide the table into two parts, one for seeds and the other for nonseeds. Have students take turns sorting items. If students cannot agree on where to place an item, put it in a separate area of the table and label the area with a question mark.
3. Ask students where seeds come from. (Many will have no idea or think they only come from stores.) Explain that they are about to play a matching game with seeds you have purchased.
4. Give each student a card with a seed glued to it. Show them where you have placed the seed packets. Tell them that they are going to move about the room, looking for the seeds which match the seed glued to their card. When they find it, they should take the seed packet and their card and return to their seats.
5. Let the students begin their search to match their seeds. If two students claim the same packet, have them examine their seeds carefully, perhaps using a magnifier, to see which seed it matches. This activity will improve the observation skills of the students since some of the seeds will look very much alike.
6. When all seeds have been matched, have students return their seed packets. Collect their seed cards in a basket or box. Mix up the cards and let students draw another seed card; if they get the same one as before, let them choose another from the box.

Closure

- Have the students sit in small groups and examine their seeds to find what they have in common. They will find that some seeds look alike, while others look very different.
- *Optional:* Show them the coconut and explain that it is the largest seed of all. Crack it open and let them taste a bite.

What's Inside a Seed?

Overview: *Students will dissect seeds to find the embryo plant inside.*

Materials

- large lima beans (two for each student)
- peanuts in the shell (enough for each student plus extras)
- magnifier for each student
- blank file cards

Lesson Preparation

- Soak lima beans for at least three hours prior to this lesson. Keep enough dry beans for all to have one for comparison.

Activity

1. Distribute a file card and dry lima bean to each student. Have them fold the card in half. Tell them to draw the outline of the lima bean on one half the card. Draw a model on the board so they will know to make outlines large enough to fill half the card.

2. Tell the students to draw within the bean outline what they think is inside the lima bean.

3. Distribute a soaked bean and magnifier to each student. Show them how to peel off the outer skin and set it aside. Ask them what they think the skin does for the seed. (*It protects the seed just as their own skin does.*)

4. The seed will now begin to open. Caution students that what they are looking for inside the seed will be very tiny and the same color as the seed. Have them look carefully between the two halves of the seed to find the tiny embyro plant. (*It will consist of a thick root and two flattened leaves with veins.*)

5. Have students use their magnifiers to examine the small plant. Help them to find details. Tell them to make another outline of the lima bean seed on the other half of their file card and draw the tiny plant which they see inside their seed.

Closure

- Ask the students if they think that a tiny plant is inside every seed. (*Many may think that only the lima bean has these.*) Distribute a peanut in the shell to each student. Ask them if peanuts are seeds. (*Most will be unsure*). Explain that all nuts are seeds. Have them open the peanut shell to find the nuts inside. Let them peel off the skin, reminding them that this is just like the lima bean skin. Have the students open the peanuts carefully to see if there is a tiny plant inside. If they look closely, they will see that in fact there is a small plant.

- Ask students again if they think that a small plant is inside each seed. Tell them that baby plants live off material inside a seed until they grow into a plant and can make food for themselves. Tell students to eat the peanuts so they can see that people can eat the food in these seeds and get nourishment from it just as the baby plant would.

- Give students their original seed drawings and have them make new drawings on the same card. Let them compare what they have learned about seeds since they made the first drawing.

Where Do Seeds Come From?

Overview: *Students will examine a variety of plants to find seeds. They also eat some seeds.*

Materials

- assortment of nuts
- variety of fresh fruits and vegetables (e.g., banana, apple, orange, avocado, corn, tomato)
- knife
- paper plates and clear plastic wrap
- mixture of seeds, nonseeds, and sorting sheets from Is This a Seed? activity (pages 154–155)

Lesson Preparation

- Lay the nuts and fruits on a table where students may gather to see them. Have these on display as students enter the classroom and allow them to look at these before beginning.

Activity

1. Divide the students into small groups and have each of them think of three things they have learned about seeds. Tell them to take turns sharing these in their groups. Discuss some of the major concepts about seeds which they described in groups.

2. Gather the students around the table with nuts and fruits displayed. Ask them where they think seeds come from. Tell them that everything on the table is a seed or has a seed inside it.

3. Show the nuts and let students eat them. Ask them to tell what is inside each nut (*embyro plant*).

4. Show them the fruits and vegetables and ask what is inside them. (*Not all students will realize that seeds are found in them*). Cut each of these open, wrap them in plastic wrap, and put them on separate paper plates. Pass them around so all the students can examine them. Be sure they find the location of the seeds in each of the samples.

5. Have the students tell which seeds they have eaten along with fruits and vegetables (e.g., banana or tomato) and which seeds are removed rather than eaten (e.g., orange or pumpkin). If you use an ear of corn as an example, point out that the only parts we eat are the kernels—seeds.

6. Cut small pieces of the fruit and vegetables which can be eaten raw and let the students taste these.

Closure

- Distribute the mixture of seed and nonseeds to the students along with the sorting sheet used in Is This a Seed? at the beginning of this study. Let them sort the materials again and compare this with the first time they did this activity.

- As homework, ask students to look for seeds they might eat with their evening meal or tomorrow's breakfast. Have them write to their parents saying that they are to tell the class what seeds they eat for dinner or breakfast. Include an invitation to the parents to help them identify these and perhaps send a sample of the seeds for their child to show the class.

How Do Seeds Grow?

Overview: *Students will plant various seeds to observe them grow.*

Materials

- pinto beans
- lima beans
- clear plastic cups (9–10 oz)
- paper towels
- soldering iron or other tool which gets hot

- metric ruler
- permanent ink marker
- copies of the data sheet Seed Growth Record (page 161)

Lesson Preparation

- With a hot tool such as a soldering iron, melt several holes in the bottom of the clear plastic cups. These are drainage holes since the cups will be used for growing seeds.
- Soak the lima beans and pinto beans for an hour prior to beginning. Each student will need one of each of these beans.

Activity

1. Distribute the file cards with the seeds drawn on them. Review with the students what they saw inside the seeds. Ask them what they think happens to a seed when it is planted. (Do not describe a growing seed; they will discover this on their own.)

2. Divide the class into groups of two or three students. Distribute a lima and a pinto bean (seed) to each student. Give each group a plastic cup and three paper towels. Have the students fold one paper towel in thirds lengthwise and line the wall of the cup with it. They should form a ball with the other two towels and push it into the center of the cup to support the first towel. Add enough to dampen the paper towels, letting excess water drain off.

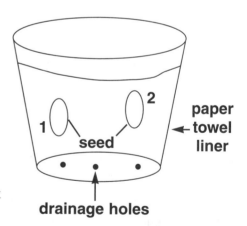

paper towel liner

seed

drainage holes

3. Have each child push the two seeds about halfway down the cup between the paper and the wall but still visible through the cup. Number the seeds in each cup, using the permanent felt pen.

4. Distribute the Seed Growth Record to each student and have each complete the information. Have them place today's date under the first cup and then draw their seeds.

5. Students should make drawings every day to show the growth of their seeds. Give each a folder to keep this record in, as well as other data they will be keeping during the study of plants. These will be placed in a plant journal at the end of the study.

Closure

This project will take several weeks. During that time, students should continue their records of the growth of the plants. Discuss what happens as the plants grow, such as the development of the two leaves which were inside the seeds and the withering of the original seed once it is no longer needed.

Seed Growth Record

Name: _____ Lima Bean Seed #_____ Pinto Bean Seed #_____

To the Student: Make a drawing each day to show what happens to your seeds as they grow. When the stems begin to grow, measure them and write their length under the containers.

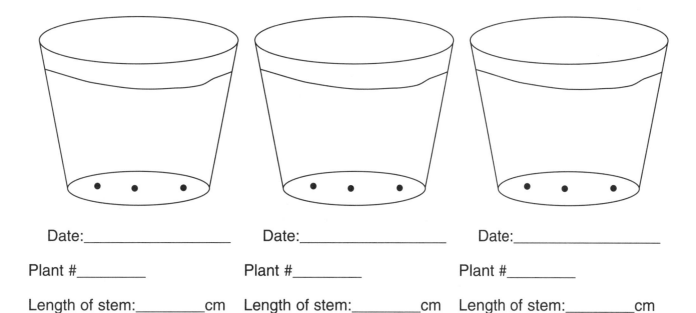

Date:_____   Date:_____   Date:_____

Plant #_____   Plant #_____   Plant #_____

Length of stem:_____cm   Length of stem:_____cm   Length of stem:_____cm

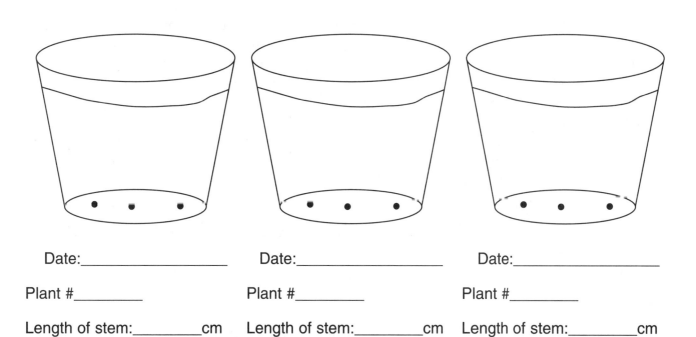

Date:_____   Date:_____   Date:_____

Plant #_____   Plant #_____   Plant #_____

Length of stem:_____cm   Length of stem:_____cm   Length of stem:_____cm

How Do Plants Grow?

Overview: *Students will graph the growth of bean seeds and plant other seeds.*

Materials

- bean seeds planted in previous lesson
- data sheet Graph of Seed Growth (page 163)
- magnifier for each student

Lesson Preparation

- Keep students in the same groups throughout this study of plants so they continue to work together to record plant growth. This activity should be done when the stems on most of the plants are at least two centimeters long.
- If any seeds begin to rot, remove them so they will not contaminate the remaining seeds.

Activity

1. Have students compare the growth of their plants. Be sure they notice that although all seeds were planted at the same time, not all plants have grown to the same height. Remind them of what happened when they raised butterfly and silkworm larvae.

2. Let students compare the growth of leaves on their plants to see what is alike and what is different for the two plants. Have them compare leaves on all plants being raised by the groups.

3. Distribute a copy of the data sheet Graph of Seed Growth to all students. Show them how and where to place today's date on the graph. Let them add the rest of the dates, including nonschool days, to their graph.

4. Demonstrate how they should plot the length of the stem for each of their plants on the same date line. Let them use a different colored pen to represent each of the plants. They should make a line beside the pinto and lima bean words to show the color being used for each of them. This same color should then be used to go over the dots on the graph that represent each plant.

5. The growth of each plant should be measured daily and plotted on the graph. When there are nonschool days, data is extrapolated by plotting the plant's growth on the next school day following the holiday(s). The points for the two data are then connected. Students will realize that growth took place, even though they were not there to measure it. They can read the growth which took place during the holiday(s) from the graph.

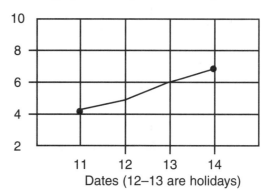

Dates (12–13 are holidays)

Closure

- Have students make drawings of their plants on their Seed Growth Record chart. Make additional copies as needed.
- Have students measure and plot each plant's growth daily. Compare these with plants grown by other groups. This comparison lets them realize that plants do not all grow in the same way.

Graph of Seed Growth

To the Student: Your teacher will help you make a graph of the lima and pinto bean plants you are growing. Compare how these plants grow.

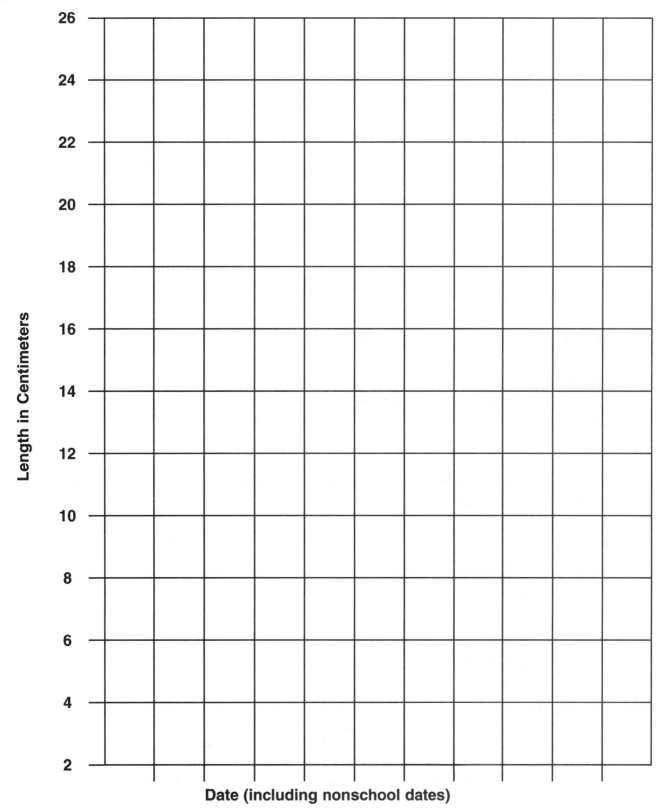

Length in Centimeters

Date (including nonschool dates)

How Does Your Garden Grow?

Overview: *Students will plant a small garden of birdseed on a sponge.*

Materials

- untreated birdseed
- untreated sponges (one per group)
- aluminum pie pan (one per group)
- How Does Your Garden Grow? data sheet (page 165)
- magnifier for each student

Lesson Preparation

- Label the pie pans with a number which is assigned to each group of students. Hot-glue one sponge to each pie pan to keep it in place. Add enough water to soak the sponge and leave a thin covering of water on the bottom of the pan.

Activity

1. Have students get into their groups. Distribute a magnifier to each student and a sample of birdseed. Let them examine the birdseed and describe what they see. Tell them that these seeds are too small to open up to see if each has a baby plant inside it. Ask them to think of a way to find out if there is a baby plant inside. Tell them that one way is to plant them in a small garden where they can be observed.

2. Provide each group with a pie pan, sponge, and about a tablespoon of birdseed. Let the students sprinkle their birdseed over the top of the sponge. Tell them they have just planted a small garden. Explain that these will be collected and placed on a table but will be returned to each group daily during the time they measure their lima bean and pinto bean plants. Explain that they will keep a daily record of changes they see in their gardens.

3. Distribute a copy of the data sheet How Does Your Garden Grow? to each student to begin the record of the sponge garden.

Closure

- Record the growth of the bean seeds.

- Discuss what the students have learned thus far.

Extender

- Soak an avocado seed to soften it and split it open so the students can see the small seedling inside.

- Grow an avocado seed for students to observe. It takes several months for the seedling to appear. Use a one-pint (.5 L) water bottle cut to half its length. Push two toothpicks or T-pins into opposite sides of the seed about halfway between the ends. Cut two slits on opposite sides of the bottle and put the toothpicks in the slits. The seed should be suspended so the stem end is below water level. Replace the water as it evaporates.

How Does Your Garden Grow? *(cont.)*

Name:_____ Date:_____

To the Student: You have just planted a small garden of birdseed on a sponge. Since you are doing an experiment to see if there is anything inside the seeds, it is important to make a record of what happens during the next few days. Begin your record on the chart below.

Birdseed Growth Record		
Date	**Tell what the seeds look like today.**	**Draw some of the seeds.**

Let's Experiment with Plants

Overview: *This activity is done when the bean plants are at least three inches (8 cm) high and the birdseed has developed sprouts. Students will conduct experiments with their plants to see how they grow under various conditions.*

Materials

- bean plants
- sponge gardens
- dark closet
- stack of books (or ring stand)
- two large shoeboxes
- pieces of tagboard

- liquid plant fertilizer
- bottle for water with liquid fertilizer
- plant record sheets begun in previous activities
- access to a refrigerator
- *optional:* video camera

Lesson Preparation

- Use books or a ring stand to support one of the cups upside down with bean plants in it. Put clear tape across the cup opening to avoid having the paper towels drop out. The sponge garden will be supported in the same way. Since the sponge is glued to the pie pan, it will not fall out when it is inverted over the books. Place a pie pan below each of these to catch the run-off water. Turn the planters over only to water them.

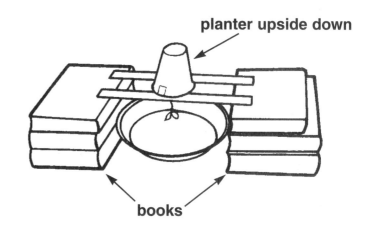

planter upside down

books

- The plants will begin to grow upward within 24 hours and should grow straight up within three days. Gravity causes this effect on plants, which is called *geotropism*. This experiment demonstrates what happens to trees growing on hillsides.

- Use one shoebox to create a container for one cup of bean plants. Put a hole in one end of the box, and two tagboard shelves on opposite sides of the walls of the box. The first should be just above the level of the top leaves, the second about halfway between this distance and the top of the box. Put the lid on the box. Open the box only to water the plants and for students to make drawings of the plant's growth.

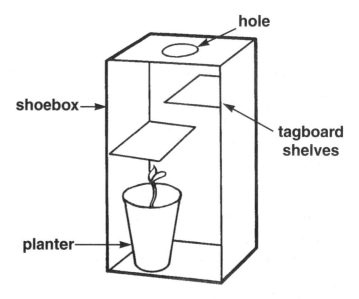

hole

shoebox

tagboard shelves

planter

Let's Experiment with Plants *(cont.)*

Lesson Preparation *(cont.)*

- Use the other shoebox to make a container for the sponge garden. The box should lie flat. These plants will not grow to the height of the beans, but this darkness test will show which direction plants grow in order to reach light. Use a nail and poke four or five holes in one end of the box. Put the garden in the box and put the lid on the box. Open it only to water the garden and for students to make drawings of the plants' growth.

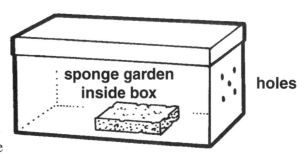

Activity

1. Divide students into their groups with their bean plants and birdseed gardens. Let them complete their records for these.

2. Ask students what plants need in order to be healthy. List these needs on the board, including light and water. Include other suggestions, even if not correct. Students will learn as they conduct their experiments what is needed by the plants.

3. Tell students that they are going to conduct some experiments to see what happens when plants are grown under different conditions. Explain that one of the cups of bean plants and a sponge garden will have no changes made (*control*)—that is, they will get the same amount of water and sunlight as they have thus far. Students will compare these with plants which are used in the experiments.

4. Write the list of changes (*variables*) to be used in the plant experiments on the board.

   - no sunlight
   - hanging upside down
   - inside a shoebox
   - inside a refrigerator

   - lying on one side
   - no water
   - fertilizer added
   - no change (*control*)

5. Discuss the various experiments which will be done. Explain that throughout the experiments, students will be keeping records of their plants' growth. They will also be watching the other plants to see what changes are occurring. Explain to students that the same experiments will be done with both the bean and birdseed plants to compare what happens.

6. Assign each group to do two different experiments. Use a different variable for each groups' plants (e.g., no light and inside shoebox). On their bean and birdseed record sheets, have the students write the variable they will use with each plant.

7. Place the plants in the locations where they will be kept during the experiment (dark closet, shoebox, etc.) Mix fertilizer with water according to the directions on the container and pour it into a bottle. Label the bottle "Water with Fertilizer." Make this bottle available for the groups conducting that experiment.

Let's Experiment with
Plants *(cont.)*

Closure

- *Optional:* Make a time-lapse videotape of some of the changes taking place. The bean plants hanging upside down will be the best ones to use for this recording. The gradual change of the bean stems will be dramatic as the videotape is played back.
- Conduct these experiments for at least two weeks. Chart plant growth and changes daily. Periodically, have each group share what they see happening with their plants.

Bean and Birdseed Plant Experiments	
Variable	**Expected Results**
no sunlight	• Stems will grow very long. • Leaves and stems will be pale.
lying on one side	• Stems will begin to grow upright. This is caused by gravity and is called *geotropism*.
hanging upside down	• Plants will gradually turn and then grow straight up. Compare this with the plants lying on their sides.
no water	• Plants will wither and leaves may change color.
inside shoebox	• Plants will grow toward the light.
fertilizer added	• Plant will grow rapidly and should look healthier than control plant.
inside refrigerator	• Plants will grow slowly and become pale. Compare these with the plants grown in the dark.

Cloning Plants

Overview: *Students will discover that new plants can sometimes grow from a parent plant without the need of a seed.*

Materials

- ripe whole pineapple
- whole yam (or sweet potato)
- carrot
- toothpicks
- two jars with openings, one to fit the yam, the other for the carrot

- healthy begonia leaf
- sand and potting soil
- untreated sponge
- aluminum pie pan
- flower pot with drainage hole
- knife

Activity

Have students observe the growth of new plants from parent plants. The plants to be used are a yam, carrot, begonia, and pineapple. This activity may extend over the entire school year. Prepare the plants as students watch. Place the plants where students can observe. Discuss the plants' growth periodically with students.

1. **Yam:** Place the yam in a container of water which has a mouth slightly larger than the yam's diameter and enough room for roots that form. Push four toothpicks into the yam about halfway between the tips. Half of the yam should be covered with water when placed in the jar. Change the water periodically. The roots will appear first, followed by the roots which emerge from the other end of the yam.

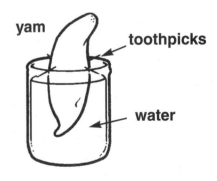

2. **Carrot:** Cut off all but two inches (5 cm) of the carrot. Trim off the sprouts on top of the carrot, leaving the green base. Follow the same directions used for the yam and suspend the carrot in a jar of water. The water should cover the bottom $\frac{1}{2}$ inch (1 cm) of the carrot. Add water as needed. Within a week feathery, green sprouts should appear from the top of the carrot.

3. **Begonia:** Place the sponge in the pie pan and add enough water to soak the sponge and just cover the bottom of the pan. Use a large, healthy begonia leaf and make five cuts in the leaf from the outer edge into the main vein. Lay the leaf on top of the sponge, underside down. Place a few pebbles on the leaf to keep it near the damp sponge. Add water to the pan periodically to keep the sponge wet. New plants should emerge from the cuts within several weeks.

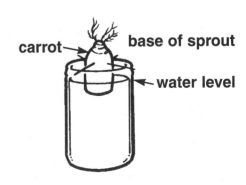

Cloning Plants *(cont.)*

Activity *(cont.)*

4. **Pineapple:** Cut the top off a ripe pineapple to get a tuft of leaves and a bit of stalk. Carefully peel some of the lower leaves from the base of leaves to reveal more stem and some small bumps, perhaps even some baby roots which have started to grow beneath the leaves. Place the stem portion of this into a flower pot filled with potting soil which is about one-half sand. The potting soil will hold the water, and the sand will allow it to drain readily and allow sufficient oxygen into the soil.

Place the pot and plant in a white plastic garbage bag which is loosely sealed at the top. Put the plant where it will get six hours of sunlight, if possible. The bag keeps the humidity high and diffuses the light so the plant doesn't burn in the sunlight. If less sunlight is available, use a clear plastic bag. Water sparingly as the soil dries. Don't overwater, but don't let it go completely dry. Fertilize once or twice a month with a house plant fertilizer. New growth should appear at the top of the plant after about two months. If the base looks like it is rotting, start again with a new pineapple top and fresh potting soil and add less water.

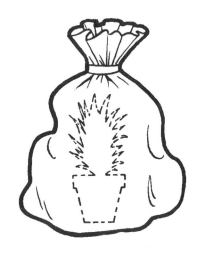

When the plant gets large, place an apple in the bag. The ripening apple produces ethylene gas which will induce flowering in the pineapple. You will have to continue these treatments for a couple of months, replacing the apple several times. It may take up to a year to get a new tiny pineapple.

Closure

- Have students make drawings to place in their plant journals to show how these plants looked when first planted.

- After the plants have begun to sprout new growth, have the students make other drawings to record the changes they observe.

Flower Power

— Teacher Information —

Some plants produce two kinds of flowers on the same plant. One will have only stamens, the other only pistils. These are *incomplete flowers*. There are also composite flowers (such as dandelions and marigolds) which consist of many complete flowers clustered into one. The flowers used for this activity should have both stamens and a pistil, known as a *complete flower*. These include flowers like the lily, gladiola, tulip, and fruit blossoms. Select the largest flowers for this lesson and provide a variety of them.

Overview: *Students will dissect flowers to discover where seeds originate.*

Materials

- complete flower (e.g., lily, gladiola, or tulip)
- data sheets Flower Dissection and Parts of a Flower (pages 172 and 173)
- clear tape
- magnifier
- transparency of How Flowers Reproduce (page 174)
- several apples

Activity

1. Ask the students if they know how seeds are produced. Tell them they are about to take a flower apart so they can see where seeds are formed. If the students are too young to dissect flowers alone, do this activity as a demonstration.

2. Distribute data sheets, flowers, magnifiers, and clear tape to students and let them follow the data sheets as they dissect the flower.

Closure

- Use the transparency How Flowers Reproduce to explain the reproduction process to students. Tell them bees are the best pollinators of flowers. When a bee goes to a flower to get nectar and pollen, some pollen drops off the bee's body onto the sticky stigma on the pistil. Beekeepers often rent hives to farms with apple orchards or other trees needing to be pollinated. Other insects which visit flowers also pollinate them. Pollen can also be transferred to the stigma by wind and by some birds and bats.

- Explain that fruits and vegetables are really swollen ovaries of a blossom that grew on the plant. Show students an apple and point out the leftover blossom and stem on opposite ends. Cut the apple open to expose the seeds formed inside the ovary. Let the students examine the seeds.

- Save the students' flower parts to be used in the next lesson and in the plant journal.

Extender

- Take students on a walk to search for fruit-bearing plants that show blossoms and fruit. Try to find examples of the transition from blossom to fruit on a plant. Cut open a blossom to expose the swollen ovary inside, the beginning of the fruit.

- Have students examine a dandelion flower and one which has gone to seed. This is a great example of a composite flower. Each seed is formed in its own flower but combined with others.

Flower Dissection Instructions

To the Student: Follow directions as you carefully dissect the flower.

- Snip off a piece of the stem. Examine it with the magnifier and then tape it in the box marked "stem" on the Parts of a Flower data sheet. Complete the rest of the information in the box.

- Locate the *sepals*, *petals*, *stamens*, and *pistil*. Count their number and write this in the boxes.

- Gently pull off the sepals and tape a specimen in the sepal box. Describe how it feels.

- Smell the flower; if it has a fragrance, describe it in the petal box. Carefully remove the petals and tape one to the data sheet. Answer the question about the flower's color and fragrance.

- Examine a stamen, the male part of the flower. Look at the top of the stamen (*anther*) with a magnifier to see the pollen grains. Put your fingertip against the anther. Did the pollen stick to your finger? This is what happens when a bee touches it. Rub the pollen between your fingers and then describe what it feels like in the pollen box.

- Take a sample of pollen grains using the sticky side of a piece of clear tape. If you have a microscope, place the tape on a glass slide and examine it. Put a sample of pollen grains in the pollen box. Draw what the pollen grains look like when magnified.

- Remove the stamens and tape one of them in the box. Describe what you see on the anther and draw a magnified view of it.

- Study the pistil, the female part of the flower. Feel the stigma, the top of the pistil. Describe how it feels. At the bottom of the pistil is a swollen area (*ovary*). Try to cut it open with your fingernail. Use your magnifier to see if you can find any tiny seeds inside the ovary. You may be able to split the stem of the stigma (*style*) lengthwise to see if you can locate the pollen tube which has grown from the stigma to the ovary.

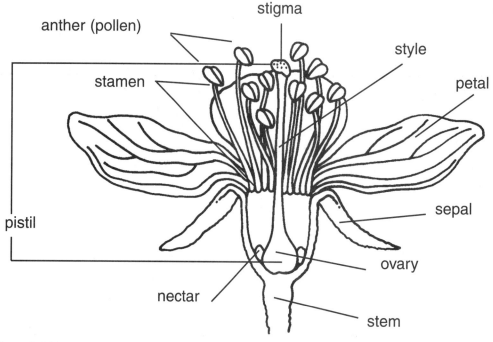

Parts of a Flower

To the Student: Tape the parts of the flower in the correct boxes below and then complete the information.

Stem

Description:

Magnified view
of the tip of the stem:

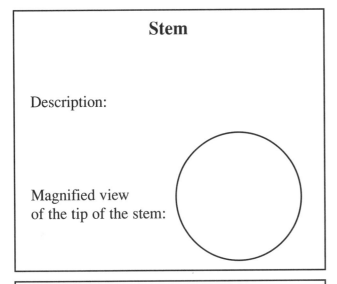

Sepal

Number of sepals:
Description of how it feels:

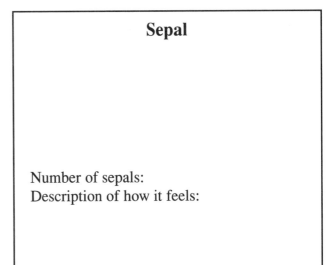

Petal

Number of petals:
Why do flowers have colored petals and
sometimes have a fragrance?

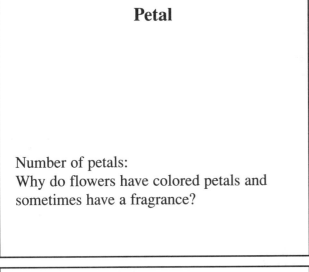

Pollen

Describe how it feels:

Magnified view
of pollen grains:

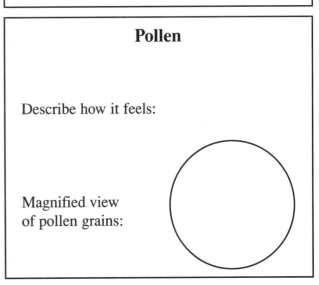

Stamen

Number of stamens:
Describe what you saw on
the anther:

Magnified view
of anther:

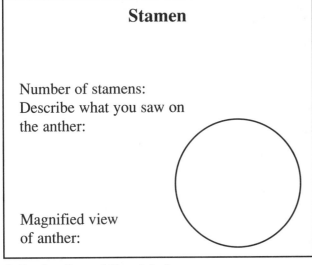

Pistil

Number of pistils:
Describe how the stigma feels:

Magnified view
inside the ovary:

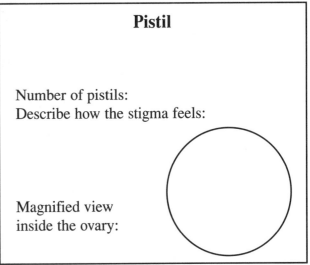

How Flowers Reproduce

1. Each pollen grain is a single cell. Pollen forms on the top (anther) of the stamen.

2. Pollen is carried by insects, wind, or birds to the stigma, the sticky top of the pistil.

3. Once on the stigma, the pollen grain absorbs moisture from the pistil and breaks open.

4. Its contents form a pollen tube, growing down into the pistil.

5. The pollen tube grows until it reaches the ovule containing an egg cell.

6. Sperm from the pollen travels down the tube to the ovule and unites with the egg cell.

7. A seed now begins to develop inside the ovary.

8. An ovary may have a single seed (avocado) or more than one seed (apple).

9. The ovary develops into a fruit enclosing the seed(s).

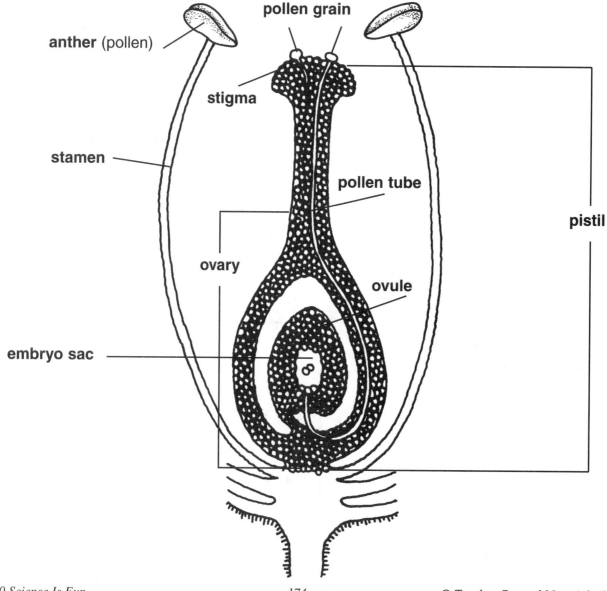

Let's Make a Flower

— Teacher Information —

Students will each create their own model of a flower. They will make a cross section of the flower and glue or tape it to a piece of construction paper. This should be included in their plant journal.

Overview: *Students will make a model of a flower.*

Materials for the Flower Model

- green construction paper (stem and leaves)
- construction paper (petals)
- cotton swabs (stamens)
- variety of ground spices such as mustard, nutmeg, cinnamon (pollen)
- poppy seeds (seeds)
- 3" x 5" (8 cm x 13 cm) colored, unlined file card

Other Materials

- data sheets Flower Dissection Instructions and Parts of a Flower (from previous lesson)
- transparency of How Flowers Reproduce (from previous lesson)
- scissors
- clear tape
- white glue

Activity

1. Review the parts of a flower, using the transparency and student data sheets from the previous lesson. Discuss what students found as they dissected their flowers. Tell the students that they are going to make a model of a cutaway view of a flower.

2. Divide the students into small groups and provide them with the flower materials. Explain how the materials are to be used to represent the parts of the flower. The cotton swabs (stamens) should be dipped into white glue, and then one of the ground spices is sprinkled over the glue. These are left to dry before being added to the flower. The stigma should be drawn as an outline on the file card and be 5 inches (13 cm) long.

3. Tell them that they should follow the picture of the cutaway view of the flowers on their data sheets. The flowers should be at least nine inches (25 cm) in length so details can be shown. They should glue all parts of the flower onto a sheet of construction paper.

4. Each student should make his or her own flower model. Encourage the students to be creative rather than making their flowers look exactly like the picture or another student's flower.

5. Have students put labels beside their flower with arrows to show where each part is located.

Closure

- Have students make models of their bean plants using construction paper. They should create their own leaves, stems, and roots and paste these to a sheet of paper.
- Post the flower and plant models on the bulletin board so the students can enjoy them.

Making a Plant Journal

Teacher Information

This is the culminating activity for the study of plants and will serve as a means of assessing student understanding.

Overview: *Students will create a cover for their plant journal.*

Materials

- light-colored file folder for each student
- colored pens or crayons
- all data sheets completed by the students from this study
- flower and plant models

Lesson Preparation

Draw a large circle on the outside of each file folder.

Activity

1. Discuss what the students have learned about the life cycles of plants. Remind them of their observations of plant growth as they grew beans and birdseed. Also, remind them of what they learned about how seeds are formed as they dissected the flowers. Compare the life cycle of plants to those of insects so students see that there are similarities.

2. Tell them that they are going to make a cover for a plant journal in which they can place all the data sheets they have made during their study of plants. Distribute a file folder to each student. Tell them to draw the life stages of a plant around the circle, beginning with a cutaway view of a seed. Explain that their drawings of each stage should be large enough to show details.

(*Note:* If the students are not capable of doing this alone, divide the task into segments. Have them draw the seed, young plant, mature plant, and flower as you monitor their progress.)

Closure

- Let students share their pictures of the life cycles of plants. Have them add the title "My Plant Journal" to the covers of their journals.
- Have students make drawings of some of the plants which were cloned (e.g., carrot) on the back of their covers.
- Enclose all the data sheets and models in the plant journals.

Fun with the Body Introduction

Learning about how their bodies function is both fun and fascinating for children of all ages. They can benefit from developing a basic understanding of their body functions at an early age. This chapter covers a wide range of topics. Since young children grow during the school year, the first activities are taking measurements of their heights, hands, and feet. This should be done at the beginning of the school year and repeated just before school ends. Students will match classmates with their baby pictures. As a result of these activities, the children will realize that, like the plants and insects studied in earlier units, they also grow from young to adult.

Next begins a study of the body. The children check to see what teeth they presently have. They will learn how the eye adjusts to bright and dim light, as well as discover the parts of the eye. The brain is investigated through a variety of activities, including testing reflexes, relaying a message, and relearning how to write their names. Muscles will be investigated by examining a chicken thigh and leg, as well as watching what happens when the muscles in their own faces are used to make expressions.

The study of the skeleton leads students inside the body. Bones found in owl pellets are used to help students see the shapes and placement of bones. These are compared to their own. Breathing is investigated through the construction of a lung model and blowing bubbles. The study moves on to the heart where students learn how blood circulates through the body by following a blood cell through this important muscle.

Children are always curious about what happens to the food they eat. The activities on walking through the digestive system and simulating the trip of a banana through the intestine will help them understand this process.

As a culminating activity for this study, students will place the internal organs and bones inside a body outline. The senses were explored in the Physical Science Activities in this book. There are many other topics about the human body which the teacher is encouraged to add to this study, such as activities to lay a foundation for good nutrition.

So Big!

Teacher Information

Do this series of activities at the beginning of the school year.

Overview: *Students' body measurements will be made and compared.*

Materials

- two-inch (5 cm) wide adding machine tape (at least 4 feet/120 cm per student)
- permanent felt marker
- one or two measuring tape(s)

Lesson Preparation

- For each student, cut a strip of adding machine tape at least 6" (15 cm) longer than the height of the tallest child.
- Write each child's name and the date at the top of the strip.
- Punch a hole in the top of each strip. Hang the strips of tape in one bundle so they reach the floor. This may be done using a bulletin board and a long thin nail. Place each strip on the nail so it will hang vertically. Trim the ends so the strips will be level with the floor.
- Hang a measuring tape beside the strips so the bottom of the tape is at floor level.

Activity

1. Discuss growth by asking students to show how big they were when born. Ask if they will always be the size they are now.
2. Explain that one way to find if they are growing is to measure themselves now and at the end of the school year. Tell them that you are going to mark each height on a strip of paper today and then use a measuring tape to see how tall they are.
3. Demonstrate how the measuring will be done by calling up the first child. Have him or her stand straight, back against a strip of paper. Mark the height on the paper. Let the student compare this mark with the measuring tape to find the height. Write that height (or let the child do so) on the paper strip. Remove that strip and call the next child. As measurements are being done, the remaining students may do another activity.
4. When all students have been measured, distribute their strips to them and have them fold along the mark showing their height. Explain that the strip is now exactly their height. In an open area, have them lay their strips on the floor side by side and then sort them according to height. Have the students line up according to the way their strips were sorted and see if they agree with the arrangement.
5. Let them realize that although they are all close in age, they are not all the same height. Remind them of the varied rates of growth they discovered in butterfly larvae and bean plants.

Closure

Explain that the strips students made today of their height are just the beginning of the study of body measurements. Ask them to help you make a list of other measurements which can be made of their bodies (e.g., length of arms).

So Big! *(cont.)*

Overview: *Students will measure and compare the sizes of their arms, hands, legs, and feet.*

Materials

- 1–1 ½-inch wide adding machine tape
- white construction paper
- Look at Us Grow graph (page 182)
- magnifiers (one per student)

- measuring tapes and yard or meter sticks
- pencils
- 3" x 5" (8 cm x 13 cm) file cards

Lesson Preparation

- Spread the activities for this lesson over several days.
- Cut the adding machine tape into strips for students to measure lengths of their arms and legs. The lengths of the strips should be several inches longer than the longest arm and leg.

Activity #1

1. Tell students that they are going to learn more about the sizes of their bodies.
2. Have students remove one shoe. Divide them into pairs and say they are going to compare the lengths of their arms, legs, and feet. Give them the following instructions:
   - Sit on chairs side by side with their shoulders pressing together. Stretch out their arms and compare the overall length. Bend their arms at the elbow and compare the lengths from elbow to wrist. Press the palms of opposite hands together to compare sizes.
   - Sit on the floor side by side with hips pressing together. Compare the length of their legs. Compare the length of the leg from ankle to knee and then knee to hip. Press the opposite feet together at the bottom to compare their size. (*Optional:* They may do this with or without socks on. The teacher should judge which is best.)
3. Discuss what the students have learned in this comparison. Remind them that their body heights were different, so it is to be expected that the body parts would also be different.
4. Tell them that they are going to measure their arms, legs, hands, and feet in the next lesson.
5. Collect these measurements to be saved for use at the end of the year.

Activity #2

1. Divide students into pairs and give each student a length of adding machine strip to measure the length of an arm from shoulder to wrist. Tell the students to write their names and the date on their strips. Have one student lie down and hold one end of the strip against his or her shoulder. The partner should stretch out the strip from shoulder to wrist and mark the strip with a pencil to show this length. The partner should also mark the location of the elbow on the strip. Partners now exchange places and repeat the measurement.

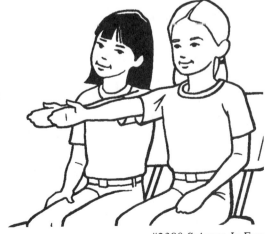

So Big! *(cont.)*

Activity #2 *(cont.)*

2. Each student should measure the length between the shoulder and wrist and record it on the strip. Tell the students to bend their arms at the elbow and compare the length of their upper arm bone with the lower bones. Have them fold the paper strip at the elbow and compare the lengths of the upper and lower arm bones. Discuss the difference.

3. Give each student a paper strip to measure their leg with their partner. Tell the students to write their name on the strip. Have the children stand on one foot while supporting themselves on a chair. Let them swing their leg and feel for the joint where it connects to the hip. Explain that this is where they will hold the strip while their partner measures the length of their leg. Let the partners take turns standing (or lying down) and pressing the strip to the leg/hip joint while the other child measures and marks the location of the knee and ankle on the paper.

4. Have each student measure the length of their leg from hip to ankle and write it on the paper. Let them bend the strip at the knee and compare the length of the upper and lower leg. Discuss how this is alike or different from their arm measurements.

5. Collect these to be saved for use at the end of the year.

Activity #3

1. Divide the students into pairs and distribute a piece of white paper to each student. Explain that they are going to trace around their partner's right hand. Tell them this should be done carefully so the size and shape of the hand are accurate. Show the students how to spread out their fingers and thumb so it will be easier for the partner to make a better drawing of the outline of the hand. Have the students mark where the finger and thumb joints are on the outline.

2. Distribute a file card to each student. Have them use the side of the lead in a pencil to make a black patch on the paper about the size of a silver dollar. The graphite from the pencil will be used to create fingerprints on their hand outlines. Show the students how to get the graphite on their fingertips by pressing and rolling each finger and then transferring it to the same finger on the hand outline. Have them rub more graphite on the card after making two or three fingerprints. Help them make clear prints. (*Optional*: Have older students or adults help with this process.)

3. Distribute magnifiers to students and let them examine their fingerprints. Have them compare the prints of the thumb and each finger with a partner. Discuss the differences seen and have students draw some examples of fingerprints they have on the board.

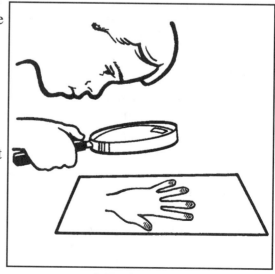

4. Have students write their names and the date on the palm of their hand outlines. Have them draw lines on the outlines of each hand from the wrist to the tip of the longest finger and side to side across the palm. Let them measure these spans and write the lengths on the lines.

5. Let each student cut out his or her hand outline. Collect these to be saved for use at the end of the year.

So Big! *(cont.)*

Activity #4

1. Divide the students into pairs and distribute a piece of white paper to each student. Explain that they are going to trace around their partner's right foot. Tell them this should be done as carefully as they did the hand, but the toes will not be shown individually. Have each partner remove a shoe and sock and stand on the paper while the other partner draws around the foot.

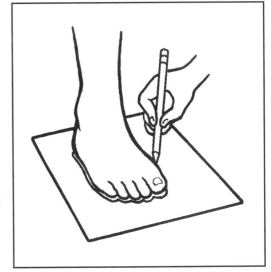

2. Use the same file card from the previous activity and add more graphite to it. Let the students press their toes to the graphite and then kneel so they can place the right foot inside the outline on the paper. They should press down on each toe to leave the print. (*Optional:* Have older students or adults assist.)

3. Have the students use magnifiers to examine these toe points and compare them with their partner's. Let each student cut out his or her foot outline.

Activity #5

1. Give students their height strips and a small self-adhesive note. Have them write their names and heights on the note.

2. Use the transparency of the height graph Look at Us Grow to project and trace on the board. Put the range of height measurements for the students along the horizontal axis. Have the students place their notes in a row above the height which matches their measurements.

3. Add the numbers of students along the vertical axis. This completes the bar graph of the data.

4. Make a simple analysis of the data. Some suggestions for analysis are given below.

   • Find the height of the majority of students. (*the longest bar*)

   • Find the average height of the students. (*halfway between the shortest and tallest heights*)

5. Transfer the data to the transparency and save this bar graph to use at the end of the year.

Closure

Collect all the measurements and file them for each student for use at the end of the year.

So Big! *(cont.)*

Look at Us Grow

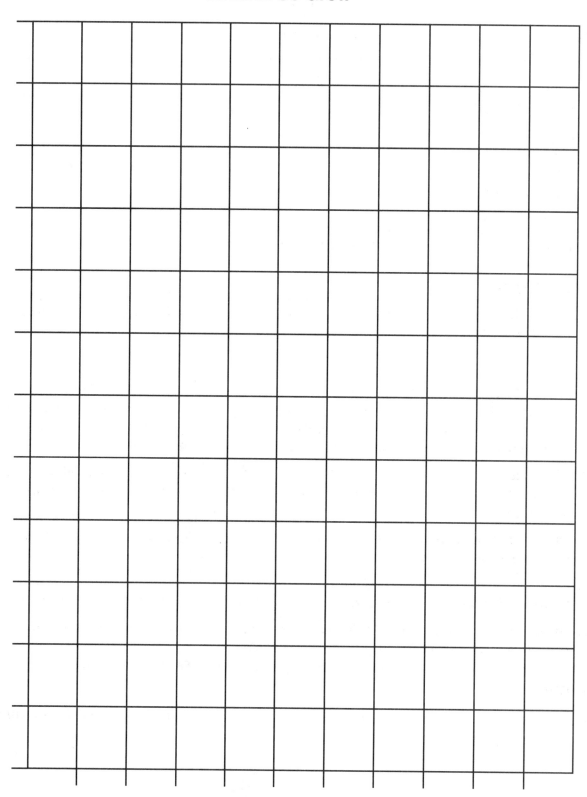

Number of Students

Height of Students

So Big! *(cont.)*

Teacher Information

This lesson should be conducted at the end of the school year.

Overview: *Students will remeasure themselves and compare these measurements with those done at the beginning of the year.*

Materials

- paper records of students' measurements done at the beginning of the school year
- unlined paper
- measuring tapes
- Look at Us Grow graph made at the beginning of the school year.

Lesson Preparation

Hang the height strips on the bulletin board so they reach the level of the floor. Place the measuring tapes on the board beside the tapes.

Activity

1. Use the height strips to measure the students again and update their height. Mark the location of the neck and hip joint on each strip. Give each student his or her height strip and tell all to compare their present height with that at the beginning of the year. Have them measure how much they have grown and mark it on their strips.

2. Distribute a self-adhesive note to all students and have them write their name and present height on the note. Compare it with the one made earlier in the school year. Remind students that not everyone grows at the same rate nor are we all the same height.

3. Distribute the arm and leg strips. Let the students compare these to their present size and update the length measurements if needed.

4. Distribute their hand and foot outlines and let the students compare these with the sizes of their hands and feet today. If their hands and feet have grown, let the students draw new outlines.

5. Attach the hand and foot outlines to the arm and leg strips. Connect the arm strip to the body strip at the neck and the leg strip at the hip location.

Closure

Let the students take these home for their parents to keep as a record of their growth this school year.

Connecting Body Parts

Overview: *Students will learn the names of external body parts and then create funny bodies.*

Materials

- transparency and copies of the body parts (pages 185 and 186)
- permanent colored felt pens
- pens or crayons for the students
- scissors and glue
- construction paper

Lesson Preparation

- Make a transparency of body parts. Color the eyes, hair, and clothing with a permanent felt pen. Cut them out and place them in an envelope for safekeeping.
- Make a set of these pictures for each student.

Activity

1. Ask the students to stand and play a body game with you. Tell them that when you call out the name of a body part, they are to point to it. Call these parts in the following order: *head, arms, hands, chest, abdomen, legs, feet.* Call out the parts of the face for them to point to in the following order: *eyes, nose, lips,* and *ears.*

2. Change the game to check for comprehension by telling the students to give the name of the body and face parts you point to on your own body. Have them point to this part on themselves and say its name. Point out the body and face parts in order at first and then at random to be sure all know what the parts are called.

3. Distribute a piece of construction paper and the copies of the body parts to the students. Write the names of the body parts (not face parts) on the board and have them label their pictures. Let them color the eyes, hair, and clothing and then carefully cut them out, placing them on their construction paper as they do so.

4. Place the transparency pieces of the body and face parts on the overhead and ask two students to come up and assemble them. Leave the overhead projector light off as they do this and have the students assemble their body and face parts on their construction paper. Once all students have put their bodies together, turn on the overhead projector so they can see if they agree with the arrangement.

5. Turn off the projector light and tell the students that you are now going to make a new body from these parts. Turn on the light to show what this funny figure looks like. Tell them to rearrange their body parts to make a new body which is different from the one you did. Encourage them to make each body different from their neighbor's so they can see how many different ways there are to rearrange the body.

Closure

Have the students glue the parts of the newly created bodies on the construction paper. Place these on the bulletin board for them enjoy.

Body Parts

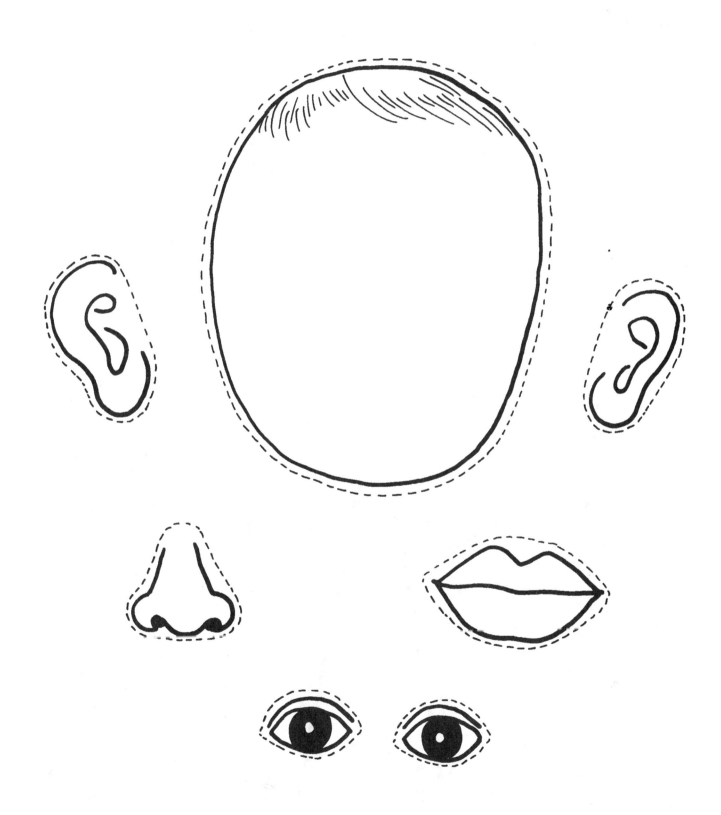

Body Parts *(cont.)*

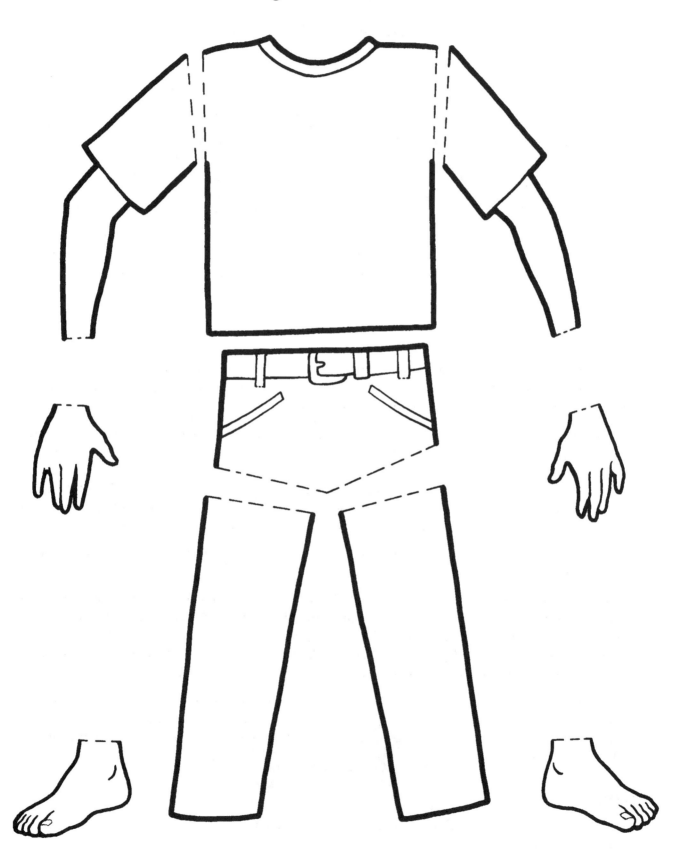

Can You Find Me?

Overview: *Students will match baby pictures with their classmates' present photos.*

Materials

- baby photographs of each student
- bulletin board
- parent letter (page 188)
- present-day picture of each student
- alphabetical list of students' names

Lesson Preparation

- Make a bulletin board with the present-day pictures of each student. Place their names below their pictures.
- Add the baby pictures to the bulletin board after most of them are brought to class. It may be best to divide the photos into small groups to make it easier for students to match them.
- Make an alphabetical list of student names for the game.

Activity

1. Ask students if they have changed in appearance as well as size since they were babies. Have them discuss some of the differences. If any students have baby brothers or sisters, let them tell how the baby's appearance is different from their own.

2. Point out the bulletin board display of student photographs. Tell students they are going to play a guessing game to see if they can match pictures taken of the class this year with the appropriate baby photos. Explain that you will need to have a baby picture from each child to put on the bulletin board in order to play this game. Distribute copies of the parent letter and read it aloud to them. Emphasize that they should not show anyone their baby pictures so as not to give away the answer. Encourage them to bring the pictures as soon as possible so the game can begin.

3. When most students have brought baby pictures to school, put them on the bulletin board and place a letter below each.

4. Show the students the bulletin board and tell them the game can now begin. Distribute a copy of the student names and explain that they should write the letter of the baby picture beside the name of the student they think matches that photo. They are not to tell anyone their choices nor ask others to point out their baby pictures. Let them know it is important to look closely at the baby photos and present-day photos to match them.

5. After students have been matching pictures a few days, give them another student list. Explain that you will begin to move pairs of photos to another bulletin board, a few at a time. They can write the answers on the new list and begin to match the remaining photos. Continue this until all photos are matched.

Closure

Let students discuss how they were able to match the photographs. Ask them which were most difficult for them to match and why.

Parent Letter for Student Photographs

Date_____

Dear Parents:

We are learning about our bodies and how they grow. All students have measured their height, length of their arms and legs, and drawn outlines of their hands and feet. They imprinted their finger and toe prints on the outlines of their hands and feet and compared them with prints made by the other students. The students' measurements will be saved to compare with new measurements we will make at the end of the school year to see how much they have grown.

The students are going to match baby pictures with a present-day photograph of each child in our classroom. The baby and present-day photographs will be placed on a bulletin board and will not be handled by the students.

Each child has been asked to bring a photograph of himself or herself as a baby, preferably one which shows the face clearly. Please write the name of the child on the back of the photograph and send it to school in an envelope. Remind your child not to show the photo to anyone. We need to keep these secret so students may compare the pictures to make their own decisions of the matching sets.

Thank you for your willingness to send the baby picture to school. All photographs will be returned when we finish this activity.

Cordially,

Look at My Teeth

─── Teacher Information ───

Look at the drawings and information about primary and permanent teeth on page 190, provided for the teacher as background. It is not important that students learn the terminology or predicted age of emergence of the teeth.

Overview: *Students will learn about their teeth and make a record of their present teeth.*

Materials

- x-rays of teeth (Ask your dentist for these.)
- examples of actual teeth
- mirrors (one per student)
- toothpicks
- activity sheet Here Are My Teeth (page 190)
- transparency of Inside a Tooth (page 191)

Lesson Preparation

- Ask your dentist for x-rays of teeth from children and adults.
- Also request teeth specimens, molds, and photographs, as well as booklets on growth and care of the teeth.

Activity

1. Ask students to feel their teeth with their tongues to see if all of them are exactly alike. Discuss the differences. Ask them if they have any missing teeth. If so, let them feel with their tongues to see if they can feel the new tooth pushing up through the gum. Discuss what it feels like to lose a tooth. Tell them that this is a natural part of growing up.

2. Give each student a mirror and the activity sheet. Show the transparency of this sheet and use it to show students how to place an X on primary teeth which are missing. Explain that they should use the toothpick along with the mirror to locate their teeth, counting from the center front to know where these are on the chart.

3. Let students begin to examine their teeth and record those which are missing. If any of the students have begun to grow adult teeth (e.g., central incisors), have them circle these on the permanent teeth drawing. Use the transparency of this chart to show the most frequently missing teeth for the students. Place an X on those teeth on the transparency.

4. Show and discuss the transparency Inside a Tooth. Show the actual teeth specimens.

5. Show the teeth x-rays on the overhead projector. Point out the roots of the teeth which are hidden below the gum line and go deep into the jawbone. If any primary and adult teeth are on the x-rays, point these out to the students so they realize that the teeth they now have are mostly primary (baby) teeth which will be pushed out as the adult teeth grow into place.

Closure

Have a dentist or dental assistant visit the class to tell them about how their teeth grow and demonstrate how to care for the teeth.

Here Are My Teeth

Name:_____ Date:_____

To the Student: Place an X over the teeth in the drawing which are missing from your mouth.

Permanent (Adult) Teeth
7–21 years of age

Primary (Baby) Teeth
8–33 months of age

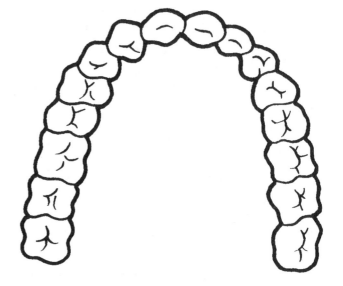

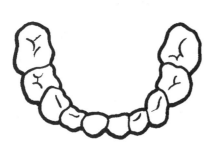

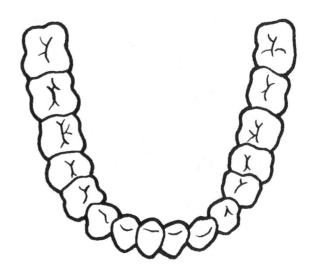

Inside a Tooth

The tooth is held tightly in the jawbone.

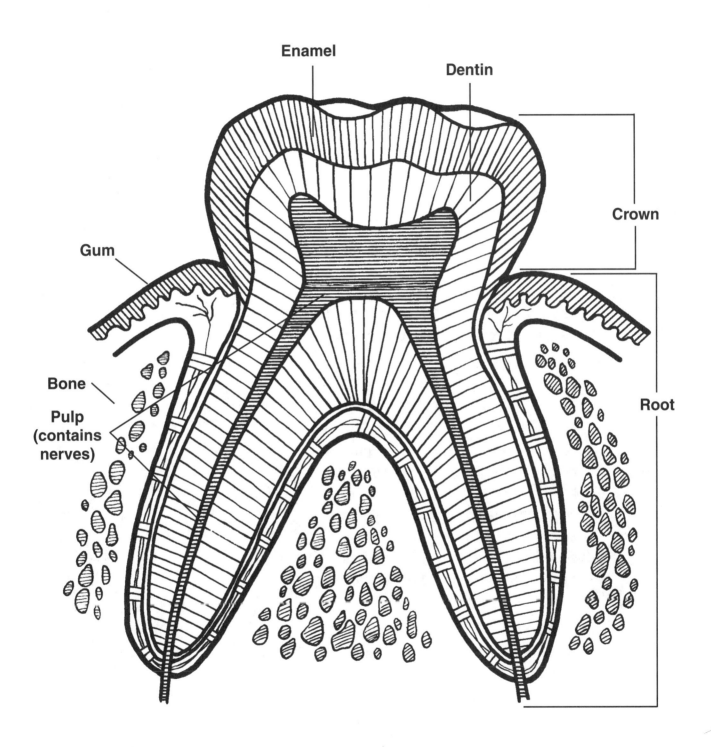

Sequence of Eruption of Teeth

central incisor	8–12 months
lateral incisor	9–13 months
cuspid	16–22 months
first molar	13–19 months
second molar	25–33 months

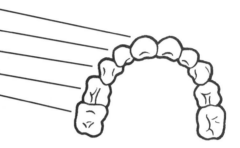

Primary Teeth

second molar	23–31 months
first molar	14–18 months
cuspid	17–23 months
lateral incisor	10–16 months
central incisor	6–10 months

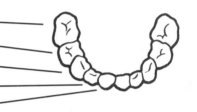

central incisor	7–8 years
lateral incisor	8–9 years
cuspid	11–12 years
first bicuspid	10–11 years
second bicuspid	10–12 years
first molar	6–7 years
second molar	12–13 years
third molar	17–21 years

Permanent Teeth

third molar	17–21 years
second molar	11–13 years
first molar	6–7 years
second bicuspid	11–12 years
first bicuspid	10–12 years
cuspid	9–10 years
lateral incisor	7–8 years
central incisor	6–7 years

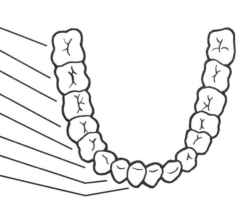

Look into My Eyes

Overview: *Students will investigate how their eyes work.*

Materials

- mirror for each student
- transparency of The Parts of the Eye (page 194)
- *optional:* cow eyes (These may be purchased through Carolina Biological Co. See Resources section.)

Activity

1. Tell students that for several days they are going to try various tests to learn how the eyes work. Distribute a mirror to each student and explain that they are to look carefully at one eye. Pair them with other students to compare their eyes and discuss what they see. Discuss what students find as they examine their eyes. They should notice the following:
   - Colored ring and black circle in the center of the eye.
   - Most of the eye is white.
   - Tiny blood vessels may be seen (reassure them this is normal).

2. Have them close their eyes and gently feel the skull around the eyes to see how it protects the eye. Tell them to gently press on the eye to see what shape it is and if it is hard or soft. Explain that the eye is a ball shape but most of it is deep inside the skull to protect it. Tell them the eye is filled with fluid, like a water balloon, and thus feels somewhat hard.

3. Tell the students to look up, down, sideways, and then roll their eyes. Explain that muscles attached to the eyeball make it possible for this motion, just as other muscles move their legs and arms.

4. Explain that there is a hole in the center of the eye, covered by clear skin. Light enters the eye through this hole, and when it is dark, muscles enlarge the hole to let in more light. Explain that they will experiment to see the pupil change size.

5. Tell students to hold a mirror in front of one eye and look at the dark circle in the middle, the hole called the *pupil*. Tell them to continue to hold the mirror where it is and to close their eyes. They should then place a hand over both eyes to make it darker. Say that you are going to count to 10 very slowly and then they should take their hands away from their eyes and quickly look in the mirror at the hole. It may be necessary to repeat this several times for students to see the change in the pupil.

6. Show students the transparency of The Parts of the Eye. The full explanation of the functions of these parts is provided for teacher background. Students should not memorize the correct terms but, rather, have a basic understanding of their functions.

Closure

If appropriate for your students, dissect a cow's eye to show the parts. The skin of the eye is tough, so sharp cuticle scissors are suited for opening it and easier to control than a scalpel. The eye parts can be seen, including the pupil, lens, muscles, optic nerve, and the fluids which fill the eye. Use the transparency to show the location and name of the parts during the dissection.

The Parts of the Eye

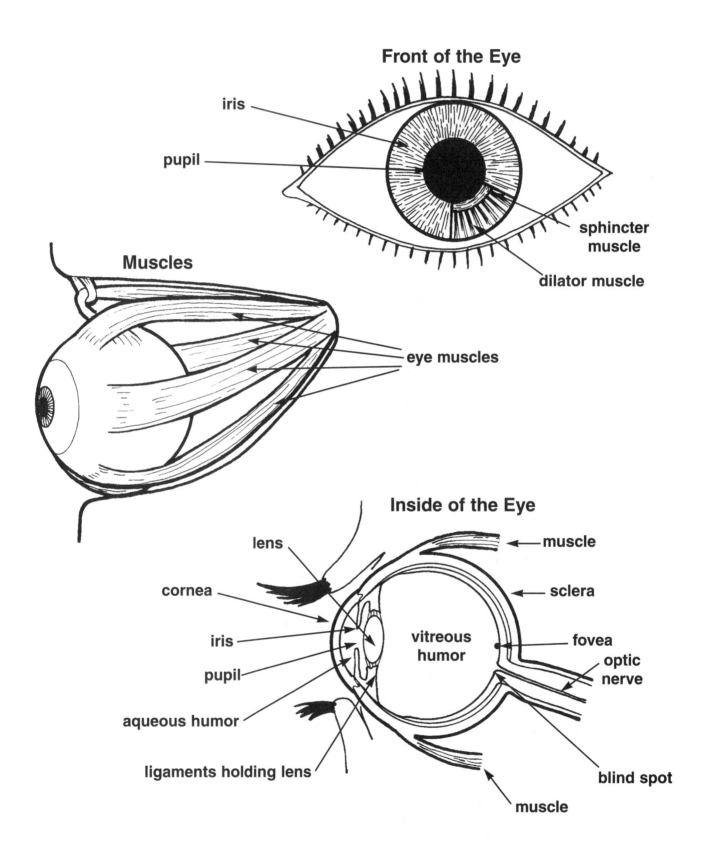

Front of the Eye

iris

pupil

sphincter
muscle

dilator muscle

Muscles

eye muscles

Inside of the Eye

lens

cornea

iris

pupil

aqueous humor

ligaments holding lens

vitreous
humor

muscle

sclera

fovea

optic
nerve

blind spot

muscle

Functions of Parts of the Eye

Note: This information is provided as teacher background. It defines the terms used on The Parts of the Eye diagrams. If appropriate, it may be shared with the students in a simplified form which they can understand.

Aqueous Humor: This is a clear watery fluid between the cornea and the pupil. It nourishes and lubricates the cornea and lens and fills the area between them.

Blind Spot: This is the area where the optic nerve leaves the retina. No vision cells are in this location, thus leaving a *hole* in what we see. This is so tiny that it does not affect the image we see.

Cornea: This is clear, tough tissue covering the front of the eye. It lets in light and does 80% of the image focusing.

Dilator Muscle: This enlarges the pupil in dim light.

Fovea: This is a dimple in the retina where light focuses after entering the lens. It is located directly opposite the lens. Cones are concentrated here, and vision is most acute.

Iris: This is a colored disk just under the cornea. Its color comes from melanin, just like our skin. The iris absorbs light. People with light-colored eyes are more sensitive to light.

Lens: This is a flexible structure about the size of an aspirin and shaped like a magnifying lens. The lens focuses 20% of the light after it passes through the cornea. Muscles (*ligaments*) surround the lens and pull or relax to adjust the thickness of the lens to focus and project an upside-down image on the retina.

Optic Nerve: This transmits the electrical impulses to the brain. The ability of the brain to interpret the image right-side up and in depth comes from experience that begins at a person's birth.

Pupil: This is a hole in the center of the iris. Light enters the eye here and is regulated by the size of the hole.

Retina: This is the innermost layer of the wall of the eyeball. It is as fragile as wet tissue paper. Light-sensitive cells (rods and cones) in the retina absorb light rays and change them into electrical signals.

Sclera: This is a tough leather-like skin covering about $\frac{5}{6}$ of the eyeball. The eyeball is about one inch (2.5 cm) in diameter.

Sphincter Muscle: This makes the pupil smaller in bright light. The pupil also becomes smaller when focused on nearby objects to create a sharper image. Six muscles surround the eyeball to move it. Both eyes move together.

Vitreous Humor: This is a clear jelly-like substance which gives the eyeball its spherical shape and holds the retina on the back of the eye.

Control Center: The Brain

Overview: *Students will do three activities to learn how the brain functions.*

Materials

- three bowls
- ice
- peppermint candy
- water
- lined paper and pencil

Lesson Preparation

Heat water and pour it into one bowl; place ice water in the second and room-temperature water in the third.

Activity #1

1. Show students bowls with hot and cold water in them. Ask them if they can tell by looking which bowl holds hot water and which cold. (*They can't tell by just looking.*) Ask them how they can tell the different temperatures of the water. (*Feel it.*) Have several students put a hand in each bowl to distinguish hot from cold. Discuss how their brains helped them know the temperatures.

2. Add a bowl of room-temperature water. Tell students that this water is between hot and cold. Call for a volunteer to place a left hand in the cold water and a right hand in the hot water. After about three minutes tell the child to remove the hands and put both into lukewarm water. Have the child tell if the water feels cold or hot. (*It feels cold to the hand which was just in hot water but hot to the hand just in cold water.*) Explain that sometimes the brain gets mixed signals and can get confused. In this case, the extremes in cold and hot water made the nerves in the hands more sensitive to a change to a moderate temperature.

Activity #2

1. Tell students that the brain relays information from all parts of our body by electrical impulses that travel to the brain or other sensors before we react. Have a student sit on a table with legs hanging over the edge without touching the floor. Explain that you are going to tap a knee to see what happens to the leg. Stretch out your hand, palm up, and gently tap on the soft tissue just below the kneecap. The leg should jerk. Repeat this on the other leg. Ask students how the child knew to jerk his or her knee since you didn't say to do that.

2. Explain that the nerves in the area below the kneecap feel the tap and send a message to the nerves in the spine. The message is immediately relayed to muscles which jerk the knee.

3. Have students make a large circle with their backs toward the center of the circle. The teacher should join the circle and have everyone hold hands. Explain that you are going to squeeze the hand of one of the students holding your hands. Tell them that when that child feels the squeeze, he or she should squeeze the child holding the other hand and so on until it gets back to you. Do not let the students know when you squeeze the child's hand. When you feel the squeeze, let the students know.

Control Center: The Brain *(cont.)*

Activity #2 *(cont.)*

4. Repeat this and time how long it takes for the squeeze to make its way around the circle. Divide the circle into two circles and have the students repeat the process, this time beginning with a designated child in each circle and beginning on your cue. This should take much less time. Relate that to the knee jerk by telling them that it would take far longer if the impulse had to be relayed through the brain than through a receptor in the spinal cord.

Activity #3

1. Distribute lined paper to each child and have each write his or her name 10 times. Now, have them write their names again, this time writing them backwards. After they have finished, ask them which was quicker for them. Ask them why they think it took less time to write their names forward than it did to write them backwards.

2. Explain that they have trained their brains to remember the order of the letters in their names so they don't have to spend time thinking about the order of each letter when writing their names forward. When they are writing the letters backward, the brain needs to take more time to think which letter comes next.

Closure

- Tell the students that their brains also control their senses. Remind them of the hot and cold water test they did which required the use of the sense of touch. Explain that they are going to test how this works with taste. Distribute a peppermint candy to each child. Tell them not to place it in their mouths until you tell them to do so. Explain that you will give them three signals (see below) and they are to respond to each of them.

    ✓ One clap—pinch the nose closed.

    ✓ Two claps—place the candy in the mouth.

    ✓ Three claps—let go of the nose and breathe through it.

- Ask the students what happened when they let go of their nose. (*They got a strong sense of the flavor of the candy.*) Explain that to taste the candy, the sense of smell is needed to help relay to the brain information which is added to the impulse arriving from nerve sensors on the tongue.

Muscle Power

Overview: *Students will learn about their muscles through activities and examples of muscles on a chicken leg.*

Materials

- a chicken leg with the skin and muscles attached (chilled until ready to use)
- single-edged razor blade
- mirror for each student

Activity #1

1. Ask all students to "make a muscle." Ask them what happened to their arms when they did this. (*The muscle on the upper arm bulged, and the lower arm bent up to touch the upper arm.*)

2. Tell them to do this again and use the other hand to feel the muscle on top of the upper arm. Have them tell what the muscle felt like as the lower arm was rising.

3. Have them repeat this but have them feel the muscle just under the upper arm. They should feel the muscle under the upper arm bone relax as the arm rises and stiffen as it stretches out.

4. Explain that muscles beneath the skin of the arm are working in pairs to raise or lower the arm. Top muscles contract (become tight) as the lower arm is raised, while the lower muscle relaxes. The opposite happens when they lower the arm.

5. Show students the chicken leg. Peel off the skin to reveal tendons and muscles. Bend the leg to show how the muscles contract and relax. Compare this to what students just did.

6. Have students open and close a fist, explaining that tendons attached to the finger bones are pulled by the muscles in the palm of the hand. On the chicken leg, show the tendons connected to muscles and the base of the leg. Explain that tendons tie muscles to bone. Carefully cut the tendons at the bone and bend the leg again. Discuss the difference without the muscles being held to the bone. Separate the muscle groups and then count them. Look for the large vessels which supply blood to the muscles.

7. Carefully cut between the thigh and drumstick to show the joint. Show the tough bands of ligaments (white sheets) and cartilage caps. Let students feel how smooth this is. Ask how it would feel if these were rough surfaces (*painful and difficult to move the joints*). Have them feel a finger joint and keep feeling it as they bend the finger. Can they feel the bone and tendons?

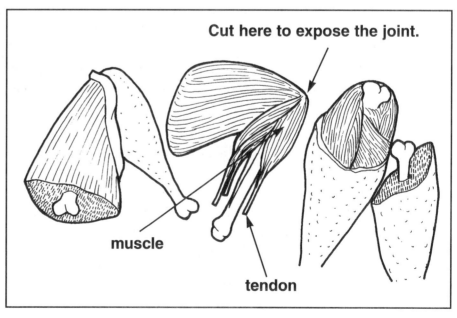

Cut here to expose the joint.

muscle

tendon

Muscle Power *(cont.)*

Activity #2

1. Explain that there are muscles beneath the skin in one's face to control facial expressions. Have them close their eyes and place their hands on their foreheads as they frown. Ask them to describe what they feel. (*The skin and muscles move.*)

2. Distribute mirrors to students and tell them they are going to watch what happens as they use muscles in their faces. Tell them to do the following:

   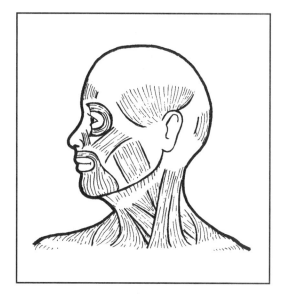

   ✓ Open and then close the nostrils.

   ✓ Raise and then lower the eyebrows.

   ✓ Raise and lower the ears.

   ✓ Wink one eye and then the other.

   ✓ Open the mouth as wide as possible and then close it.

   ✓ Stick out the tongue and then roll it.

   ✓ Push down the lower lip.

   ✓ Push up the lower lip.

   ✓ Turn the corners of the mouth up and then down.

   ✓ Make faces which show they are happy, sad, mad, and scared.

3. Discuss how they used their muscles to do all of this with their faces.

Closure

- Do this activity with the students so they can follow. Tell them each to sit in a chair some distance from their desks. Have them stand up. Ask them to repeat this and see how their thigh muscles feel as they rise. Discuss this so they realize that their bodies push forward and thigh muscles contract as they stand.

- Repeat this activity but this time have them fold their arms across their chests and stand while keeping their backs straight. Have them try again, checking to see if the thigh muscles are contracting. (*They are.*)

- Ask students what happens when they try to stand with arms folded. (*They can't stand.*)

- Ask what is different about the positions in the two experiments. (*They lean forward in the first but not in the second.*)

- Explain that gravity pulls us down, even when sitting. When we stand, we lean forward, shifting the pull of gravity over our feet. The thigh muscles contract and pull the legs to a standing position. If we keep the back straight, the pull of gravity is over the hips. The thigh muscles contract but can't pull hard enough against gravity to make us stand.

Dem Bones

Teacher Information

Owls are birds of prey which eat rodents, birds, and some insects whole but cannot digest the bones, fur, or hard insect exoskeleton. These indigestible items collect in the stomach and are regurgitated periodically in the form of a ball. The ball (pellet) consists mostly of fur. When the pellet is dissected, tiny bones, parts of insects, and feathers may be found. These bones look very much like those of humans and can therefore serve as an excellent way of teaching about our skeletons. Owl pellets can be handled without gloves, which makes it easier to locate tiny bones such as vertebrae. (Wash with soap and water after dissecting one.)

This activity requires at least two days. Teachers may dissect the pellets and clean the bones for very young students to use.

Overview: *Students will learn about the bones in their bodies by examining those in owl pellets.*

Materials

- one-ounce plastic cups with lids
- trays (one per group)
- small cups of water
- tweezers
- toothpicks
- paper towels and newspaper
- one quart of water mixed with two tablespoons of bleach
- tea strainer
- colored construction paper

- copies of the Vole Skeleton (page 203) run on colored paper
- transparencies of Bone Identification Key, Vole Skeleton, and The Human Skeleton (pages 202–204)
- x-rays of human bones (Check with hospitals for these.)
- owl pellets, one for each group of two or three students (Owl pellets may be ordered from Genesis, Inc. See Resources section.)

Lesson Preparation

- Place the owl pellets in a flat container and add a small amount of water. Cover the container so moisture will be absorbed by the pellets and they will soften.

- Number the one-ounce cups, using a permanent marker. Assign a corresponding number to each student group.

- For each group, make up a tray containing the following:

  ✓ newspaper and paper towels   ✓ pair of tweezers

  ✓ one-ounce numbered cup and lid   ✓ toothpicks for each child

  ✓ softened owl pellet   ✓ small cup of water

- Once the bones have been extracted from the pellet, they need to be cleaned and dried for use on the next day. This is done as follows:

    Cut four-inch newspaper squares and put the number which corresponds to each cup of bones on them. This will help to identify the bones as they are cleaned. Lay these on a tray.

Dem Bones *(cont.)*

Lesson Preparation *(cont.)*

Pour bleach mixture into each cup of bones and let sit at least an hour. Dump the contents into the tea strainer and rinse with clear water. Put bones on the newspaper with that group's number. Turn the cup upside down to dry overnight along with the bones. When the bones are dry, pour them back into the cups and put on lids.

Activity: Day One

1. Have students stand and remove shoes. As you lead them, have them feel the shape of bones in their fingers, arms, ribs, back, hips, legs, ankles, and toes. Show them the transparency of the human skeleton and x-rays of the human skeleton.

2. Tell them they are going to look at tiny bones which look very much like those in their bodies. Use the Teacher Information to explain the owl pellets and what they might find in them.

3. Divide students into pairs and distribute a tray of materials to each group. Explain that they are to pull the owl pellet into two or three parts to distribute among the group. Tell students to search the pellet, using fingers to feel for the bones. When bones are found, they should be placed in the small cup.

4. If skulls or other hollow bones are found, they may need to be dipped into water and washed. This is done by using tweezers to hold them and then picking out the fur with toothpicks.

5. When all bones are found, tell students that you will clean them so the next day they can find out just what they are.

Activity: Day Two

1. Divide students into their groups again and distribute the bones and a piece of dark construction paper. Tell them to sort the bones on the paper according to shape.

2. Use the transparency and x-rays to have them compare these bones with those of humans.

3. Use the transparency Bone Identification Key to help them recognize bones, especially skulls which identify the animals.

4. Select some bones to place on the Vole Skeleton transparency so students can see where they belong. Distribute a copy of this skeleton to each group and have them select bones which they can lay on the matching bones in the drawing.

5. Find a *femur* (leg bone) and a *pelvis* (hip bone) that match. Put the ball of the femur into the socket of the pelvis to show the joint. Use the overhead projector so all can see. Have students stand and place a hand on top of their leg where it joins the hip. Move the femur back and forth as they stand on one leg, feeling at the hip to sense the ball-and-socket joint moving.

Closure

Provide white glue, waxed paper, and toothpicks so each group can glue samples of bones to matching bones in the vole skeleton drawing. The glue will dry clear so the bones will be visible. Even the skull and jaw bone can be glued on the diagram. Place on cardboard, cover with plastic wrap, and display so students can compare the bones which have been found.

Bone Identification Key

	Voles and Rats	Mice	Shrews	Birds
Skull and Jaws	Teeth	Tooth	Tooth	No Teeth
Hips (pelvis)				
Shoulder (Scapula)	The shoulder blade is similar in all of these animals.			
Other	Mole Skull and Jaw	Beetle Wings / Insect Leg	Fish Bones / Scales	Bird Breastbone / Wing Bone

Vole Skeleton

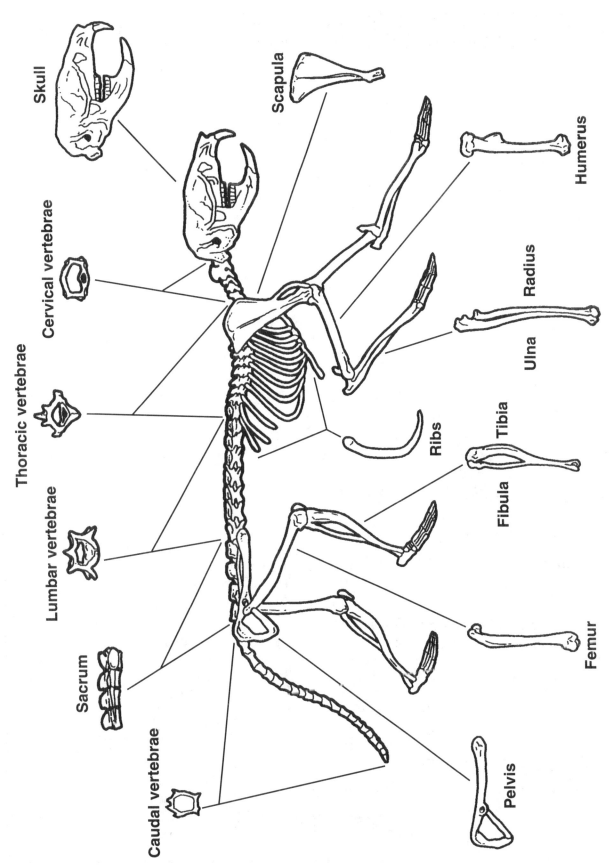

The Human Skeleton

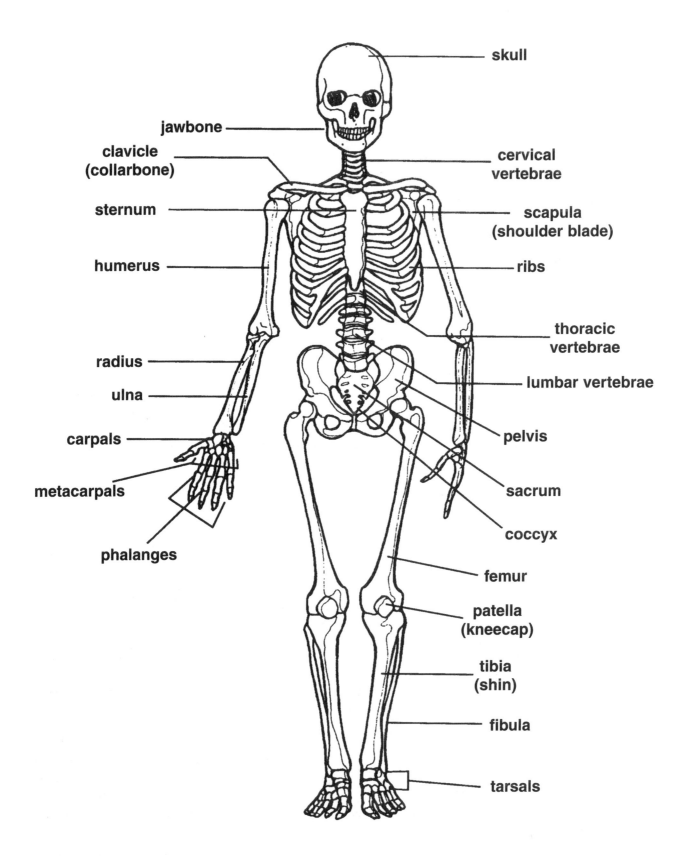

How Do We Breathe?

Overview: *Students will learn how their lungs work and make a model of the lungs.*

Materials per Child

- one pint (.5 liter) clear plastic drinking-water bottles
- round balloon
- rubber band
- pint or quart-size clear plastic bag (Cut off any zip-lock edges.)

Other Materials

- transparency of How You Breathe (page 207)
- scissors

Lesson Preparation

- Cut off the bottom of the water bottle about two inches (5 cm) from the bottom.
- Make a model of the lung as described in #3 below so students will know what their finished product should look like.

Activity

1. Tell students to take a deep breath and then slowly exhale. Ask them what parts of their body they used to do this. (Most will say their mouth or nose and lungs.) Ask them to show you how large they think their lungs are. Demonstrate how to place one hand on the collar bone and the other at the bottom of the ribs. Explain that is the length of their lungs and that there are two of them, one on either side of the chest. Tell them that the lungs fill the chest cavity and are therefore quite large.

2. Tell students you want them to feel what happens when they breathe. The teacher should demonstrate for students so they can follow. Sit straight on a chair without pressing the back against the chair. Point flattened fingers of each hand down and place them just below the breastbone. As you breathe deeply through the mouth, press gently to feel movement up and down. This is the diaphragm, a muscle beneath the lungs. Have students run in place for a minute and then repeat this. They will feel the diaphragm moving higher into the chest as they breathe deeper.

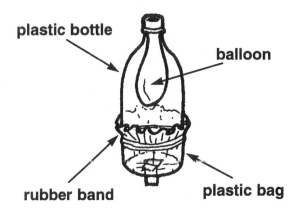

plastic bottle **balloon** **rubber band** **plastic bag**

3. Tell students they will make a model of the lungs. Distribute a water bottle and balloon to each. Show your finished model as an example of what theirs will look like. Have them put the balloon into the mouth of the bottle and turn the edge of the balloon over the lip of the bottle to hold it in place. Put the plastic bag over the bottom of the bottle and secure it with the rubber band (or clear packing tape). Leave some of the bag hanging so it acts as a handle that lets you push and pull the bag.

How Do We Breathe? *(cont.)*

Activity *(cont.)*

4. Let students "play" with their models by pushing air in and out of the balloon, using the plastic bag. Explain that the balloon is like a lung but a real lung is not hollow like the balloon. A lung would look like a sponge, full of tiny air sacs. Tell them the plastic bag is the diaphragm which is a muscle in our body that pulls air into the lungs and pushes it out again.

Closure

• Show the transparency of How You Breathe and have the students pull down on the bag and watch the balloon inflate. Point to the diagram showing the person breathing in and the diaphragm being down. As they push the plastic bag up, the air is forced out of the balloon. Point to the next drawing showing the breathing-out position of the diaphragm. Have them notice that when the bag is pulled down, there is more space inside the bottle than when it is pushed up. Point out that this can be seen in the diagrams of the chest cavity also. The diaphragm pushes up, and the chest cavity becomes smaller so the air is pushed out of the lungs. When the diaphragm drops, it makes the space in the chest bigger and air is pulled into the lungs.

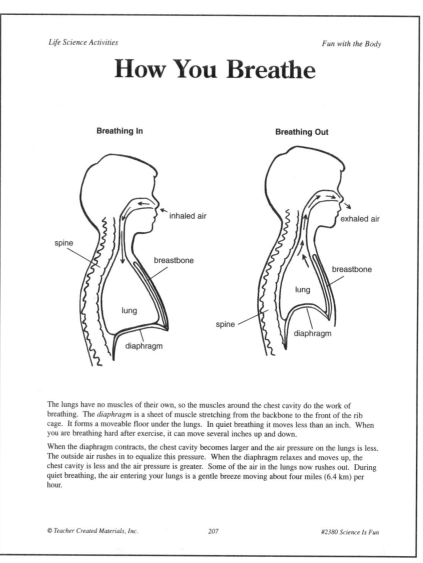

Life Science Activities   *Fun with the Body*

How You Breathe

Breathing In

Breathing Out

The lungs have no muscles of their own, so the muscles around the chest cavity do the work of breathing. The *diaphragm* is a sheet of muscle stretching from the backbone to the front of the rib cage. It forms a moveable floor under the lungs. In quiet breathing it moves less than an inch. When you are breathing hard after exercise, it can move several inches up and down.

When the diaphragm contracts, the chest cavity becomes larger and the air pressure on the lungs is less. The outside air rushes in to equalize this pressure. When the diaphragm relaxes and moves up, the chest cavity is less and the air pressure is greater. Some of the air in the lungs now rushes out. During quiet breathing, the air entering your lungs is a gentle breeze moving about four miles (6.4 km) per hour.

© *Teacher Created Materials, Inc.*   207   *#2380 Science Is Fun*

• Tell the students to put the opening of the balloon near their faces so they can feel the air rushing out when they push up on the bag.

• As they pull down on the bag, have the students take a deep breath to feel what is happening to their lungs. As they push the bag up, tell them to breathe out and feel the diaphragm doing its work for them. Have them repeat this several times as they use their lung model and their own lungs to breathe in and out.

How You Breathe

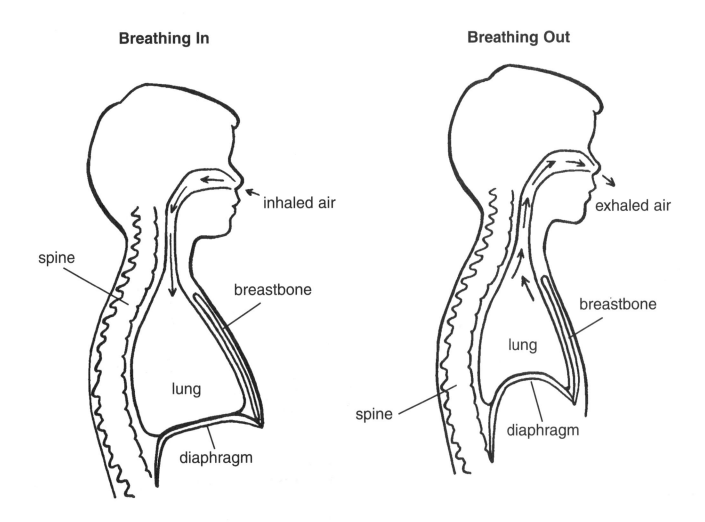

The lungs have no muscles of their own, so the muscles around the chest cavity do the work of breathing. The *diaphragm* is a sheet of muscle stretching from the backbone to the front of the rib cage. It forms a moveable floor under the lungs. In quiet breathing it moves less than an inch. When you are breathing hard after exercise, it can move several inches up and down.

When the diaphragm contracts, the chest cavity becomes larger and the air pressure on the lungs is less. The outside air rushes in to equalize this pressure. When the diaphragm relaxes and moves up, the chest cavity is less and the air pressure is greater. Some of the air in the lungs now rushes out. During quiet breathing, the air entering your lungs is a gentle breeze moving about four miles (6.4 km) per hour.

Take a Deep Breath

Overview: *Students will learn more about the structure of the lungs and experiment to measure the amount of air in their lungs.*

Materials

- bubble solution
- drinking straws
- rulers
- transparency of The Lungs (page 210)
- transparency of Graph of Air Exhaled from Our Lungs (page 211)

- large soft sponge
- large clear container of water
- 3" x 5" (8 cm x 13 cm) lined file cards
- trays (*optional:* sheets of waxed paper)

Lesson Preparation

- For each group prepare a tray of materials: a container of bubble solution, straws, file cards for each member, and a ruler.
- This activity must be done indoors to prevent the wind from breaking the bubbles.

Activity

1. Have students use the lung models to tell what they have learned about lungs and how much air their lungs will hold.

2. Use the transparency The Lungs to show students what their lungs look like and learn more about their function.

3. Show students the sponge and explain that lungs look much like a sponge. Pass the sponge around so students can see how light it is. Cut it in half to show that the holes are throughout the sponge. Let students know that these are really air sacs in the sponge, not holes, and that their lungs have these as well. Place one half the sponge in the water and let them see that it floats until water enters the air sacs, forces out the air, and makes the sponge so heavy that it begins to sink.

4. Tell students that they are going to see how much air their lungs can hold. Divide students into small groups and give each group a tray of bubble materials. Let each student write his or her name on a file card and then write **1**, **2**, and **3** at the beginning of the first three lines. Have them remove all items from the tray and pour about a tablespoon (15 mL) of bubble solution on the tray. They should spread it around with their hands to make the entire surface wet with the solution.

5. Show them how to dip one end of a straw into the bubble solution and blow a bubble through it. After they have been successful, show them how to take a very deep breath and this time blow the biggest bubble they can on the surface of the tray. When the bubble pops, use a ruler to measure its diameter and write it on a file card. Do this until three trials have been completed. Tell all the group members to take turns blowing one bubble and then repeat this until three trials have been made.

Take a Deep Breath *(cont.)*

Closure

- Tell the students to circle the measurement of the largest bubble they blew. Use this data to help students see how to construct a graph. Distribute a small self-adhesive note to each student and have each write his or her name and bubble size on it.

- Ask the students to tell you their bubble sizes. Find the largest and smallest bubbles. Project the transparency of the Graph of Air Exhaled from Our Lungs on the board. Write the bubble sizes in order from smallest to largest on the horizontal axis.

- Have each student place his or her note on the line which represents the size of that bubble. Ask the students to help you count the notes for each measurement and then complete the vertical axis.

- Let students have the experience of analyzing this data by asking them the following:

    ✓ What was the largest bubble size?

    ✓ What was the smallest bubble size?

    ✓ What was the size of the bubble most of the students blew? (Explain that this was the average-size bubble for the class.)

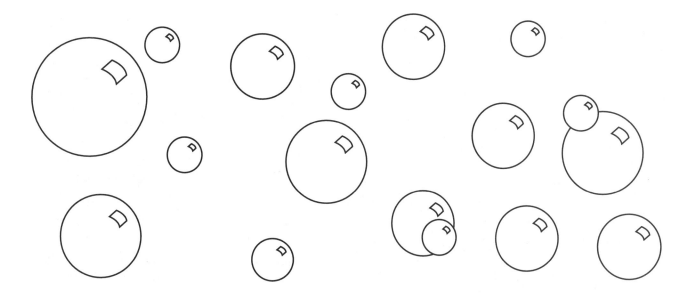

- Tell the students your largest bubble size and compare it with the size of theirs. (*The teacher's bubble should be larger.*) Find the bubble measurements for the tallest students in the class and see if they blew larger bubbles than the shortest students.

- Explain to the students that our lungs grow as we grow and the bigger we are, the larger our lungs become. Therefore, if their lungs did not hold as much air as someone else's did, they may have smaller lungs. Tell them also that we can never squeeze out all the air in our lungs.

The Lungs

The respiratory center in the brain stem controls the diaphragm, telling it how fast to pull in air. It tells the heart to beat faster if you need more oxygen. It does this automatically.

The tubes leading into the lungs look like an upside down tree. Air comes in through the nose or mouth into the windpipe (*trachea*), which branches into two main tubes (*bronchi*). These continue to divide into smaller and smaller branches until they reach the tiny air sacs (*alveoli*).

Your lungs contain hundreds of millions of tiny air sacs (*alveoli*). Tubes no thicker than a hair carry blood cells past the air sacs. Carbon dioxide gas collected by the blood cells from your body passes through the walls of these tubes, and oxygen passes out of the sacs and into the blood cells. These blood cells return to the heart and take blood to all parts of the body.

When you breathe, a trapdoor (*epiglottis*) which is attached to the root of your tongue allows air to enter the trachea. When you swallow, the epiglottis closes over the trachea so no food can get into your lungs. If food does get past this trapdoor, it can be forced out by pressing hard under the diaphragm so it pops out.

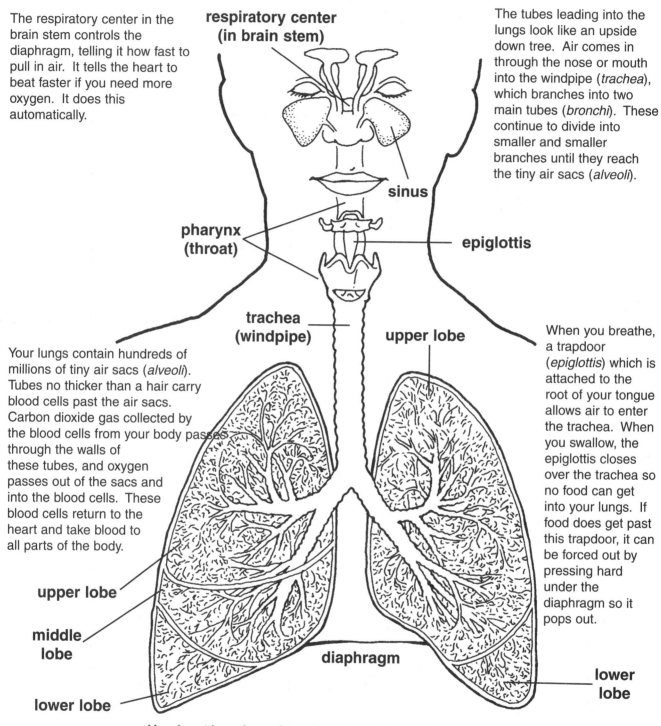

respiratory center (in brain stem)

sinus

pharynx (throat)

epiglottis

trachea (windpipe)

upper lobe

upper lobe

middle lobe

lower lobe

diaphragm

lower lobe

Your heart is under and mostly centered between the two lungs. Your right lung has three lobes, each with its own section of the bronchial tree. Your left lung has only two lobes, with a notch to fit the bottom of your heart. If one lobe is damaged, the others keep functioning. Healthy people do not use their entire lung capacity, and so they have extra breathing power. You exhale only about $\frac{1}{6}$ of the air in your lungs. That means most of the air is left in your lungs.

Graph of Air Exhaled from Our Lungs

Number of Students

Bubble Diameters

This Is Your Heart

Overview: *Students will learn how their heart functions through a series of activities.*

Materials

- regular-sized white bedsheet
- black, maroon, red, and pink permanent felt markers
- maroon and red construction paper
- stethoscopes (cardboard tubes will work but not as well)
- transparency of This Is Your Heart (page 214)
- copy of The Blood Cell's Journey (page 215)
- small juice boxes with red drink (one per student)
- small paper cups (one per student)
- tennis balls
- picture of the circulatory system of the human body (See Resources section.)

Lesson Preparation

- Pin the bedsheet to a wall and project the transparency of the Journey Through the Heart on it, making it as large as possible. Trace the drawing with pencil. Lay it on a table and trace over the lines with permanent felt pen. Trace the veins leading into the heart (the right atrium and ventricle) and the arteries leading right and left into the lungs (see arrows) in purple or maroon pen. Trace all other parts of the heart in red. Outline the lungs in pink. Use black to trace the captions.
- Cut out ovals about three inches (7.5 cm) long and nearly circular from the construction paper to represent blood cells.

Activity #1

1. Ask the students if they have ever been cut. Have them tell you what color their blood was. Tell them to look at the veins in their wrists and hands and tell what color they see. (*Most will say they see blue.*) Explain that this is blood flowing through their wrists and hands, and although it looks blue, it is really a dark purple.

2. Tell students that you want them to do an experiment. Have them raise one arm straight up above their heads and let the other hang straight down. They should hold this position for one minute. At the end of the time, have them compare the hands. They should see that the one held high is much lighter than the other. It will also feel slightly colder than the other hand. Ask them to explain what was happening. (*Do not correct them if they offer wrong ideas.*)

3. Give students unlined paper and have them draw how they think blood travels through their bodies. (*This is a check of their level of understanding, so do not give any answers.*) Have students share some of the ideas with the class or in small groups.

This Is Your Heart *(cont.)*

Activity #1 *(cont.)*

4. Explain that the heart is a muscle which pumps blood throughout the body. Tell them that they are going to make a heart from a juice container. Distribute a juice container and a cup to each child. Help them push the straw into the container. Tell them the container is the heart and the straw is the artery leading from the heart. Have them squeeze the container and watch the drink flow into the cup. Explain the red drink is like their blood. Let them continue squeezing the container, forcing the juice into the cup.

5. Tell students that the heart muscle is actually harder to squeeze than the container. Divide the students in small groups and give each group a tennis ball. Have them squeeze the ball and explain that this is how hard it is for their hearts to pump blood through their bodies.

6. Let the students listen to another student's heart through the stethoscope. This needs to be done in a quiet room.

Activity #2

1. Tell students that they are going to take a trip through the heart. Place the bedsheet with the heart on the floor. Have students gather around it so you can explain the parts of the heart. Point out that they are looking down on the heart so the left and right sides are reversed.

2. Select three students to help with the demonstration of blood traveling through the heart. Two will be stationed in each of the lungs and will hold red blood cells. The third will carry a maroon blood cell and stand at the *inferior vena cava* ready to enter the heart. They represent blood and will follow the arrows moving through the heart as directed by the script you read aloud.

3. Begin to read The Blood Cell's Journey and help the student with the maroon blood cell move along toward the lungs. The blood cells should each go to the left lung, where they exchange their maroon blood cell for a red one and then reenter the heart on the other side. Finally, they exit the heart to the upper or lower body.

4. Let other students take this journey so they can see how their blood travels through their heart and lungs and out into their bodies. They may enter from above or below the heart and go to either lung before going to the other side of the heart. They can leave the heart to pass to the upper or lower body.

5. Show the students a picture of the circulatory system in the body so they can see how the blood travels from the heart throughout their bodies.

Closure

Return the drawings students made earlier about how blood passes through their bodies and let them make another drawing to show what they have learned.

This Is Your Heart *(cont.)*

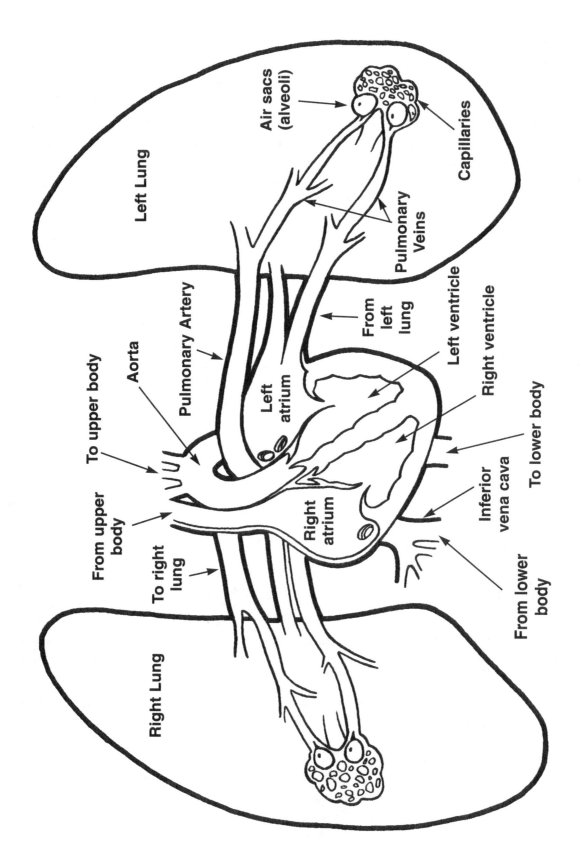

Air sacs (alveoli)

Capillaries

Left Lung

Pulmonary Veins

Pulmonary Artery

From left lung

Aorta

Left ventricle

Right ventricle

To upper body

Left atrium

From upper body

To lower body

To right lung

Right atrium

Inferior vena cava

From lower body

Right Lung

The Blood Cell's Journey

(Script)

You are a blood cell just entering the heart from below the heart. The blood pressure has forced you on your journey all the way through this body to the heart. You are dull red (maroon) in color now since you don't have much oxygen but a lot of carbon dioxide that you picked up from cells along your way. You moved faster as you got nearer the heart, and now you are swept into the . . .

Inferior Vena Cava, a large vein which lets all blood return from the lower body. The heart relaxes and blood rushes into the . . .

Right Atrium. Now you find yourself in a small pocket which has a white bulging floor made of three triangular flaps of a valve which suddenly spring open, pouring you into the . . .

Right Ventricle. This is a large chamber in the lower right side of the heart. Just when you thought you were safe, there is a loud BOOM as the heart beats, squeezing this chamber hard. You go racing up through a valve into the . . .

Pulmonary Artery. This tube leads into the left and right lungs. You are forced into the left lung where this tube narrows into thin capillaries again. You join the line of blood cells in single file, passing through the thin walls of the . . .

Alveoli. These microscopic air sacs make up the sponge-like lungs, which are filled every time you breathe in. Our air has many different gases in it. About $1/5$ of it is the gas oxygen. You give off the carbon dioxide gas molecules and take oxygen molecules through the alveoli walls, which are much thinner than tissue paper. (*The blood cell exchanges the maroon cell for a bright red one.*) The lungs will exhale the carbon dioxide and bring in fresh air with oxygen in it.

This journey isn't over yet! You now flow into the pulmonary vein. As the heart relaxes, you flow into the . . .

Left Atrium, located in the upper left part of the heart. The atrium is a small sack that fills with blood cells as the heart relaxes. It waits for a split second for the valves below to open, and then the blood cell pours into the lower chamber, called the . . .

Left Ventricle. The blood doesn't stay in this chamber long either. Once again, the heart squeezes (beats), forcing the blood cells through the valve in the top of this chamber and into the thick walled tube called the . . .

Aorta. This thick tube splits into three large arteries. Some blood flows to the upper body, going to the arms, fingertips, and the brain. The rest of the blood goes to the lower body, traveling all the way to the tips of the toes.

Your blood circulates everywhere, including the kidneys, brain, and the heart itself. It removes wastes from the body and carries nutrients and oxygen to all your cells. What wonderful life-giving "juice" your blood is! You can help it do its job by eating healthy food and getting plenty of exercise every day to keep your body in good shape.

Where Does the Food Go?

Overview: *Students will take a walk through the digestive system to see how food passes through the body.*

Materials

- twin-size white bedsheet
- transparency of The Digestive System (page 217)
- copy of Food Travelogue (page 218)

- various colored permanent pens
- measuring tape
- string and thick yarn

Lesson Preparation

- Pin the bedsheet to a wall and project the transparency of The Digestive System. Trace the picture with pencil and then lay the sheet on a table. Trace over drawing and labels with colored felt pens.
- Cut a length of string eight yards (7.2 meters) long. Measure two yards (1.8 meters) of thick yarn. Use tape to label it the "Large Intestine." Tape the yarn to the string and measure seven yards (6.3 meters) from where they join. This part is to be labeled "Small Intestine." The remaining string is the distance from the mouth through the stomach and into the small intestine.

Activity

1. Conduct this lesson following lunch. Give each child unlined paper to draw where they think their lunch goes after it is swallowed. Have them begin their drawings at the mouth and show its journey to the point where it leaves the body. (*Do not give any information since this is a pretest.*)

2. Tell students they will journey through the digestive system to follow food through the body. Lay the bedsheet on the floor to see the parts of the digestive system. Ask for a volunteer to walk through the body as you read the script. The underlined terms in the script are the labels found on the drawing. Point these out as the student moves through the digestive system.

3. Ask students how long they think the entire digestive system is from mouth to anus in an adult. Say you are going to walk from the front of the room and they are to hold up a hand when they think you have gone as far as the digestive system would stretch. Begin moving slowly and stop when most hands are up.

4. Let a volunteer hold the "mouth" end of the string and begin to stretch it out. Stop to show the distance to the stomach and then the small intestine. Let students update predictions on the length of the digestive system by having a volunteer stand at the point they think you will reach when all string is unwound. Unwind the string and show students the full length of the system. Explain that this is what would be found inside a six-foot person; their digestive systems would be shorter since they are smaller.

5. Have them look at the small and large intestine and explain how they got their names. (*The small intestine is longer but thinner than the large intestine.*)

Closure

Distribute students' original drawings of the digestive system and let them draw another.

The Digestive System

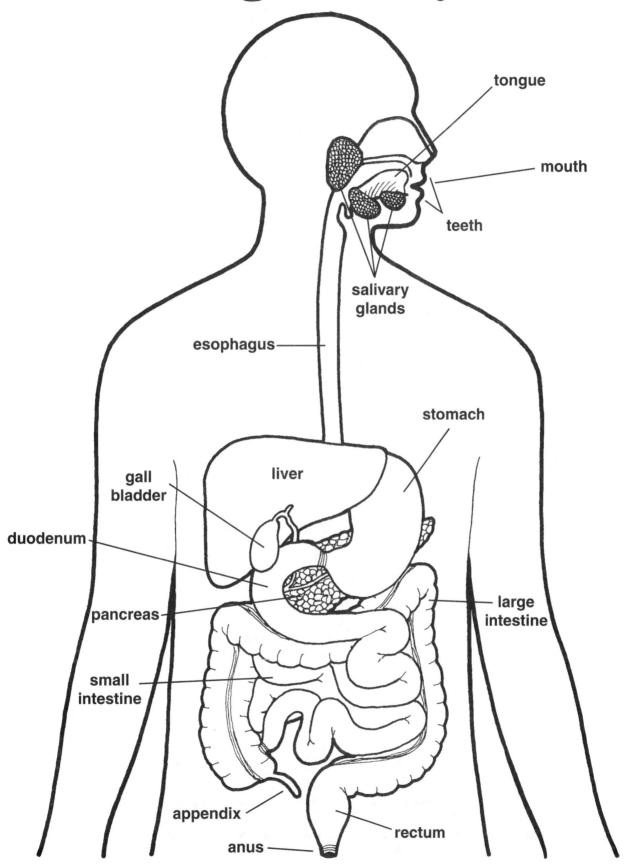

tongue

mouth

teeth

salivary glands

esophagus

stomach

gall bladder

liver

duodenum

pancreas

large intestine

small intestine

appendix

rectum

anus

Food Travelogue

The tongue and teeth work together, breaking food apart and pushing it around. Saliva pours into the mouth from salivary glands to begin digesting food, softening and lubricating it on its way. The tongue pushes against the roof of the mouth as you swallow, helping push food down the . . .

Esophagus, which is about 10 inches (25.4 cm) long in an adult. It lies behind your windpipe (trachea) and is flattened when empty. As you swallow, you stop breathing for a moment. A trapdoor called the epiglottis automatically closes the opening to your voice box and lungs, and the soft palate at the back of the roof of your mouth swings up to shut off the passage to your nose. If you swallow too fast, the epiglottis may not have time to close, causing you to cough to clear out any food that might enter the trachea. The muscles in the esophagus ripple to push the food into the . . .

Stomach, where gastric juices made of hydrochloric acid and the enzyme pepsin are released to break down protein in food. These acids are strong enough to eat through the wall of the stomach. Normally, these acids are not manufactured until food is in the stomach and a protective mucus coats the stomach. Like a balloon, the stomach expands with food. The muscles which surround it begin to churn the food back and forth. Carbohydrates move out first and then proteins. Fats are the last to leave the stomach. Some food may remain in the stomach for two to five hours. The food is now called *chyme*; it is a thick liquid. The chyme squeezes into the . . .

Duodenum, the first 10 inches of the small intestine where the digestive process will be completed by other juices. Like a large salivary gland, the pancreas produces pancreatic juice. One to two pints (.5–1 liter) of pancreatic juice per day pour into the duodenum to digest carbohydrates, proteins, and fats. Bile is made by the liver and stored in the gall bladder. Bile works like a detergent to break down fats so they can be dissolved in water and absorbed into the body. Pancreatic juices and bile flow into the duodenum through the bile duct. The partly digested food now moves into the . . .

Small Intestine where about five pints (2.1 liters) of digestive juices enter through the walls daily. Completely digested food has been changed to nutrients which can now be absorbed through tiny fingers (*villi*) that line the walls of the small intestine. Tiny blood and lymph vessels are inside the villi. They take in the vitamins, minerals, and other nutrients and carry them to all parts of the body through the blood and lymph systems. The average adult absorbs about 10 quarts (9 liters) of digested food and liquid each day. The journey through the small intestine may take four to eight hours. What remains undigested passes into the . . .

Large Intestine where it spends 10 to 12 hours losing large quantities of water and nutrients. At the end, the solution is fed on by a colony of bacteria which decay the remains (feces). The feces are brown because they contain dead blood cells. What is left of your meal passes to the rectum, ready to leave the body through the opening called the anus. The entire journey lasts about 15 to 48 hours.

Moving Out

Overview: *Students will simulate the movement of food through the intestines.*

Materials

- one pair of pantyhose
- one banana
- one plastic bag
- transparent packing tape
- green food coloring
- two tablespoons (30 mL) of water
- *Everyone Poops* by Taro Gaomi and *Your Insides* by Joanna Cole

Lesson Preparation

- Cut the pantyhose in half; only one leg of the hose will be used. Cut off the toe of the hose.
- Mix the food coloring and water.

Activity

1. Review the steps of the journey through the digestive system which students took during the previous activity. Tell them that they are going to see what happens when food has passed out of the stomach and into the intestines.

2. Hold up the banana and explain that it will be the food they have just eaten. Peel it and place it in a plastic bag. Add the colored water and tell them this will be the gastic juices from the stomach. Roll the bag around the banana and seal it with tape. Be sure to squeeze all the air out of the bag and wrap the tape around the bag to strengthen it. Mash the banana slightly to simulate the stomach muscles squeezing it.

3. Show the students the panty hose and explain that it represents the intestines. Have them line up in a double line, facing a partner. Give them the pantyhose to stretch out and hold. Place the bagged banana inside the top end of the pantyhose. Show the students how to use their hands to massage the banana on its way through the hose. Each child should give the banana a squeeze to keep it moving and to mash it further. Continue moving the banana along until it reaches the toe of the pantyhose. Take the banana out of the bag and unwrap it to show your children the "digested" banana.

Closure

Read aloud *Everyone Poops* and *Your Insides* or similar literature about the digestive system.

This Is My Body

Overview: *As a culmination of this unit, students will make a paper model of the body.*

Materials

- Body Parts (page 221)
- colored pens or crayons
- glue
- transparency of the human skeleton (page 204)
- picture of muscles of the human body (See Resources section.)
- cardboard or tagboard

Activity

1. Now that they have completed their study of their bodies, tell the students they are going to make a paper copy of what they look like inside.

2. Distribute copies of the body outline and body parts to each child. Have them color the body parts as follows:
   - **brain**—gray
   - **esophagus**, **stomach**, and **duodenum**—yellow
   - **heart**—red
   - **lungs**—pink
   - **liver**—brown
   - **gall bladder**—green
   - **small intestine**—yellow
   - **large intestine**—pink

3. The students should cut out the body outline and glue it to cardboard.

4. Have students cut out the body parts and place them on the body outline. Let them check with other students to see if they agree with the placement and then glue these in place.

5. Show the students the skeleton transparency and let them sketch in the bones of the arms, hands, legs, and feet.

6. If available, show the picture of the muscles found in the human body and have students add some of those found in the arms and legs to one side of their body outline.

   (*Note:* See the Answer Key for the completed body pictures.)

Closure

- If appropriate for these students, have them label their body parts.
- Cover the finished picture of the body with plastic wrap. Have the students take these home with the assignment of sharing them with family members and explaining some of what they learned from this study.

Body Parts

Body Parts　　　　　　　　　　　**Body Outline**

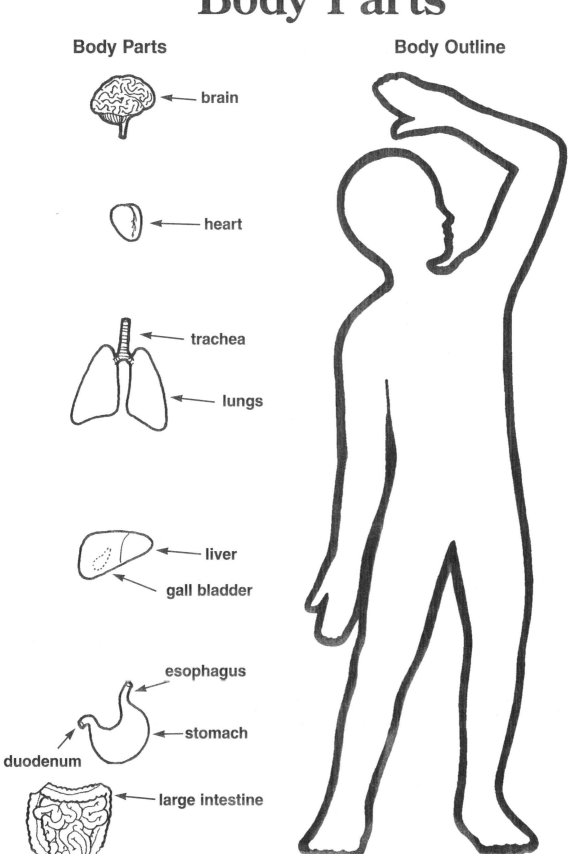

← brain

← heart

← trachea

← lungs

← liver

gall bladder

esophagus

← stomach

duodenum

← large intestine

← small intestine

Fun with Rocks and Minerals Introduction

Rocks cover the entire surface of Earth, even beneath every body of water and the polar ice caps. This rock covering is referred to as the *crust* of Earth. Dirt or soil, which consists of crushed rock and pieces of once living (*organic*) material, covers some areas of the crust.

Earth's crust consists of three types of rock—*igneous*, *sedimentary*, and *metamorphic*. These rocks do not remain as one type but are continuously being recycled from one type to another.

Igneous: Melted rock beneath the crust, called *magma*, is under tremendous pressure and sometimes rises through cracks in the crust. Magma may cool underground within the crust or break through the crust and pour onto the surface in the form of liquid rock called *lava*. When the magma or lava solidifies, it is called *igneous* rock. The crust is cracked into large sections called *plates*. The edges of some crustal plates are forced beneath other plates, melting and recycling the leading edge of rock as it comes into contact with the hot magma.

Sedimentary: These rocks consist of crushed rocks which were once igneous, metamorphic, or sedimentary. This crushed rock material is deposited in layers by wind, water, or ice. As the layers build up, the pressure packs the material together until it compresses into solid rock layers. These sediments may consist of rock fragments ranging in size from large boulders to fine grains of sand and silt. Sedimentary rocks may also be deposits of minerals in the form of crystals or organic material such as shells.

Metamorphic: This type of rock changes or undergoes a *metamorphosis* due to tremendous pressure when it is buried deep in the earth's crust. It can also be changed due to the heat of magma when it comes close to the rock layer but not close enough to melt the rock. Metamorphic rock began as igneous, sedimentary, or metamorphic rock. The original rock changes in appearance and often in mineral composition. For example, the igneous rock *granite* changes to the metamorphic rock *gneiss*, and the sedimentary rock *limestone* changes to the metamorphic rock *marble*.

The activities in this section will enable students to develop an understanding of the rock cycle and the differences between rocks and minerals. They will also learn how to identify minerals.

An Ant's Eye View of Soil

Overview: *Students will examine a variety of soil samples.*

Materials (for each student)

- snack sized zip-lock bags
- magnifying lenses
- transparency and copies of the worksheet What Is Soil? (pages 225 and 226)

- parent letter (page 224)
- plastic spoons

Lesson Preparation

- Make copies of the parent letter and attach a plastic bag to each note. Write students' names on the bags.
- A day or two before doing this activity, give each student a plastic bag and parent letter. Explain what they are to put in the bag and when they need to return the sample to school. Send home the letter and bag.

Activity: Day One

1. Ask the students what they call the "stuff" which is found on the ground (*dirt*). Explain that this can also be called *soil* and that they are going to go on a walk around the school area to collect different samples of soil.

2. Take the students into the schoolyard to find different types of soil samples. Look for a variety of areas to dig up samples, such as a grass area, a field of native plants, or dry soil without any vegetation. Collect samples in bags and write where each was found.

3. Return to the classroom and explain that these specimens will be used during the next science class. Explain that the students will need to bring in their soil samples from home so that the different specimens can be compared with those collected around the school area.

Activity: Day Two

1. Divide students into groups of four. Give each student a magnifier, plastic spoon, and a copy of the two worksheets. Have the students put a plastic spoon into each bag with the soil specimen.

2. Discuss the difference between living or once-living things and things which were never alive. Give them examples of these two categories and write some of these on the board.

3. Use the transparency of the worksheet to demonstrate how to use the spoon to place a small sample of one soil specimen in the circle. Show how to write the location where the sample was collected.

4. Monitor students as they complete the data for their first specimen.

5. Have students examine three other specimens and write their observations. Give them clear tape to place over their specimens to preserve their samples.

Closure

- Discuss what students found in their soil samples. Compare these with the materials found in the school soil samples. Save the worksheets for the students' rocks and minerals journals.

Parent Letter for Soil Samples

Date_____

Dear Parents:

We have begun a study of rocks and minerals, and our first activity will be to look at different samples of soil. The students will examine these samples with magnifiers to see if they can find out what makes soil.

Please help your child partially fill the attached small bag with a soil sample. This may be taken from the yard or a houseplant. Write where the sample was collected and your child's name on the label below and place it inside the bag.

It is important that the child bring the bag back to school by_____ so the soil can be examined during our science class time.

Be sure to ask your child what he or she learned from this activity after we have looked at the specimens. You are welcome to join us. We will be examining our specimens on_____at_____.

Thanks for helping your child add to our science study of dirt.

Cordially,

Soil Sample

Collected by _____
                                      student name

Collected from _____

_____

_____

What Is Soil?

Name:_____ Date:_____

Fill in the information needed below:

Location: _____

Color:_____

Smell:_____

Feel:_____

Living or once-living things which
I found in this soil:

_____

_____

Things which were never alive which
I found in this soil:

_____

_____

Sample #1

Location: _____

Color:_____

Smell:_____

Feel:_____

Living or once-living things which
I found in this soil:

_____

_____

Things which were never alive which
I found in this soil:

_____

_____

Sample #2

What Is Soil? *(cont.)*

Name:_____ Date:_____

Fill in the information needed below:

Location: _____

Color:_____

Smell:_____

Feel:_____

Living or once-living things which
I found in this soil:

_____

_____

Things which were never alive which
I found in this soil:

_____

_____

Sample #3

Location: _____

Color:_____

Smell:_____

Feel:_____

Living or once-living things which
I found in this soil:

_____

_____

Things which were never alive which
I found in this soil:

_____

_____

Sample #4

Let's Eat Dirt

Overview: *Students will use edible materials to simulate dirt.*

Materials

- chocolate cookies, two per student
- one cup (240 mL) powdered sugar
- four cups (1L) milk
- two cups (480 mL) raisins
- eight-ounce (240 mL) package of softened cream cheese
- $\frac{1}{2}$ cup (120 mL) margarine or softened butter
- jellied sugar worms, one per student
- chocolate sprinkles
- two 4-ounce (120 mL) packages of instant chocolate pudding
- eight-ounce (240 mL) container of whipped topping
- clear plastic drinking straw, one per student
- clear plastic 6-ounce (180 mL) cup
- snack-size resealable plastic bag for each student
- small paper bowls, two per group
- plastic spoons, one per student

Activity

1. Discuss what the students found in their soil samples in the previous lesson. Tell them that in this lesson, they are going to make dirt which they can eat.

2. Distribute to each student one plastic bag and two chocolate cookies. Tell them to place the cookies inside the plastic bag, press out the air, and then zip it closed.

3. Have each student place a book over the plastic bag and press hard until the cookies are crushed into small pieces. Tell them the cookies are rocks which they are breaking into tiny pieces to make dirt.

4. Divide the students into groups to assist in preparing the following:

   - Cream together the softened cream cheese, butter, and powdered sugar.
   - Fold the whipped topping into the creamed mixture.
   - Beat the milk into the instant pudding.

5. Distribute separate bowls of the creamed and pudding mixtures to each group.

6. Give each group raisins, jellied worms, and chocolate sprinkles. Explain that the raisins are small rocks, the jellied worms are earthworms, and the chocolate sprinkles are small insects like ants.

Let's Eat Dirt *(cont.)*

Activity *(cont.)*

7. Give every student a plastic cup and have each place a thin layer of crushed cookies at the bottom of the cup. Have them spoon alternating layers of the creamed and pudding mixtures. They should also add thin layers of crushed cookies, raisins, and sprinkles between the layers. The worm can be added to any layer and covered over. The last layer should be of cookie crumbs.

8. Chill the cups of "dirt" until they are set.

Closure

- Distribute the chilled dirt to the students and give each of them a drinking straw. Have them push the straw into the mixture and pull out a sample. Have them look at the different layers they see inside the straw. Explain that this is just what they see when they drive through a road cut—the layers of rock and dirt that were laid down over millions of years.

- Let the students enjoy eating their "dirt" samples.

Mini-Rocks

Overview: *Students will examine a variety of sand samples to learn where they come from.*

Materials

- transparency and two copies per student of Teeny Tiny Rocks worksheet (page 231)
- magnifying lens for each student
- scissors
- double-sided tape (*optional:* rolled clear tape)
- sand samples
- parent letter (page 230)
- snack-size resealable plastic bags (one per student)

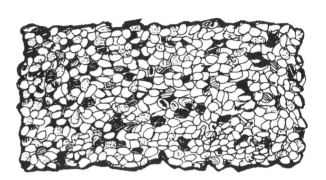

Lesson Preparation

- Make copies of the parent letter and staple a bag to each of them. Distribute these at least a week prior to doing this lesson.
- Contact construction supply stores to see if they can provide some unusual sand samples. Collect some sand from the school sandbox. Label all the bags of sand specimens with the location from which they came, including those brought to school by students.

Activity

1. Review what students found soil is made of and ask them what they think sand is.

2. Distribute a copy of the worksheet to each student. Divide the students into small groups and give each of them sand samples.

3. Use the transparency to show students how they will place the double-sided tape on the worksheet. Show them how to place a pinch of sand on top of the tape and press on the sand to be sure it sticks to the tape.

4. Demonstrate how they should use their magnifiers to make the sand grains as large as possible and then make a drawing of some of the sand grains to show their shapes. Tell them to write the colors they see in the sand.

5. Show them how to label the location from which the sand was taken.

6. Let the students examine at least four different sand samples.

Closure

- Have students share what they saw when they examined the sand.
- Ask them how they think sand is made. (*Rocks are broken into smaller pieces by water, wind, and pressure.*)

Parent Letter for Sand Samples

Date_____

Dear Parents:

We appreciated the soil samples you sent to school for our science class. The students learned that soil is made up of crushed rocks, as well as things which at one time were alive, such as insects or leaves. Now, we are ready to take a closer look at sand to see if we can find what it is made of.

If you have any sand samples to offer, please put a small amount in the attached bag. On the label below, write where the sample was collected and your child's name and place it inside the bag.

It is important that the child bring the bag back to school by_____ so the sand can be examined during our science class time.

Be sure to ask your child what he or she learned from this activity after we have looked at the samples. You are welcome to join us. We will be examining the sand on_____at_____.

Thanks for helping your child add to our science study of sand.

Cordially,

Sand Sample

Collected by _____
                                student name

Collected from _____

_____

_____

Teeny Tiny Rocks

Name:_____ Date: _____

Fill in the information below:

I see the colors _____.

This sand feels _____.

This sand came from _____.

Put the tape across the box and put a pinch of sand on it.

When I looked at the sand through a magnifier, it looked like this.

Fill in the information below:

I see the colors _____.

This sand feels _____.

This sand came from _____.

Put the tape across the box and put a pinch of sand on it.

When I looked at the sand through a magnifier, it looked like this.

Crust of the Earth

Overview: *Students will discover that Earth is made of layers, somewhat similar to a hard-boiled egg.*

Materials

- hard-boiled egg
- permanent black marker

Activity

1. Have each student draw what they think Earth would look like if it were cut in half.

2. Save these drawings to be used again after this lesson is finished.

Demonstration

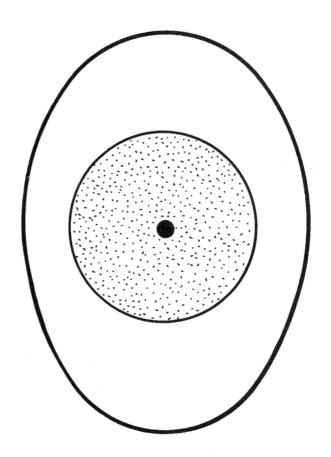

1. Cut a hard-boiled egg in half lengthwise and use the black marker to make a dot in the center of the egg.

2. Explain that Earth is somewhat like this egg, with the crust being the egg's shell, the white layer representing the mantle, the yolk representing the core, and the black dot being the inner core.

3. Crack the shell to show how Earth's crust is cracked. Tell the students that this is due to pressure of the mantle pushing upward against the crust, cracking it in some areas.

4. Tell students that the egg shell is actually too thick to represent Earth's crust. Remove the shell and color the outside of the egg with a felt pen. This layer of coloring would represent the actual thickness of the crust in comparison to the rest of Earth.

Closure

Do the Earth Pizza activity.

Earth Pizza

Overview: *Students will make a model cross section of Earth, formed by spirals of colored ropes of modeling compound.*

Materials

- small containers of red, yellow, blue, and brown tempera paint
- five toothpicks or T-pins for flags
- Earth's Layers Flags (page 235)
- ruler
- compass (for drawing circles)
- round pizza cardboard at least 14 inches (36 cm) in diameter
- transparency of Earth's Layers (page 237)
- one pound of Crayola Model Magic® Modeling Compound (available at craft store)

Activity

1. Use the chart below to see how many students to assign to each section.

Scale Model of the Earth

Section	Number of Ropes	Size	Color
Inner Core	1 to form a disk	2.5 inch diameter	red
Outer Core	9–10	2.1 inch band	red-yellow = orange
Core/Mantle Boundary	1.5–2	thin band	red-blue = purple
Lower Mantle	35	2.1 inch band	yellow
Upper Mantle	7	.5 inch band	pink (slightly red)
Crust	none	thickness of paint	blue (oceans) some brown (land)

2. Draw circles on the cardboard, beginning in the center for the inner core. Mark distances for the other sections from the outside edge of the last band. Keep the point of the compass in the center to draw the next circle. Continue until the four circles are drawn.

3. Make each rope from a ball (about one-inch diameter) of modeling compound. Flatten the ball and place drops of one or two colors to create the desired tint. Fold and knead the compound to distribute color. Take a pea-size piece of the ball and roll into a very thin rope. Link each rope to the previous one, coiling out from the center.

4. The inner core is made first and laid in the center of the cardboard. Add orange ropes to the outer edge to fill the circle for the outer core. Smooth the coils to join them together.

5. Add colored ropes until all sections are filled.

6. The crust layer is painted on the outer edge, using blue for oceans and some brown for land above sea level.

Earth Pizza *(cont.)*

Closure

- Discuss the thickness of each section with the class to help them realize how thin the crust is compared to the rest of the earth.

- Place a marker for each section, using a flag made from a small triangle cut from a file card. This flag should have the name of the section, its thickness, temperature, and state of matter (e.g., solid) of the material. Hold the flags in place with toothpicks or T-pins.

- Use tempera paint to illustrate subduction of crustal plates and fountains of hot spots as shown in the illustration below.

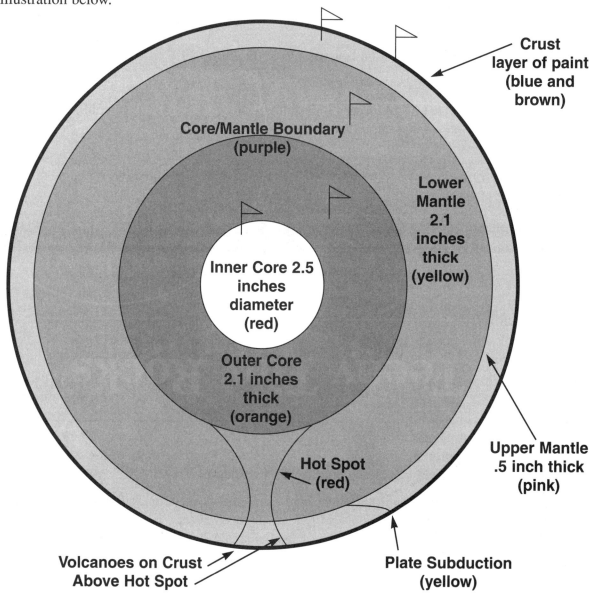

Crust layer of paint (blue and brown)

Core/Mantle Boundary (purple)

Lower Mantle 2.1 inches thick (yellow)

Inner Core 2.5 inches diameter (red)

Outer Core 2.1 inches thick (orange)

Upper Mantle .5 inch thick (pink)

Hot Spot (red)

Volcanoes on Crust Above Hot Spot

Plate Subduction (yellow)

Extender

The model will dry within 24 hours but remains soft and flexible. This "Earth Pizza" can be divided into sections with a knife or pizza cutter for each student to keep.

Earth's Layers Flags

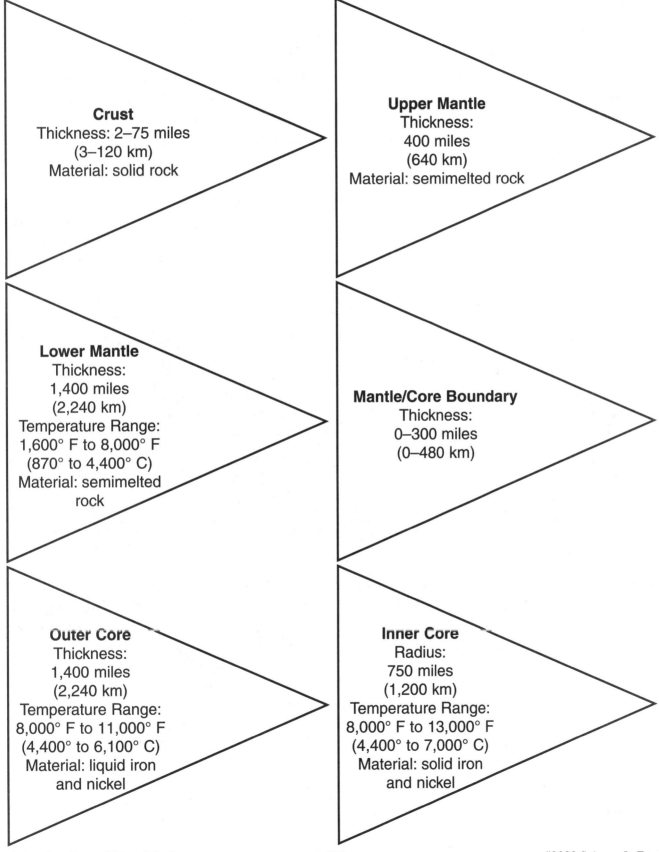

Crust
Thickness: 2–75 miles
(3–120 km)
Material: solid rock

Upper Mantle
Thickness:
400 miles
(640 km)
Material: semimelted rock

Lower Mantle
Thickness:
1,400 miles
(2,240 km)
Temperature Range:
1,600° F to 8,000° F
(870° to 4,400° C)
Material: semimelted
rock

Mantle/Core Boundary
Thickness:
0–300 miles
(0–480 km)

Outer Core
Thickness:
1,400 miles
(2,240 km)
Temperature Range:
8,000° F to 11,000° F
(4,400° to 6,100° C)
Material: liquid iron
and nickel

Inner Core
Radius:
750 miles
(1,200 km)
Temperature Range:
8,000° F to 13,000° F
(4,400° to 7,000° C)
Material: solid iron
and nickel

Earth's Layers

Teacher Information

Earth is about 7,928 miles (12,685 km) in diameter. Most scientists believe Earth is divided into five layers: crust, upper mantle, lower mantle, outer core, and inner core. The inside view of Earth shown on page 237 gives information about these layers. The thinnest part of the crust is beneath the ocean; the thickest is beneath the continents.

Scientists know what the interior of Earth must be like from studying earthquake data. They measure how fast the earthquake waves travel through Earth and in what directions. The temperature and density of the material inside Earth can be calculated from this information. The mantle/core boundary is a division between the mantle and core. It varies in thickness as it is pulled and pushed by the lower mantle, moving in a swirling pattern caused by convection currents.

These convection currents are created when magma in the mantle gets near the core and is heated. It becomes less dense and, therefore, rises. Eventually, it meets the undersurface of the crust where it loses its heat and begins to descend again toward the core. This is just like a conveyor belt. The crust sits on top of the mantle and is pushed around by this action. Where weak spots occur, the magma can push through the crust, creating volcanoes. On the floor of the ocean there are cracks where magma pours out like toothpaste squeezed from a tube. The magma becomes lava which cools on contact with the ocean water and adds to the rock layers. The force of the convection currents in the magma also pushes the plates of the crust around, creating earthquakes as the plates push against each other and force up mountains at the contact point. The plates may also push under other plates; this is called *subduction*. The solid rock on the leading edge of the plate being subducted melts on contact with the magma in the mantle and is recycled.

It may seem strange that despite the inner core being the hottest layer of Earth, it is solid iron and nickel—not liquid as in the outer core. The pressure of the rest of Earth on the inner core is so great that the molecules of iron and nickel are packed so tightly they form solid crystals.

To the Teacher: Use the information on this page along with a transparency of the diagram on page 237 to teach students about the inside of Earth.

Earth's Layers *(cont.)*

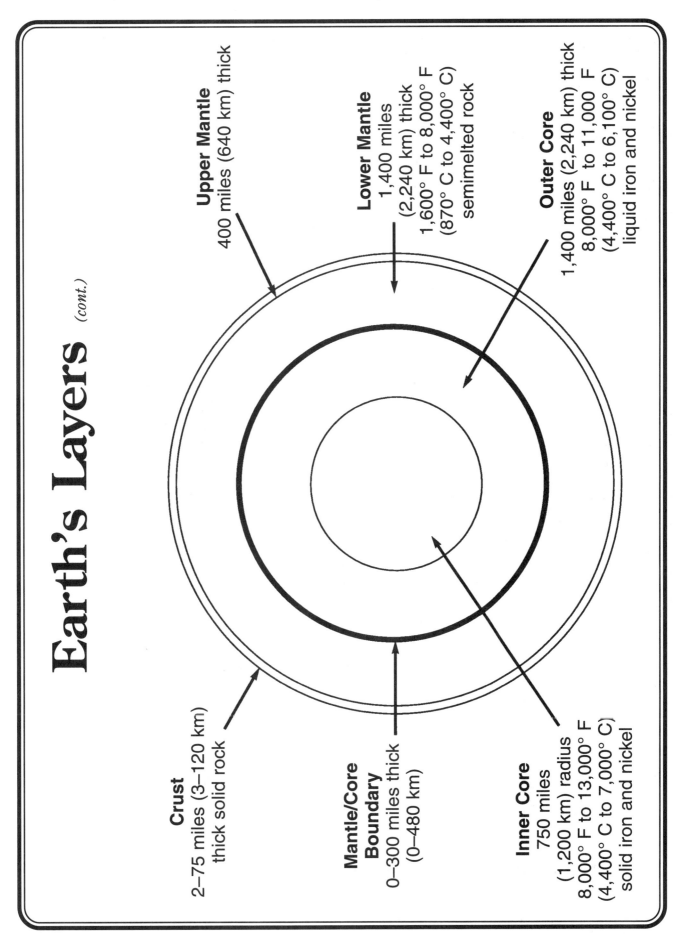

Upper Mantle
400 miles (640 km) thick

Lower Mantle
1,400 miles
(2,240 km) thick
1,600° F to 8,000° F
(870° C to 4,400° C)
semimelted rock

Outer Core
1,400 miles (2,240 km) thick
8,000° F to 11,000° F
(4,400° C to 6,100° C)
liquid iron and nickel

Crust
2–75 miles (3–120 km)
thick solid rock

**Mantle/Core
Boundary**
0–300 miles thick
(0–480 km)

Inner Core
750 miles
(1,200 km) radius
8,000° F to 13,000° F
(4,400° C to 7,000° C)
solid iron and nickel

Walk Through the Rock Cycle

Overview: *Students use a model of the rock cycle to walk on as they discover how the three types of rocks are created and recycled.*

Materials

- large white bedsheet
- permanent ink felt pens
- transparency of The Rock Cycle (page 240)
- Walk Through the Rock Cycle script (page 239)
- five pieces of 5" x 8" (13 cm x 20 cm) cardboard

Lesson Preparation

- Pin the sheet to a wall and project the transparency on it so that it fills the bedsheet. Using pencil, trace the picture, including captions and numbers.
- Lay the sheet on a table and trace over the outlines and captions with black permanent pen.
- Color the igneous rock gray, the sedimentary rock brown, and the metamorphic rock green. The lava and magma should be red.
- Make signs on the cardboard to read as follows: ***Igneous Rock***, ***Sedimentary Rock***, ***Metamorphic Rock***, ***Lava***, and ***Magma***.

Activity

1. Place on the floor the bedsheet with the rock cycle diagram on it.
2. Gather the students around the sides and bottom of the diagram.
3. Select one student to walk through the diagram. Give the student the card which is labeled ***Magma***.
4. Have the student stand on #1 and read aloud the script. The child should move as directed in the script. Give the child the proper signs that are mentioned in the script.

Closure

Let additional students walk through the rock cycle. This can be done without the script so the students can tell the story in their own words.

Assessment

Have students write an illustrated summary of what they have learned about the rock cycle.

Walk Through the Rock Cycle Script

1. You are *magma* under Earth's crust, below the floor of the ocean. Since your temperature is 1,600° F (870° C), you are semiliquid rock. You are under tremendous pressure from the hot magma below, as it rises from deep near the center of Earth. Now, you are being squeezed like toothpaste from a tube, and you flow out of a crack in the crust and onto the ocean floor.

2. As you break through the crust and meet the ocean water, you begin to cool. You are *lava* now, still hot enough to be semiliquid, so you ooze across the ocean floor getting thicker and thicker as you cool off.

3. You have cooled enough to become *igneous rock*, and you are added to the top and sides of the crustal plate under the ocean. Shells from dead animals fall to the floor of the ocean and pile up on top of you. More and more and more layers of shells and sand are piled up on you until they are squeezed together and turn into sedimentary rock. Since you are being pressed so hard by the sedimentary rock, you change from igneous rock to *metamorphic rock*.

4. The plate you are on is gradually moving, pushed along by more magma coming up through the crust just as you did. In many millions of years, you travel to the edge of the continent which is on another plate. Now the plate you are on begins to dive under the continental plate.

5. It is getting much hotter again, and you start to melt back into *magma*. You flow under the crust until you reach another large chamber.

6. You are inside a large chamber deep under a volcano. The pressure of the magma under you is pushing on you again, forcing you to rise up the throat of the volcano.

7. As you rise in the volcano, you begin to lose some of your heat and become thicker and turn into lava, but you are still not rock. Suddenly, the pressure is building behind you, and you are rising faster and faster!

8. You are pushed out of the top of the volcano and begin to flow down its steep side toward the ocean. Some of the material that came out with you has turned to fine ash and rises in a huge gray cloud over the volcano.

9. As you roll down the volcano's side, you run into the ocean. Oh! That feels better. Since you are still hot lava, you turn the water to boiling temperature, and it hisses and gives off steam. Your temperature changes very quickly, and you turn into pieces of rock. This is *igneous rock*, but you are in the form of sand because you cooled so quickly.

10. Millions of years later you are rolled to the ocean floor and begin to pile up with other sand and shells. As more layers are added, you are pressed into *sedimentary rock*. Your journey does not end here, however. You are on a plate going under the continental plate where you will be remelted and may have a trip to the center of Earth before rising through the crust again.

The Rock Cycle

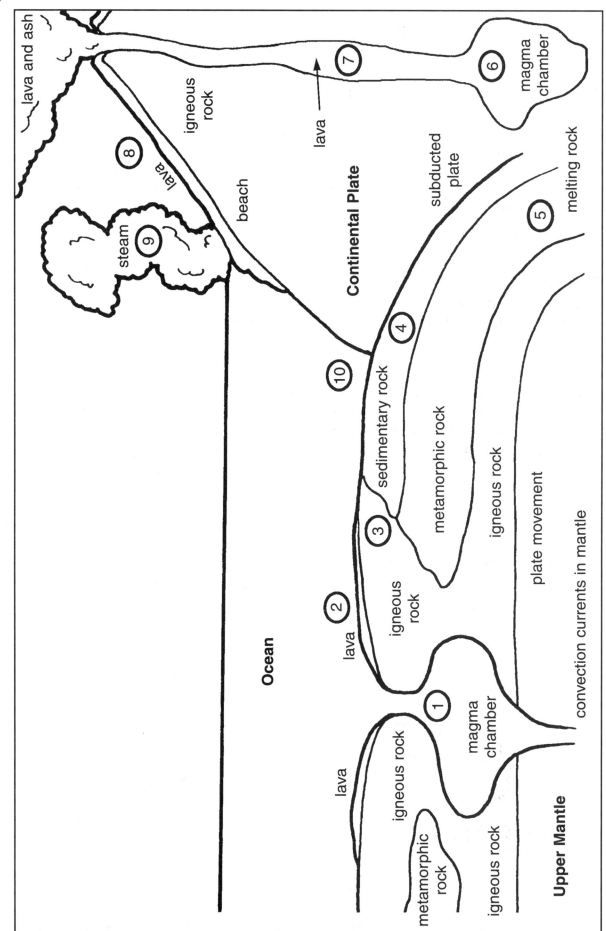

Rocks or Minerals?

Overview: *Students will discover the difference between rocks and minerals by using cookies.*

Materials

- cookies containing a variety of ingredients (e.g., colored M&Ms, raisins, chocolate chips, nuts)
- transparency and copies of the worksheet What's in My Cookie? (page 242)
- mineral specimens
- rock specimens

Activity

1. Show students the examples of minerals and rocks. Tell them we often call all of these rocks but that the activity they are about to do will show them the difference.

2. Distribute a cookie and worksheet to each student. Explain that the cookie is like a rock, made up of many minerals.

3. Have students divide their cookies in half and put one half aside, to eat later. Let them begin to look in the cookie for ingredients which represent the minerals (e.g., raisins). Use the transparency to demonstrate how they pull the minerals out of the cookie and place them in different boxes on the worksheet.

4. After all the "minerals" have been placed on their worksheets, have the students tell you what they found. List the names on the board and have the students write these on their worksheets.

Closure

- Show the students the rock specimens and point out some of the different minerals which they can see in them.
- Let the students eat their "rocks."

What's in My Cookie?

Pretend your cookie is a rock and pull it apart to find the "minerals" inside it. Put each different mineral in a box. After you have taken out all the "minerals," write what they are on the line in the boxes.

Homemade Rocks

Overview: *Students will make simulated rocks.*

Materials

- parent letter (page 244)
- play dough (Each child needs an amount about the size of a golf ball.)
- materials to mix into the play dough
- 10 inches (25 cm) of string
- rock specimens which students bring from home

Lesson Preparation

Several days prior to doing this activity, send home the parent letter requesting materials to use to make the simulated rocks.

Activity

1. Distribute a lump of play dough to each student and have each knead the lump until it is soft.

2. Tell students to slowly mix the play dough with the things they brought to represent minerals.

3. Each student should add another thin layer of play dough to the rocks. This represents the weathering which takes place in nature, often hiding the minerals which are inside the rocks.

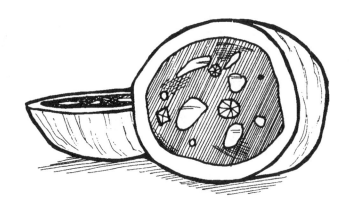

Closure

- Give each student a piece of string. Have each student tie each end to a separate pencil so that about four inches (10 cm) of string is left between the pencils. Show them how to use this device to cut their rocks in half.

- Let students examine the cross section of their rocks and look at the minerals which they can now see that were not visible on the surface before. Have them compare their simulated rocks to the classroom rock collection.

Parent Letter for Simulated Rock Materials

Date_____

Dear Parents:

Our class has studied the difference between *rocks* and *minerals*. The students learned that a rock is made up of two or more minerals, while a mineral is all the same material. We used cookies to represent rocks and pulled them apart to find all the "minerals" in them

Our next activity is to make simulated rocks from play dough and things students bring from home. These items should be small since the lump of play dough will be about the size of a golf ball. Items which would be good to use are as follows:

- small chips of rocks, such as aquarium rocks

- synthetic jewels from old jewelry

- marbles

- small pebbles

- charcoal pieces

- scraps of aluminum foil

The students also need a variety of actual rock specimens to compare with their simulated rocks. If you have any interesting rocks you are willing to lend our class, we would appreciate having them for our display table. Of course, these will be returned to you as soon as our study ends.

When the students are finished making their rocks, they will cut them open and compare them with the actual rock specimens. They will keep their simulated rocks at the end of our study.

Thank you for your help in making this an exciting activity for your child.

Cordially,

Identifying Minerals

———— Teacher Information ————

Rocks are made up of two or more minerals. Minerals are created from elements on Earth and are found in soil and rocks. Many of these same minerals make up the crust of the rocky planets of Mercury, Venus, Mars, and moons of the planets in our solar system.

Mineralogists define minerals as substances which . . .

- formed naturally.

- are made of materials that were never alive.

- have the same chemical makeup wherever they are found.

- have atoms which are arranged in regular patterns and form solid units called crystals.

By this definition, substances such as coal, petroleum and natural gas, or pearls and coral are not minerals since they were formed by once living plants and animals. Substances such as calcium, iron, and phosphorus, which are found in food and water, are often called minerals, but mineralogists do not consider them minerals.

Minerals are usually a compound of two or more elements. Some minerals, such as gold and sulfur, however, are made of only one element. The most common elements which form minerals are oxygen and silicon. Others include aluminum, iron, sodium, potassium, and magnesium. There are about 2,000 known minerals. Common minerals can be recognized by some characteristics such as the following:

Color: Minerals are found in a variety of colors due to the chemicals in them. For instance, quartz occurs in many hues but may also be colorless. Some minerals are always the same color—e.g., galena is metallic gray, sulfur is yellow, azurite is blue, and malachite is green. A fresh surface is needed to see the true color since weathering may hide it.

Luster: The amount of light reflected from a mineral's surface is its luster. Luster may be described as glassy, metallic, shiny, dull, waxy, satiny, or greasy.

Streak Color: Some minerals leave a colored streak when rubbed across a piece of unglazed white tile. The streak color may not be the same as the mineral's color. For example, hematite may be black to brown, but its streak is red-brown.

Texture: Texture is the "feel" of the mineral's surface when it is rubbed. This may be rough, smooth, bumpy, or soapy.

Hardness: Although all minerals are hard, the surface varies in resistance to scratching. The Mohs hardness scale of 1 to 10 is applied to minerals. The hardness test is done with common materials which vary in hardness, such as a fingernail, penny, steel knife or nail, and glass. The hardness number is assigned depending upon which item will scratch the mineral's surface.

The activities in this section will develop the students' skills in identifying minerals through careful observation and by gathering data about the characteristics described above.

The Sorting Game

Overview: *Using their shoes, students will learn how to sort by one characteristic.*

Materials

- one shoe from each student and one from the teacher
- decks of cards

Activity

1. Tell students you are going to sort them into groups and that you want them to see if they can guess how you are sorting them. Divide the students into groups by sex without letting the students know your system. Do this by calling one student at a time to a specific area in the room so they will join the boys' or girls' group.

2. After you have selected five students, ask the students if they have guessed the characteristic you are using to sort the students. Ask the students if they know of any other way to sort people.

3. Tell the students that they are going to learn how to sort their shoes. Seat the class in a large circle on the floor and have each remove one shoe. Place these in the center of the circle, along with a shoe from the teacher, so that all can see the shoes. Have the students talk to their neighbors to discuss ways in which the shoes could be sorted (*color, size, material,* etc.).

4. Ask the students to tell some of the ways they thought of for sorting the shoes and list these on the board. Choose one of the characteristics suggested by the students and have volunteers sort the shoes by this method.

5. Select another characteristic but show the students that it would make the job of sorting very difficult if they used both the new and old characteristics to sort the shoes. Place the shoes in the center again and have other volunteers sort the shoes again by the new characteristics.

Closure

- Divide the students into groups of three or four and give each group a deck of cards from which the jokers have been removed. Tell the students to sort their cards by one characteristic chosen by the group. Have them share the different ways each group discovered for sorting the cards and list these on the board.

- Continue to have them use the cards to find more ways of sorting them.

Mystery Mineral

Overview: *Students will begin to develop methods for identifying minerals.*

Materials

- parent letter (page 248)
- rock and mineral specimens
- pictures of minerals
- sets of eight mineral specimens: *calcite, galena, graphite, hematite, magnetite, obsidian, quartz,* and *talc* (Mineral specimens are available from the Delta Education ESS catalog. See Resources section.)

Lesson Preparation

- Send home the parent letter to invite them to bring or send mineral specimens to school so they may be displayed in the classroom. As the specimens arrive, arrange them on a display table. Do not add identification labels at this time.
- Make up sets of the minerals listed above for small groups of students to use.

Activity

1. Review the activity of shoe sorting with the students. Tell them that in this activity they will be sorting mineral specimens.

2. Divide the students into groups of three or four. Distribute a set of minerals to each group. Tell them to look at and handle the minerals and decide how they can be sorted, using only characteristics chosen by the group. Explain that they should place the minerals in different areas on their table, according to the characteristics. Let them know that when they have finished they will be moving to another group's area to see how they sorted their minerals. Tell them that if the other group can tell how their minerals were sorted, they did a good job.

3. Let the students sort their minerals. Monitor them to be sure they are using only one characteristic and that they are setting each group of minerals apart to show how they were sorted.

Closure

- Have the students go to another group and determine what characteristics they used to sort the minerals. Write these on the board.
- Let each group re-sort the minerals done by the other group, using a different characteristic. List the new methods for sorting on the board.

To the Teacher: Do not let students sort by a characteristic which would vary, such as size of the pieces of minerals. They should discover that the minerals can be sorted by *color*, *texture*, *luster*, and possibly *density*.

Parent Letter for Mineral Specimens

Date_____

Dear Parents:

During our study of rocks and minerals, we have examined sand and soil to learn where they come from. We have also learned about *igneous*, *metamorphic*, and *sedimentary* rocks and discovered how these rocks are constantly being changed and recycled.

Now, we are going to study the minerals which make up the rocks. It would be very interesting for the children to see a wide variety of minerals. If you have any which we could display in our classroom, we would appreciate borrowing them for a short time. Please bring them to school or send them with your child. If possible, please label the minerals so the students can see their names. The minerals will be placed on a display table where students are permitted to look but not touch them, so we will take good care of the specimens.

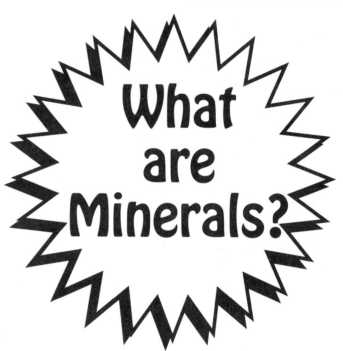

Following is a partial list of minerals, some of which you might have to help us in our study:

- pyrite
- gypsum
- agate
- amethyst
- chert
- garnet
- halite
- jade
- mica
- petrified wood
- malachite
- turquoise

Your mineral specimens will be returned to you by_____ when our study ends. You are welcome to come visit our classroom and see our display of minerals, as well as watch us in action while we do activities to learn about minerals.

Be sure to ask your child what he or she is doing in science class while learning about rocks and minerals.

Cordially,

Match My Mineral

Overview: *Students will describe mineral specimens.*

Materials

- sets of eight mineral specimens
- transparency and copies of the worksheet Match the Minerals (page 250)

Activity

1. Review the list of mineral characteristics students discovered in the previous lesson.

2. Divide the students into groups of three or four students and distribute a set of minerals and the worksheet to each group.

3. Show the transparency of the worksheet. Explain the terms *luster* and *texture* and write examples of these on the board (see teacher information on page 245). Write examples of colors students see in the eight minerals on the board.

4. Select one of the mineral specimens and show it to the students. Place it on the worksheet in the #1 position. Have the students help you write a description of its color, luster, and texture.

5. Explain that each member of the group will pick one of the minerals and write a description of its color, luster, and texture on the worksheet. Tell the students that they may not choose the mineral that was used for the demonstration. Be sure they know that they are only to describe one mineral per group member, rather than describing all eight minerals.

6. Let them know that when all have finished their work they will go to another group's table, just as in the last class, to see if they can match their minerals with their descriptions. The group will be considered successful if the other group can match all of their minerals.

7. Monitor the students as they work, assisting when needed. Be sure the students are as specific as possible with their descriptions.

Closure

- When all students have finished describing their minerals, have them put the minerals in a pile next to the worksheet and move to another group's table. They should read the descriptions and match the minerals.

- Have each group return to their own table and check on the matching to see if it was done correctly. To help students see how they can improve on their descriptions, discuss any of the minerals which were not matched.

Match the Minerals

Names of Group Members: _____

Each member of the group should pick a different mineral to describe. Next to one of the numbers, write the color, luster, and texture of that mineral.

Mineral	Color	Luster	Texture
1			
2			
3			
4			

What Is My Mineral's Name?

Overview: *Students will identify the eight mineral specimens.*

Materials

- sets of eight minerals
- transparency and copies of the Mineral Identification Key (page 252)
- streak plates (Streak plates are unglazed tiles. These may be purchased through ESS Catalog.)

Activity

1. Review what the students learned in the previous activity, Match My Mineral. Tell them that they are going to find out the names of the eight minerals they have been using.

2. Divide the students into their small groups and distribute a set of minerals and the identification key to each group.

3. Show them the transparency of the identification key and select one of the descriptions to use as a demonstration of how to use the key. Let the students find the mineral which matches the description you have selected and tell them to place that mineral on its name. Check to see if all have been able to find the mineral.

4. Tell the students to divide the remaining minerals among their group members. They should use the descriptions to find the names for their minerals and place them on the chart.

5. Monitor the students as they work to be sure they are matching the minerals correctly. If they have incorrectly matched any of the minerals, remove them from the key and have them try again.

Closure

- Have students identify some of the display minerals (if available) which are the same as the eight minerals they have been using.
- Add the labels to the display minerals so the students can now see the mineral names.

Mineral Identification Key

Match your minerals to these descriptions and then find their names.

Mineral	Color	Luster	Texture	Streak	Hardness
calcite	tan and white	shiny and glassy	smooth	white or pink	penny 3
galena	silver	metallic and shiny	smooth to rough	dark gray or black	penny 3
graphite	dark gray	dull	smooth to bumpy	black or dark gray	fingernail 1
quartz	milky white	shiny and glassy	smooth to bumpy	white	none more than 6.5
obsidian	black	glassy	smooth with sharp edges	none	none more than 6.5
hematite	reddish brown	dull	rough	red brown	fingernail to nail 1-6
magnetite	gray or black	dull	rough	black or dark gray	none above 7
talc	light gray, may have some white	dull	smooth, feels like soap	white	fingernail 1

Crystal Creations

Teacher Information

Most minerals are formed in a liquid state and develop crystal structures as they solidify. That means they have solid, regular shapes. These shapes vary from simple to complex, from very tiny to extremely large. Some minerals (gems) form beautiful crystals which we use as jewelry. The most famous gems are diamonds, rubies, and emeralds. Crystals may vary in color, depending upon chemical content. For example, diamonds may be blue, white, or pink, as well as other shades.

Overview: *Students will watch crystals form of salt, alum, Epsom salt, and cupric sulfate.*

Materials

- eight disposable five-ounce (160 mL) cups
- eight disposable spoons
- very hot water
- food coloring
- magnifying lenses (one per student)
- transparent or double-sided tape
- 3" x 5" (8 cm x 13 cm) file cards
- eight petri dishes or small saucers
- crystal forms of salt, alum, Epsom salt, and cupric sulfate

(Petri dishes are available from Delta Education. See Resource section. Epsom salt and alum are available in drug stores. Cupric sulfate is poisonous and should therefore be handled with care. It can be obtained from Flint Scientific [see Resources section] or a high school chemistry teacher.)

Lesson Preparation

Make sets of four cards, each with a different crystal specimen adhered with double-sided tape. Since cupric sulfate is poisonous, adhere it to the cards by placing the clear tape over the crystals. Label each card with the name of its crystal (e.g., alum, Epsom salt). Each group of students will need a set of cards.

Activity

1. Divide students into small groups and distribute a set of file cards and four magnifiers to each group.
2. Have students look closely at the crystal shapes. Have them draw the shape of each crystal on a piece of paper.
3. Explain that these crystals form naturally and that you are going to show them how they become crystals.
   - Pour about three teaspoons (15 mL) of hot water into a cup.
   - Add about ¼ teaspoon (1 g) of cupric sulfate to the water.
   - Stir with the spoon until it dissolves completely. If necessary, continue to add more cupric sulfate until no more will dissolve.
   - Pour all of this solution into the petri dish or small saucer.
   - Set the dish on a tray with a label nearby of the chemical used.
   - Repeat with other chemicals, using a new cup and spoon each time.
4. Tell the students that they will be watching these dishes during the next few days to see what appears.

Crystal Creations *(cont.)*

Closure

- After the water evaporates, the crystals of salt, etc., should appear in the bottoms of the dishes. The slower the evaporation rate, the larger the crystals will be. When they have formed, have students examine them with magnifiers and compare them with what they saw earlier. They should see that the same shapes appear as before the solids were dissolved.

- Explain that this is just what happens in nature. If available, show examples of natural crystals such as quartz or calcite.

- Tell students that crystals may be of different colors, depending upon what chemicals may mix with them as they form. If available, show the students natural crystals which may be the same shape but different color, such as clear, milky white, or black quartz. Tell them this can be simulated by using food coloring as the chemical added to their homemade crystals. Mix up a solution of salt and add a few drops of food coloring. Pour this into a dish to evaporate. When the salt crystals form, they will be the color which was added to them but have the cubic shape of salt. Make colored solutions of Epsom salts and alum, using different colors to show that they also can be various colors.

Crystal Shapes

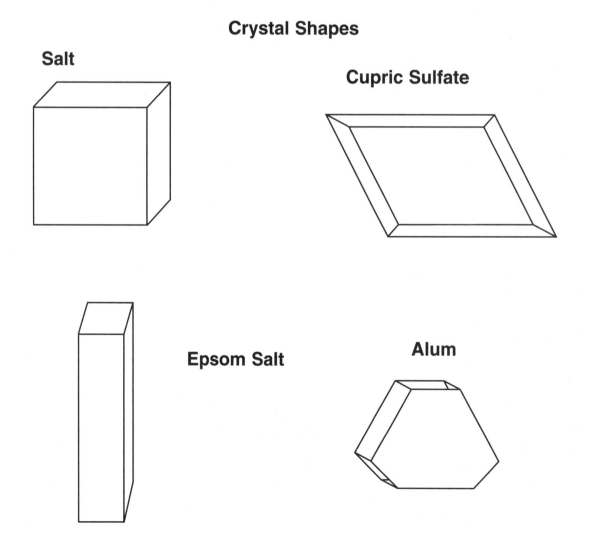

Salt

Cupric Sulfate

Epsom Salt

Alum

Simulated Geodes

Teacher Information

A very special kind of crystal formation takes place inside some rocks. When such rocks are broken open, beautiful crystals may cover the cavity within the rock. Water with dissolved mineral in it filled the hollow rock at one time. When the water evaporated, it left behind the crystals of the mineral. These rocks are usually roughly spherical and may be 2 to 6 inches (5 to 15 cm) in diameter. They are called *geodes*. Crystals of quartz are often found inside geodes. Finding a geode is like discovering a treasure chest.

Overview: *Students will make simulated geodes from nut shells.*

Materials

- walnut shell halves
- large paper cup of hot water
- salt, alum, or Epsom salt
- red, green, or blue food coloring
- spoons
- magnifying lenses
- examples of geodes

Activity

1. Divide the students into groups. Distribute a cup of hot water and salt, alum, or Epsom salt to each group. Supply them with a spoon and a container of food coloring.

2. Have them pour salt, alum, or Epsom salt into the hot water, adding the solid until no more will dissolve.

3. They should add a few drops of food coloring and then pour the solution into the walnut shell. The shell should not overflow with the liquid.

4. Have the groups set these aside and allow the liquid to evaporate for the next few days so the crystals will form.

Closure

- Have the students compare the geodes they have "grown" with examples of actual geodes.
- Explain the teacher information to the students so they can see that natural geodes form much like the ones they have just made.

Crystal Garden

Overview: *Students will observe a chemical crystal garden grow.*

Materials

- small container such as margarine tub
- piece of sponge or charcoal, about the size of a golf ball
- dropper bottles of red, green, blue, and yellow food coloring
- household ammonia
- water
- salt
- laundry bluing (found in laundry section of grocery or drug stores)
- glass jar for mixing
- measuring cup and spoons
- large spoon for stirring mixture

Demonstration

1. This demonstration needs to be done outside or in a well-ventilated classroom to avoid breathing ammonia fumes. Mix the following in a jar to make the chemical solution:
   - six tablespoons (90 mL) each of hot water and laundry bluing
   - three tablespoons (45 mL) salt
   - one tablespoon (15 mL) ammonia
2. Place the sponge or charcoal in the center of the margarine tub.
3. Mix the salt and hot water until it dissolves.
4. Add bluing and ammonia and stir into the mixture.
5. Pour this solution over the sponge or charcoal, completely covering it.
6. Place a few drops of food coloring on the surface of the sponge or charcoal. Add different colored drops in various areas, leaving some without any coloring.
7. Place the bowl in a location where it will not be disturbed but can be observed by students. Crystals will begin to form in 1 to 12 hours, depending on the amount of humidity in the atmosphere and the temperature. The slower the liquid evaporates, the larger the crystals will become. The odor of the ammonia and bluing will persist until the liquid evaporates.
8. Do not touch the crystal garden once crystals begin to form. The crystals are very fragile.

Closure

Have students compare the crystals grown in this garden with the salt, alum, Epsom salt, and cupric sulfate crystals grown in the Crystal Creations and Simulated Geodes lessons. They will see that these crystals look more like snow and are very soft.

Extenders

- Grow the chemical crystals on different surfaces, such as rock, leaf, cloth.
- Try making the solution without the salt, ammonia, or water and see if crystals will form.

Making a Rock-and-Mineral Journal

―――――――― **Teacher Information** ――――――――

This culminating activity will act as a final assessment for the study of rocks and minerals.

Overview: *Students will create a cover for their rocks-and-minerals journal.*

Materials

- light-colored file folders or heavy construction paper
- colored pens or crayons
- all data sheets completed by the students in this study
- copies of Earth's Layers (page 237) and Walk Through the Rock Cycle script and diagram (pages 239 and 240) for each student

Activity

1. Distribute a folder or folded construction paper to each student. Distribute the worksheets the students have completed during this study. Give them copies of the diagrams of the earth's layers and rock cycle (pages 237 and 240).

2. Discuss some of the things students have learned during their study of rocks and minerals.

3. Tell the students to draw pictures on the fronts and backs of their covers to show some of the things they learned.

4. Monitor the students as they work to help inspire them as needed.

5. Have each student write a brief story, pretending to be a rock going through changes to become igneous, metamorphic, and sedimentary rock. Tell them to make pictures to help them tell their stories.

Closure

Display the journals in the classroom and let students share them with their parents and other students.

Fun with Weather Introduction

Life on Earth is possible only because of the envelope of air covering the planet. We call this envelope *atmosphere*, and it is hundreds of miles thick. The atmosphere protects us from the sun's harmful rays and most meteors which may be pulled toward Earth by gravity. The atmosphere is made of gases, mostly *nitrogen* and *oxygen* but also small amounts of other gases, such as *carbon dioxide*.

Weather affects our lives in many ways—the clothing we wear, types of homes we need, how we spend our leisure time, and the ways we travel. Weather also often determines our moods—for example, sunshine puts us in a happier mood than overcast skies or rain. It also determines the types of plants and animals that can survive in various areas of the world.

Some parts of Earth receive more heat from the sun than others. The equator receives the greatest amount of sunlight, the poles the least. This uneven heating of Earth's surface causes air movement—that is, the winds. Warm air at the equator moves toward the poles, and cold air at the poles moves toward the equator. Earth's rotation deflects the winds to the west. This regular wind pattern is complicated because Earth's surface is made up of land and water. Land heats up more quickly than water but also loses its heat faster. This sets up pressure differences in the air over various parts of the world. Earth's motion around the sun, causing the seasons, further complicates matters. As a result of all these influences, masses of air wander about Earth's surface. It is these wandering air masses that are responsible for changes in weather. They run into each other and rise as they warm or sink as they cool.

The water on Earth is constantly being recycled through the atmosphere. Water on Earth's surface evaporates into water vapor, a gas, and is held in the air. When the air cannot hold any more moisture, the vapor condenses into water droplets and ice crystals. These form clouds which are carried along by the winds. Depending upon the various conditions of temperature and pressure, rain or snow or other forms of precipitation may fall. Fog is a localized cloud which is sitting on Earth's surface.

This section enables students to begin to learn about some of the instruments used to measure weather conditions. They will also do activities which teach them some of the basic concepts of weather patterns, such as the movement of wind and the cloud formations. Most importantly, the children will discover that continuous observations are needed to learn about weather conditions where they live.

Watching the Weather

Overview: *Students gather data on daily weather patterns.*

Materials

- large calendar
- weather symbols for the calendar (page 260)
- videotape of TV weather report for the day previous to the closure activity
- transparency and copy of the Student Weather Calendar for each student (page 261)

Lesson Preparation

Activity 1

1. Gather students in the morning and explain that they are going to begin a record of the type of weather they have every day for a month. *Note*: This activity works well if begun at the first of the month and incorporated into the daily calendar routine.

2. Have students tell about different kinds of weather they have experienced. List their ideas on the board. Let volunteers come forward to draw a symbol for each type of weather. Be sure to include terms such as *sunny*, *partly cloudy*, *rainy*, and *snowy*.

3. Show the class the symbols they will use on their weather chart. Compare these to symbols the students drew on the board.

4. Discuss the weather conditions today. If possible, go outside where they can see the sky and help them choose the right symbol to represent the conditions they see. Glue the symbol on today's date on the calendar. Now ask the children to predict tomorrow's weather. Their predictions will be only guesses at this point. On the calendar, pin the symbol which represents the majority predictions for tomorrow's weather.

5. The next morning, have students again report the weather condition and check to see if their predicted symbol was accurate. If not, replace it with the correct one. Repeat this all week until the children feel comfortable using symbols.

Activity 2

1. After students have posted the weather symbols for the week, distribute a Student Weather Calendar to each child. Use the transparency of the chart to help them complete information such as days of the week and dates. Begin their weather calendar with the first of the month.

2. Have students copy data from the class weather calendar onto their own calendars, drawing the weather symbol for each day.

3. Let students draw the weather symbol for the present day on their calendar and post the correct symbol on the classroom calendar. Continue to do this throughout the month. Include the weather for weekends and holidays on both calendars.

4. At the end of each week, discuss the different types of weather children have recorded.

Closure

Show a weather report recorded from the previous day's television broadcast. As it is viewed, point out some information being covered in the report. Ask students to watch the weather report that evening and be ready to tell about it tomorrow.

Weather Symbols

Sunny	Cloudy	Partly Cloudy	Rainy	Snowy

Student Weather Calendar

month _____ year _____

How Do Thermometers Work?

Teacher Information

Thermometers work on the principal of expansion and contraction of liquids at different temperatures. Thermometers are filled with alcohol dyed red for easy viewing or mercury, which is silver in color. The thermometer is a glass tube sealed at both ends and partially filled with the liquid. Thermometers are calibrated to an exact temperature scale, either in degrees of Fahrenheit (F) or Celsius (C). When it is hot, the liquid inside the thermometer will expand and rise in the tube; the opposite happens when it is cold.

Overview: *Students will learn to read and make their own thermometers.*

Materials

- hot and cold water
- ice
- room-temperature water
- clear plastic nine-ounce (270 mL) cups
- black felt marker
- clear drinking straws
- tacky adhesive (used to adhere pictures to a wall, available in most office supply stores)
- red food coloring
- rubbing alcohol (available in drug stores)

- small clear plastic water bottles with screw-on lids
- nail (the same diameter as the drinking straws)
- hammer
- easy-to-read thermometers (all the same type)
- transparency of the thermometer
- *optional:* trays

Lesson Preparation

- Use the hammer and nail to make a small hole in the center of the lid of the plastic bottle. This hole needs to hold the straw in place without pinching it closed.
- Push the straw through the hole so that it is about $^1/_2$ inch (1 cm) above the bottom of the bottle. Place tacky adhesive around the straw where it meets the cap so it is airtight.
- Fill the bottle $^1/_4$ full of alcohol and add a few drops of red coloring.
- Screw the lid on the bottle, making certain it fits tightly. Some of the alcohol may rise in the straw at this point.
- Test the thermometer in hot and ice water. If the hot water makes the alcohol rise so high that it spills out of the straw, pour some out.
- Make sets of three plastic cups, each set marked "hot," "cold," and "room temperature." Fill the cups $^3/_4$ full just before the activity. Add ice to the cold water. Be sure the hot water will not burn. These sets may be placed on trays to minimize spilling.

Note: This activity is divided into two parts which may be conducted on different days, if needed.

How Do Thermometers Work? *(cont.)*

Activity 1

1. Ask students what is used to tell the temperature of liquid, air, or their bodies (*thermometers*). Tell them that they are going to use a simulated thermometer to learn how it works.

2. Divide the students into small groups and give each group a set of cups and the bottle thermometer. Explain that the straw is like the glass tube in a real thermometer and that the liquid is alcohol which you dyed red so they could see it.

3. Have the students test their thermometers in the three cups of water and watch what happens to the liquid in the straw each time it is placed into a different temperature.

4. Discuss what they observed. Be sure they see that the liquid rises when it gets hot and drops when it becomes cold.

5. Let students try making the alcohol warm with their own hands to see if their body temperature will register on their thermometers.

6. Tell the students to place their thermometers into the hot water. Ask them what temperature the thermometer is showing. They will realize that they cannot answer the question, since the thermometers show no numbers.

7. Explain that in their next activity, they will learn about real thermometers to compare with those they have just used.

Activity 2

1. Divide the students into small groups and give each group a thermometer. Tell them to examine its parts and be ready to tell you what they see.

2. Discuss what the students saw on their thermometers.

3. Distribute the three sets of water to the students. Have them place their thermometers into the cups, watching to see what happens to the liquid as they do so. Discuss what they observe. Compare this with the bottle thermometers they used in the previous activity.

4. Show the transparency of the thermometer and point out the markings on it. Explain how to read the thermometer by using the level of the liquid in the glass tube and the markings alongside it. Have the students practice reading the thermometer as you indicate a variety of temperatures on the scale.

5. Let the students return to placing their thermometers into the water cups and reading the temperature from the scale. Move among the students to help them with this.

Closure

- Place the thermometer on the classroom wall low enough for students to read it. Take two thermometers outside and place one in the sun and the other in the shade. Help students to read these. Discuss why they are all different temperatures.

- Add the outside temperature to the classroom weather calendar, using the thermometer in the shade. Continue to do this daily until the weather calendar is no longer used. Try to record the temperature at the same time each day so it can be compared with the previous day.

Graphing the Weather

Overview: *Students will graph weather data recorded for one month.*

Materials

- Classroom and Student Weather Calendars from the previous lesson
- videotape of previous evening's TV weather report
- transparency and copies of Weather Graph (page 265)
- copies of Weather Symbols (page 260)
- piece of large white butcher paper, at least 36 inches (90 cm) square
- double-sided tape or glue sticks

Lesson Preparation

- Project the transparency of the weather graph on the butcher paper and trace it to make a large graph. Add additional columns beside the symbols, if needed, for the data to be graphed.
- Make multiple copies of the weather symbols. These will be used to paste on the weather graph, so make enough of each to represent those pasted on the classroom weather calendar. Place these on a table in the classroom.

Activity (This should be done on the last day of the month.)

1. Have students tell about weather reports they saw last evening on TV.
2. Let students post the symbol for today's weather on the classroom and their own weather calendars. Review weather students observed during the month. Tell them they are going to make a graph of the number of days of that month which were sunny, cloudy, partly cloudy, rainy, or snowy in the morning.
3. Divide the students into four or five groups. Assign each group a different week on the weather calendar.
4. Explain that each group should choose the symbols they need for each day of their week from the table where these have been displayed. They should write the corresponding date on each of the symbols. Have the students put double-sided tape or glue on the back of each symbol.
5. After all the weather symbols have been prepared, call one child from each group to post their symbols on the large graph beside the matching symbol shown in the left column.

Closure

- Have students look at the results on the graph and discuss what the weather was like during the month. They should count days for each type of weather pattern and record that on the graph at the end of the row of symbols.
- Let them find those weather patterns which happened most and least frequently during the month.
- Review the Classroom Weather Calendar to see if there were any repeating weather patterns during the month.
- Show the videotape of last evening's TV weather report. See if the predictions made in this report actually come true.

Weather Graph

month _____ year _____

☼ sunny					
cloudy					
partly cloudy					
rain					
snow					

Building a Weather Vane

Teacher Information

A weather vane points in the direction from which the wind is blowing. There are several different ways to make this instrument. Follow the directions to make a weather vane to use with your students.

Overview: *Students will use a weather vane made by the teacher to determine wind direction.*

Materials

- 2 ½ inch (6.35 cm) Styrofoam ball
- meat skewers
- long, thin knitting needle
- plastic drinking straw
- coffee can with lid
- sand

- cardboard
- tape
- magnetic compass
- scissors
- Weather Vane Patterns (page 268)
- test tube or tall olive jar

Lesson Preparation

- Drive the knitting needle straight through the Styrofoam ball.
- Push the meat skewer into the ball so it is perpendicular to the knitting needle. The ends should stick out evenly on both sides of the ball.
- Trace the weather vane patterns onto cardboard and cut them out. Tape these to the ends of the meat skewer.
- Poke a hole in the center of the coffee can lid so it will hold the drinking straw in place.
- Place the test tube or olive jar in the coffee can and pour sand into the container to hold it upright and directly below the hole in the lid.
- Push the straw through the hole in the lid until it is inserted into the test tube or jar. Place the knitting needle through the straw and into the jar.
- Test to see if the weather vane has free movement by blowing on it. It should move even in a gentle breeze.

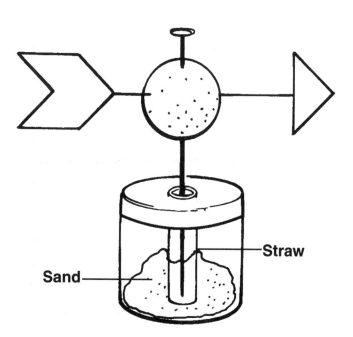

Building a Weather Vane *(cont.)*

Activity

1. Have the students look outside and tell you if the wind is moving. Ask them how they know (*trees or flag moving*).

2. Show the students the weather vane and take them outside to show them how it works. Do this on the playground or other area where buildings will not stop the wind.

3. Use the compass to find north. If available, find an area of pavement or dirt and draw the direction of north as an arrow. Place a line perpendicular to this line to show east and west. Mark this diagram with the letters **N, E, W, S**. The diagram is now a *compass rose*.

4. Set the weather vane on the diagram where the lines intersect. Have the students stand away from it and see which way it points. Explain that this is the direction from which the wind is blowing. Let them find the direction of the wind for that time.

Closure

- Return to the classroom and put the wind direction on the weather calendar, along with the other weather information.

- Have the students return to the area of the compass rose daily to find the wind direction and add this data to the weather calendar.

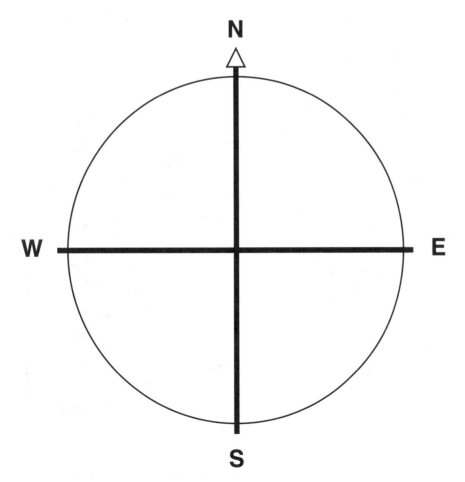

Weather Vane Patterns

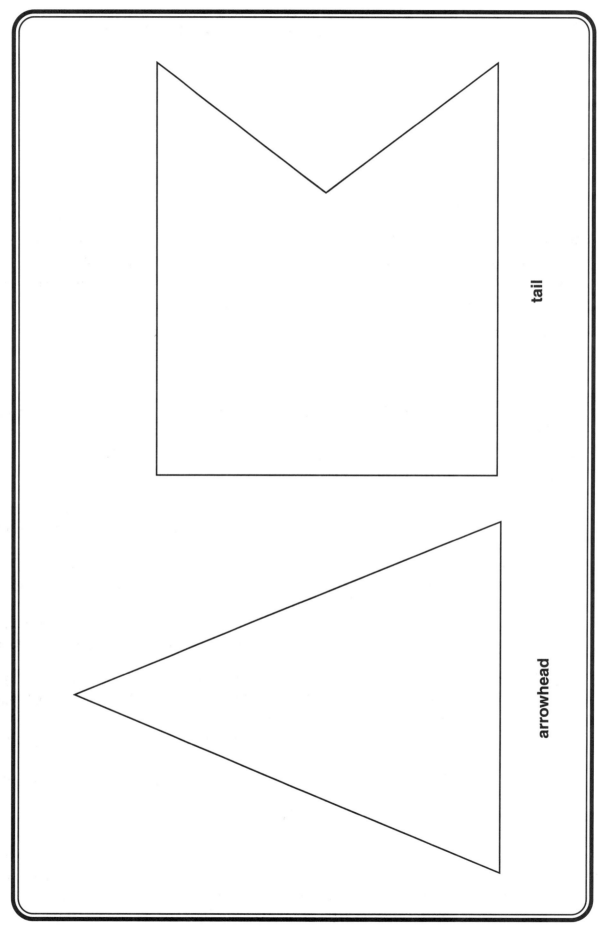

tail

arrowhead

Let's Go Fly a Kite

— Teacher Information —

Using lightweight, easy-to-fly kites is one of the best ways to let children experiment with wind currents. Although many patterns are available for homemade kites, inexpensive plastic kites work best for this activity.

Overview: *Students will use kites to study the wind.*

Materials

- inexpensive plastic kites (one for each pair of students and two extra kites)
- six-inch (15 cm) lengths of one-inch (2.5 cm) plastic irrigation pipe (one per kite)
- thick cotton string (available on a cardboard cone)
- classroom weather vane
- copies of Flying a Kite for each student (page 270)

Lesson Preparation

- Cut 50 feet (15 m) of string for each of the kites. Tie one end to the center of the kite according to the instructions on the kite, and the other to the center of the plastic pipe. Attach one kite to a string 200 feet (60 m) long. (*If possible, older students can assist in this activity.*)

Activity

1. Take students to a large field. Have them check the wind direction with the weather vane. Look at trees to see how the wind is moving the leaves and branches. Toss a handful of grass into the air so students can see the direction it blows.
2. Use the kite with the longest string to demonstrate how to fly a kite. Just as the children will do, have another person hold the kite up and release it when you are ready to run. When the kite is airborne, have students observe it move in the wind.
3. Explain that it is now their turn to fly their kites. Divide students into pairs in a line at one end of the field. The partners should stand face-to-face. The child who is to fly the kite will hold the pipe in one hand. The partner will hold the kite high by the center stick.
4. At a signal, the child holding the kite releases it, and the other partner runs down the field, gradually letting out string so the kite will climb. The other partner should run behind. Both should watch what the kite is doing as the wind catches it.
5. Have students practice in one part of the field to gain experience. It is best to let only a few practice at one time.
6. After students reach the far end of the field, they should line up again. This time, the other partner will get to fly the kite.
7. Provide time for students to observe their kites.

Closure

Return to the classroom and have students make a series of drawings showing how they flew their kites. Have them write what they did to get the kite into the air and what helped to keep it up.

Flying a Kite

Name:_____ Date: _____

Draw three pictures which show how you flew your kite. After each drawing, write what you saw and felt as you flew the kite.

1. This is how I began flying my kite.

   _____

   _____

   _____

   _____

   _____

2. My kite is beginning to fly.

   _____

   _____

   _____

   _____

   _____

3. My kite is very high now.

   _____

   _____

   _____

   _____

   _____

What Is a Cloud?

Overview: *Students will learn about clouds through a series of activities.*

Materials

- hot plate (*optional:* An electric skillet can be used in place of the hot plate and one pie pan.)
- two pie pans
- ring stand or other device to hold one pie pan over the other
- water
- ice
- glass of water

Lesson Preparation

- Place the hot plate on the table and put one pie pan on top of it. Pour in about one inch (2.5 cm) of water. Suspend the second pie pan above the pie pan with water in it. Put ice in this pan.

- This lesson will be done as a demonstration by the teacher. Arrange the students in the best position for them to observe the demonstration.

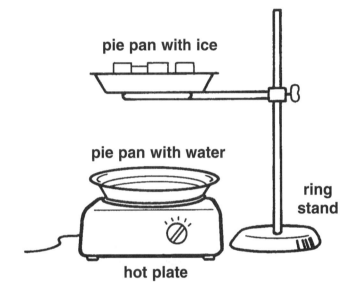

pie pan with ice

pie pan with water

ring stand

hot plate

Activity (Do this activity on a sunny day.)

1. Ask students to tell you what they think clouds are made of and where they come from. Tell them they will begin a study of clouds today.

2. Take students outside to an area where there is pavement, preferably blacktop. Show them the glass of water and explain that you are going to spill the water onto the pavement. Have them predict what they think will happen. Pour the water and have them observe it. They should see that some of the water sinks into the pavement but most will spread out, leaving a wet spot.

3. Ask them to predict what they think will happen to the water as it is left to sit in the sunlight. Outline the puddle with chalk and tell the students that they will return to the classroom but will come back to this spot in a while to see what has happened to the water.

4. Return to the classroom and tell students that you are going to demonstrate how clouds form and what they are made from.

5. Point out the hot plate, the pan of water on it, and the pan of ice above it. Show that as the water heats, it turns into steam which rises. When the steam hits the cooler surface of the pan of ice above it, it begins to cool and turns into water droplets under the pan. Eventually, the water will begin to fall back into the pan on the hot plate.

6. Return to the area where the water was spilled on the pavement. Let students discover that the water has completely disappeared. Ask them where they think the water has gone.

What Is a Cloud? *(cont.)*

Closure

- Have the students return to the classroom. Let them look at the hot water and ice demonstration again. Explain that the hot plate is like the sun which is heating the water. As the water heats, it begins to turn into steam, which is really droplets of water spread out into vapor. When it hits the pie pan above it, the vapor begins to cool off. Tell them the cold pie pan is like the upper atmosphere high above Earth. As the water vapor rises in the sky, it begins to cool and collects into clouds. If enough water vapor collects, it may begin to rain or snow, depending upon the temperature.

- Ask the children if any of them have ever flown in an airplane and flown through or near clouds. Explain that although the clouds look like cotton from the ground or from an airplane, they are really only water droplets which are very cold and thus usually in the form of ice crystals.

Where Is the Water Vapor?

Overview: *Students will learn that the air holds invisible water vapor.*

Materials

- ice
- food coloring
- clear container of water, at least one quart (1 L)
- thermometer
- white tissue handkerchief

Lesson Preparation

This lesson will be done as a teacher demonstration. Gather the students where they will able to observe the demonstration.

Activity

1. Ask the students what they learned about clouds in the previous lesson, What Is a Cloud?

2. Remind them that they saw water vapor being created by using the hot plate and the sun. Explain that today they will be able to see the invisible water vapor that is carried in the air around them.

3. Pour the water into the clear container. Add several drops of food coloring and stir until the color is mixed with the water. Show the students that the outside of the container is dry by running the tissue over it.

4. Take the temperature in the water and begin to add ice. Stir the water periodically. Add ice until water droplets begin to condense on the outside of the jar. Record the temperature on the board.

5. Wipe some of the water off with the tissue. Show the students that it is not the color of the water. Ask them where they think the water has come from. Did it leak out of the jar? (*No, or it would be colored water.*)

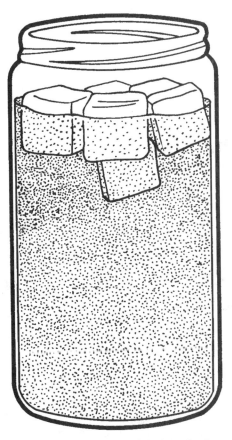

colored water with ice in it

Closure

Remind the students that the water temperature dropped when ice was added to it. Explain that when the air hit the cold jar, the water in it began to pull together in the form of water droplets on the outside of the jar. Tell them this process is called *condensation*.

Where Does Water Vapor Come From?

Overview: *Students will see that plants give off water vapor.*

Materials

- three quart (liter) sized sealable plastic bags
- tree with large leaves on it
- two clear plastic 9-ounce (270 mL) cups
- copies of Watching Water Vapor data sheet for each student (275)

Activity

1. Review what students learned about condensation of water from the atmosphere in the lessons What Is a Cloud? and Where Is the Water Vapor?

2. Ask them how they think water vapor gets into the air.

3. Explain that water vapor can come from water evaporating from any moisture which is in the open air. Tell them they are going to do two experiments to see how water gets into the air.

4. Pour the same amount of water into the two clear plastic cups. Mark the level of the water in the cups with the black felt marker. Put a plastic bag over one of the cups and tape it in place. Tell the students that this experiment will take several days and that they will record what they see happening during that time.

5. Take the students outside to the tree. Let them watch you place the bags over two different leaves, sealing them around the stem of each leaf. Have them observe that there is nothing else inside the bag. Tell them that they will observe these leaves for a few days and record what happens to them.

6. Distribute two copies of the water vapor record sheet to each student. Let them begin by writing "leaves" on one form and "cups" on the other. Next, they should put the date, time, and their comments and drawings on the chart. If changes in either experiment occur before the school day ends, let the students update their records. If the students are too young to record their own data, make a class record on an enlarged version of the chart.

Closure

After students have observed and recorded changes in the water cups and bags on the leaves for several days, discuss what they have discovered. Explain what is happening.

- *The water in the open cup will drop below the black mark. This is due to the water changing to water vapor and mixing with the atmosphere—the process of* evaporation.

- *The water level in the cup covered by the plastic bag will not have dropped, but condensation will form inside the bag. This indicates that the water is evaporating but is unable to escape through the plastic bag.*

- *Water will begin to collect inside the bags which encase the leaves. Plants give off moisture through leaves, just as an animal does through skin. Normally this moisture is not visible since it evaporates as it oozes out. The plastic bag prevents evaporation.*

Watching Water Vapor

Name: _____ Date: _____

These are my observations of the two_____.

Date	Time	Comments	Picture

What Are Those Clouds?

Overview: *Students will observe and identify clouds and record them on their weather calendar.*

Materials

- transparencies of Types of Clouds and Clouds in the Atmosphere (pages 277 and 278)
- sheets of cotton (available in drug stores) *optional:* large cotton balls
- white glue
- waxed paper
- toothpicks
- blue construction paper, 8½" x 11" (22 cm x 28 cm)
- large-tipped black felt pens

Lesson Preparation

Make copies of the altitudes shown on the right side of the Clouds in the Atmosphere chart.

Activity (If possible, do this lesson on a day when clouds are visible.)

1. Take the students outside to look at the clouds. Let them sit or lie down and watch what happens to the clouds. If the clouds are moving, point this out to the students. Help them to see familiar objects (e.g., animals) formed by the clouds.

2. Return to class and show the transparency of the four types of clouds. See if the students can find any that match what they saw outside.

3. Show the transparency of the Clouds in the Atmosphere and explain to students that some clouds are lower than others. Point out those clouds which form high in the sky and those which are at lower levels. Explain that they are going to make a model of this picture, using cotton to represent the clouds.

4. Divide students into small groups and give each member a piece of construction paper and handful of cotton. Give each group a piece of waxed paper and white glue. Have them squeeze some of the glue onto the waxed paper. Give each child a toothpick and explain that each should use it to spread glue on the paper and then place the cotton over it.

5. Distribute to each student a strip with the altitudes on it. Have them glue this to the right edge of their papers.

6. Have the students glue cotton to their papers to represent the various clouds, following the chart. The black pen should be used to darken the undersurface of the cumulonimbus cloud. These are storm clouds and frequently appear dark underneath.

7. Let students copy the names and altitudes of these clouds on their charts.

(*Note:* If the students are too young to make individual cloud charts, the teacher should make one large one for display in the classroom.)

Closure

- Post the students' cloud charts on the bulletin board.
- On the weather calendar, write the types of clouds which were seen on this day. Continue to write the types of clouds on the calendar in the coming days.

Types of Clouds

The following illustrations show the three basic types of clouds and the cumulonimbus clouds. Below the illustrations, descriptions are given, along with explanations of how the clouds were named.

Cirrus clouds are high, thin, white clouds that are made of tiny ice pieces. *Cirrus* is a Latin word meaning curl.

Stratus clouds are low, flat gray clouds which are layered. When stratus clouds lie close to the ground, they are called fog. *Stratus* is a Latin word which means layer.

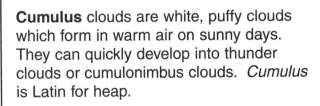

Cumulus clouds are white, puffy clouds which form in warm air on sunny days. They can quickly develop into thunder clouds or cumulonimbus clouds. *Cumulus* is Latin for heap.

Cumulonimbus clouds or thunderheads are huge, puffy, dark clouds, which are a type of cumulus cloud. *Nimbus* is Latin for rain.

Clouds in the Atmosphere

This table illustrates several types of clouds and the heights they can reach in the atmosphere.

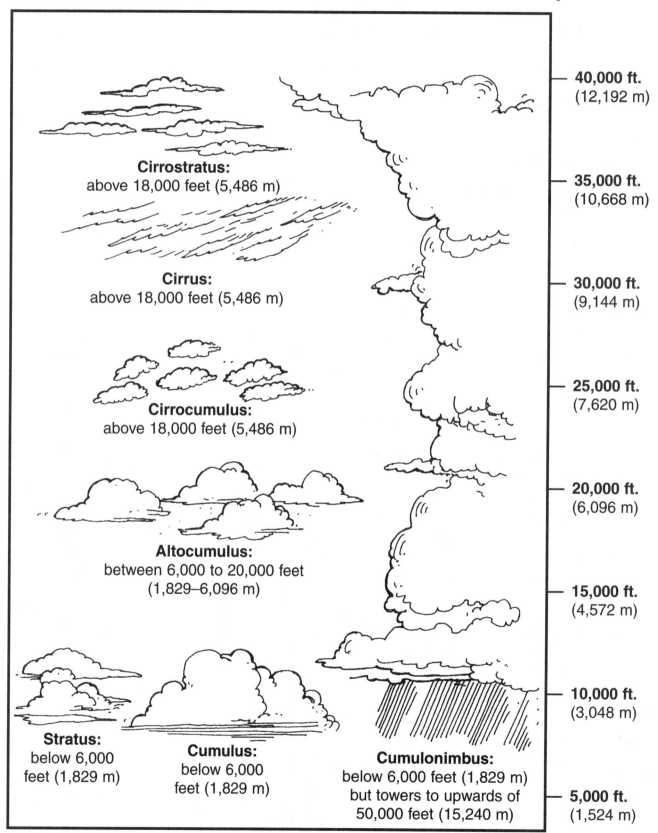

Cirrostratus:
above 18,000 feet (5,486 m)

Cirrus:
above 18,000 feet (5,486 m)

Cirrocumulus:
above 18,000 feet (5,486 m)

Altocumulus:
between 6,000 to 20,000 feet
(1,829–6,096 m)

Stratus:
below 6,000
feet (1,829 m)

Cumulus:
below 6,000
feet (1,829 m)

Cumulonimbus:
below 6,000 feet (1,829 m)
but towers to upwards of
50,000 feet (15,240 m)

— **40,000 ft.**
(12,192 m)

— **35,000 ft.**
(10,668 m)

— **30,000 ft.**
(9,144 m)

— **25,000 ft.**
(7,620 m)

— **20,000 ft.**
(6,096 m)

— **15,000 ft.**
(4,572 m)

— **10,000 ft.**
(3,048 m)

— **5,000 ft.**
(1,524 m)

Our Weather Report

— Teacher Information —

This activity will serve as the culmination of this study, as well as assessment of what the students have learned from the activities.

Overview: *Students will create their own weather reports to give to the rest of the class.*

Materials

- weather calendars
- videotape of the most recent weather report
- props selected by the students
- homemade microphone or real one
- *optional:* video camera

Activity

1. Show the students the videotape of the weather report. As it goes along, discuss how the reporter is describing the weather and point out some of the things he or she uses to show the weather. Explain that the students will be writing their own weather reports, using some of the records they have made so far.

2. Discuss some of the ways students can report the weather, possibly even taking the class outside to look at the clouds. Help them think of a variety of ways to present the report and list these on the board.

3. Divide the students into small groups and have them brainstorm what information they will present and how they will report this to the class. Monitor the students' progress, offering suggestions and assistance as needed. Allow sufficient time for students to put their reports together, bring materials from home, and practice before presenting the reports to the class.

Closure

Assign the groups to different mornings to give their weather reports. Invite the parents to visit during this time to see the results of the weather study.

Fun with Astronomy Introduction

Astronomy is perhaps one of the oldest sciences, since it was originated by the earliest civilizations. They used the stars to predict when to plant and harvest their crops and invented calendars and time according to the annual and daily motions of the sun. They invented star patterns (*constellations*) to create star maps of the sky. These ancient astronomers (*astrologers*) were interested in recording and then predicting the motions of the wandering stars (*planets*) and the moon, which they believed controlled human destinies. Modern astronomers recognize the contributions of these early scientists. Although we no longer believe in astrology, the legacy of observations made by the astrologers provided the foundation for mankind to learn about what we see in space and ultimately to venture out for a closer look.

This section is designed to help students see how easy it is to learn by observing what is happening in the sky, both day and night. It begins with a simple experiment to show students how they can use their shadows to learn about the sun's daily motion. They discover that the sun appears to move east to west, making their shadows change length and direction during the day. Proving that it is Earth which is doing the moving, and not the sun, was difficult for our ancient ancestors. For over 2,000 years they believed that Earth was the center of all we see in space, and everything—including the sun, moon, planets, and stars—revolved around our planet. Many of our young students have these same misconceptions. By following the shadow activity with a demonstration using a globe with a paper figure on it and the sun, the children can see that the shadow's changes can be created by a rotating Earth.

The mystery of why the moon changes its shape is solved through nightly observations and drawings students make of the moon from first crescent to full phase. This data is collected each night and then brought to school to be recorded on a classroom chart. The data is applied during an activity to simulate the phases of the moon, using Styrofoam balls as the moon and a bright light as the sun. Even young children can begin to solve the mystery of the cause for the phases of the moon through these activities.

Using the ancient constellations, students begin to find their way around the night sky. They look at the pictures ancient astronomers superimposed on the star patterns and then invent their own modern constellations from these same patterns. Using the dot-to-dot method, the children find the dipper and the bear hidden in the sky. They place this pattern over the outline of a bear which American Indians invented long ago for this set of stars. The students hear the Indian story which explains how *Ursa Major* and *Ursa Minor* (*Big Bear* and *Little Bear*) got their long tails.

Finally, students learn about the comparative sizes of the planets and their distances from the sun and each other. This is done using scale models created by the teacher to enable students to experience these concepts concretely.

The students' families are involved throughout these activities which take place during and after school. Thus, the child has the opportunity to show his or her family that science is really fun.

Me and My Shadow

Teacher Information

The sun appears to move east to west across the sky each day. Most young children believe this is caused by the sun's motion. This lesson is designed to help children correct this misconception. A quick assessment of their understanding of the concept is done prior to the lesson. Using their own shadows and the shadow of a paper child on a globe, students learn through a simulation how the sun's apparent motion can be caused by Earth's motion.

Overview: *Students will use shadows to demonstrate that Earth is moving, not the sun.*

Materials

- chalk
- large globe
- file card
- adhesive putty

Pre-assessment

- Distribute paper to the students and have them make drawings that describe how they think day and night occur.
- Tell them to label their drawings. Let them share these in small groups.
- Save these drawings to compare them with the post-assessment drawings.

Activity One

1. Early on a sunny day, take the students to an area where paving is available to do this activity. Have the students spread out so they can all see their own shadows. Explain that you will give them some time to play with their shadows to see what they can learn about them. Demonstrate how this can be done safely by pointing out your own shadow and how you can change its shape. Don't give too many suggestions; you want the students to discover on their own. Let students have about five minutes to investigate their shadows and then have them share what they have learned. Be sure they have discovered that their shadow looks just like their shape but shows neither color nor complete features, such as a face.

2. Divide the students into groups of three and provide a piece of chalk for two members of each group. Explain that one member of the group will create a shadow and hold the pose while the other two draw around the shadow. They should begin by drawing around the shoes so the person will know exactly where he or she is standing. The entire shadow should be outlined. Let the child whose shadow has been drawn compare it to his or her actual size by lying on it with his or her heels in the outline of the feet. (*Alternate method:* Use string which is the same height as the child to compare the length of the shadow and the student.) Tell the students they will return to this same location in a few hours to see what has happened to their shadows.

Me and My Shadow *(cont.)*

Activity One *(cont.)*

3. Return to the shadow site about noon and have each child stand on the outline of his or her shoes. Let the students discover what has happened to the shadow. (*It will have moved from west to east.*) Remeasure the length of the shadow in the same way as before. Ask the students what they observed. (*The shadow will be smaller than before.*) Have the same person pose for another shadow outline, standing in the original shoe outline in the same pose.

4. Return to the shadow just before school ends. Let the students study the shadows and measure them again. Discuss what has happened throughout the day. (*All shadows changed size from large to small to large again. They all moved from west to east during the day.*) Tell the students to think about what they observed today and to return tomorrow with ideas of why this happened.

Activity Two

1. Do this the day after activity one so the shadow outlines will still be visible. Cut a one-inch (2.5 cm) high figure of a child from a file card and use sticky putty to hold it on the globe in the location of the school. Take the globe and students to their shadow outlines at the same time in the morning as was done the previous day. Ask the students to stand in their outlines again. Let students discuss what they see. (*The shadows should be close to the outlines made on the previous day.*)

2. Set the globe in the sun and turn it so the shadow of the paper child is visible and lines up with the shadows on the ground. Tell students to pretend they are the paper child standing on the globe. Have them watch as you turn the globe west to east in a counterclockwise direction. (*The shadow will move and become shorter.*) Stop the globe when the shadow is shortest. Ask the students what caused the shadow to change. (*direction of the sun as the globe [Earth] moved*) Help them to understand that to the child on Earth, the sun appeared to climb higher in the sky, moving east to west. Continue to turn the globe to show that the shadow becomes long again and disappears as the child moves into night.

Closure

Repeat this so students will once again be able to observe the shadow change. Ask them to explain what the sun would look like to the child on Earth at various locations. Have students discuss this and let them turn the globe themselves to develop a better understanding of this abstract concept. (*Note:* Many young children have the misconception that we live beneath "the skin" of the globe. This may be because they see blue sky overhead and oceans are blue. Be sure to point out that we live on the surface of Earth and that the sky is not shown on the globe. A photograph of Earth as seen from the space shuttle or the Apollo mission would help to reinforce this concept.)

Assessment

Return to the classroom and have students make another labeled drawing to explain how day and night occur. Compare this with their pre-assessment.

What Shape Is the Moon Tonight?

Overview: *Students will gather data about the phases of the moon.*

Materials

- copies of Student Moon Record sheet (page 285)
- parent letter (page 284)
- Classroom Moon Record (page 286)

- small bulletin board covered with black butcher paper
- 16–$^3/_4$ inch (2 cm) white, self-adhesive dots

Lesson Preparation

Make a transparency of the Classroom Moon Record and project it onto the black paper. The diameter should stretch at least two feet (60 cm). Use white crayon to trace the arc and pencil to make the small marks. These represent the positions of the moon during half the month.

Pre-activity (Begin this lesson two days after the new moon. Check the weather section of the newspaper or a calendar for this date.)

1. Distribute the parent letter and Student Moon Record. Discuss these with the students so they understand how to record the phases of the moon every evening at the same time.
2. Show them the Classroom Moon Record and say that each day you will place a moon shape there showing what they report in the evening sky. Point out where the sun is shown on the record.
3. As students report the moon shape each day, cut an adhesive dot into that shape and place it on the chart. The first one will be on the first or second mark, depending upon how many days past the new phase this record is begun.
4. After three days of recording data, have students predict how the next day's phase will look. Draw all predictions on the board and check them the next day. If a night is cloudy, have students predict what the shape of the moon was, based on the phases before and after.

Closure

- Review the positions and phases of the moon relative to the sun's position. Repeat the activity with the balls and light so students can see how this represents what they are recording.
- About two days after the moon is full, look for it in the morning sky in the west. Its phase will change to gibbous, quarter, and then a crescent as it gets closer to the sun each day. Be sure they see that it is now the left side of the moon which is illuminated by the sun.

Extender

Make a daytime record of moon phases after the full moon. Project the moon record on blue paper and make the same markings. Since this is a day view, the sun should appear in the east (sunrise). Even though students will view the moon after the sun has risen, the sun can be in the east. The full moon would be in the west as the sun is rising. As the moon changes to gibbous, circles can be cut according to views seen and pasted along the arc, continuing west to east, as the moon moves around Earth. The last quarter phase would be 90° between the east and west; the final crescent would be very close to the sun as it rises in the east.

Parent Letter for Moon Observations

To the Teacher: The time for sunset can be found in most weather reports on TV or in the newspaper. Add the time to the letter which is 30 minutes after sunset, the time students should observe and draw the moon.

Date_____

Dear Parents:

We are studying the changing shapes of the moon (phases), and each child has been asked to look at the moon and draw it each evening. Please help your child with this activity. It is important that he or she observe the moon at about the same time each evening. We will be viewing the moon approximately 30 minutes after sunset which will be about_____p.m. Have your child go outside to get a good view of the moon. Ask him or her to draw exactly what is seen and bring the drawing to school the next day. We will be using those drawings to place the correct phase on a Classroom Moon Record daily.

It will take approximately two weeks for us to gather the data we need for this study. This activity will help your child understand that the moon is constantly changing its shape as well as its position every day.

Thank you for helping your child learn about the moon. You are always welcome to come visit our class to see our moon record.

Cordially,

P.S. A helpful chart of the moon's phases appears below.

Phases of the Moon

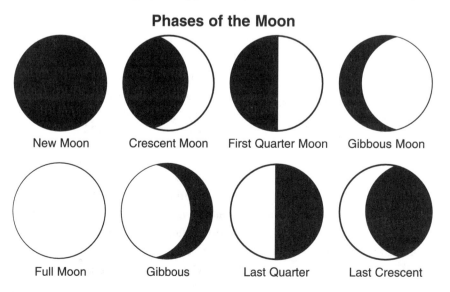

New Moon   Crescent Moon   First Quarter Moon   Gibbous Moon

Full Moon   Gibbous   Last Quarter   Last Crescent

Student Moon Record

Name:_____   Date: _____

Go outside where you can see the moon clearly. Make a drawing of the moon each evening about_____P.M. Write the date and time. Bring this record to school each day.

Date: _____ Time:_____	Date: _____ Time:_____	Date: _____ Time:_____
Date: _____ Time:_____	Date: _____ Time:_____	Date: _____ Time:_____
Date: _____ Time:_____	Date: _____ Time:_____	Date: _____ Time:_____
Date: _____ Time:_____	Date: _____ Time:_____	Date: _____ Time:_____
Date: _____ Time:_____	Date: _____ Time:_____	Date: _____ Time:_____

Classroom Moon Record

To the Teacher: Make a transparency of this page and project it onto a large piece of black butcher paper. The horizon line should be at least two feet (60 cm) long. Use white crayon to trace the arc and horizon. Trace the marks along the arc in pencil so they are not seen. These are the positions of the moon phases. The phases begin with the new moon at the western horizon, first quarter moon 90 degrees from east and west, and full moon on the eastern horizon.

Color one of the self-adhesive dots orange to represent the sun. Place it on the classroom chart in the location indicated on this drawing, to represent the sun's position 30 minutes after sunset.

The sky is represented by the arc. The view is to the south.

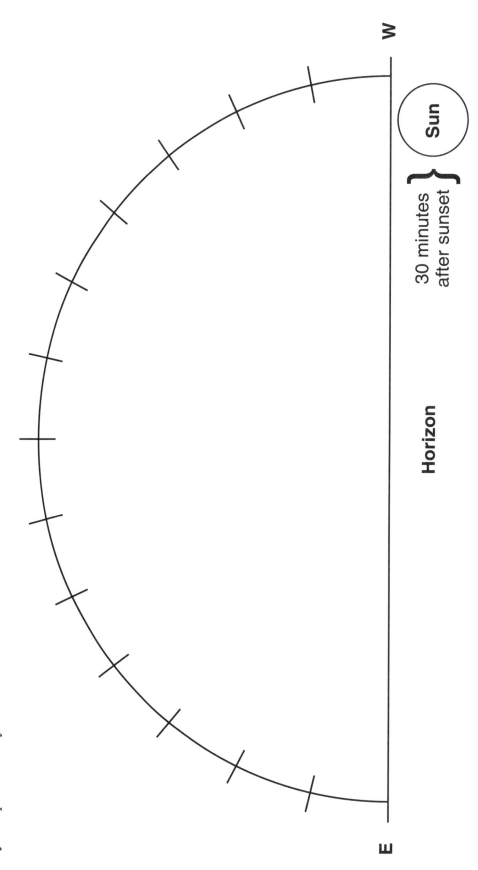

Moon Shapes

Overview: *Students will discover what causes the phases of the moon.*

Materials

- transparency of Moon Phase Cutouts (page 289)
- clamp-on light fixture with 150 watt bulb (*optional:* overhead projector)
- three-inch (8 cm) Styrofoam balls (one per student)
- sticks (one per ball)
- white glue (*optional:* hot glue)
- transparency of The Phases of the Moon (page 290)
- large ball (e.g., soccer)

Lesson Preparation

- Push a stick halfway into each Styrofoam ball, withdraw it, and pour liquid glue into the hole. Reinsert the stick and let it dry.
- Clamp the light onto the wall in the front of the room, at least six feet off the floor. Clear an area in front of the light for all students to be able to gather near but with room to spread out.
- Place a sticky note on the large ball, large enough to be clearly seen from six feet away.

Activity

1. Ask students if they have noticed the shape of the moon lately. Let them draw on the board the shapes they have seen the moon take.

2. Put the moon phase cutouts on the overhead (or board) and have the students suggest how they should be arranged in the order they are viewed. (Do not expect accuracy just yet.)

3. Ask them if they can explain why the moon changes shape.

4. Explain that they are going to do an activity which will show how the moon changes its shape. Distribute a ball on a stick to each student. Gather near the light and darken the room (the darker the better). Arrange the students so that no one is standing in another child's shadow.

5. Tell the students to watch you as you demonstrate how they are to move. Explain that the ball is the moon and their head is Earth. They are standing on Earth looking at the moon. Hold the moon (ball) so it covers up the light and have the students do the same. They should notice that they cannot see any light on the moon; this is the *new* phase.

6. Slowly turn to your left (students should follow) and have them look for the thin crescent of light on the right side of the moon. Let them know that about two days have passed since the moon was new, and it is now in the *crescent* phase.

7. Continue to turn slowly to the left, stopping to show the phases of *first quarter, gibbous, full, gibbous, last quarter, last crescent,* and back to *new.* Tell the students this whole trip of the moon around Earth takes about 29 days or one month.

8. Have the students continue to revolve slowly, holding their moons slightly above their heads and seeing the different phases as you call out the phase names. Move among the students to be sure they are seeing the correct shapes. Let them do this several times.

Moon Shapes *(cont.)*

Closure

- Ask the students to rearrange the moon phases on the overhead (or board) to show what they have learned about the order of the phases. Let them go through the motions again of creating the moon phases with the Styrofoam balls.

- Turn on the lights and have the students sit in a large circle. Use the large ball to represent the moon and let the students represent Earth. Tell the students that we see only one side of the moon but that the moon does rotate around on its axis, just as Earth does. Carry the ball around the students in a counterclockwise direction to show how the moon would look if it did not rotate on its axis. Point the sticky note toward the front of the room. Now, demonstrate how this looks as the moon rotates while orbiting Earth. Point out that the sticky note on the moon always faces the students (Earth). Be sure they see that the mark is pointing in different directions as it moves around Earth, since the moon gradually rotates on its axis. It takes about the same length of time for the moon to rotate once as it takes to go around Earth once.

Phases of the Moon

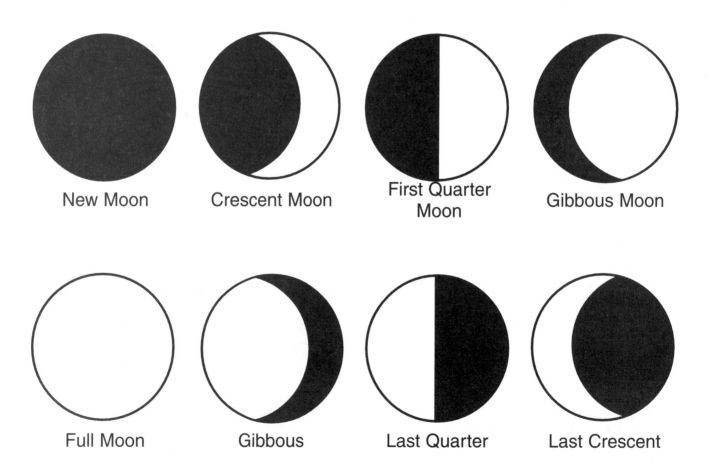

New Moon	Crescent Moon	First Quarter Moon	Gibbous Moon

Full Moon	Gibbous	Last Quarter	Last Crescent

Moon Phase Cutouts

To the Teacher: Make a transparency of this page and cut out the moon phases.
Optional: Enlarge these cutouts and add adhesive to the back of them to be used on the board.

The Phases of the Moon

Outer Circle: moon positions as viewed from outer space
Inner Circle: moon phases as viewed from Earth

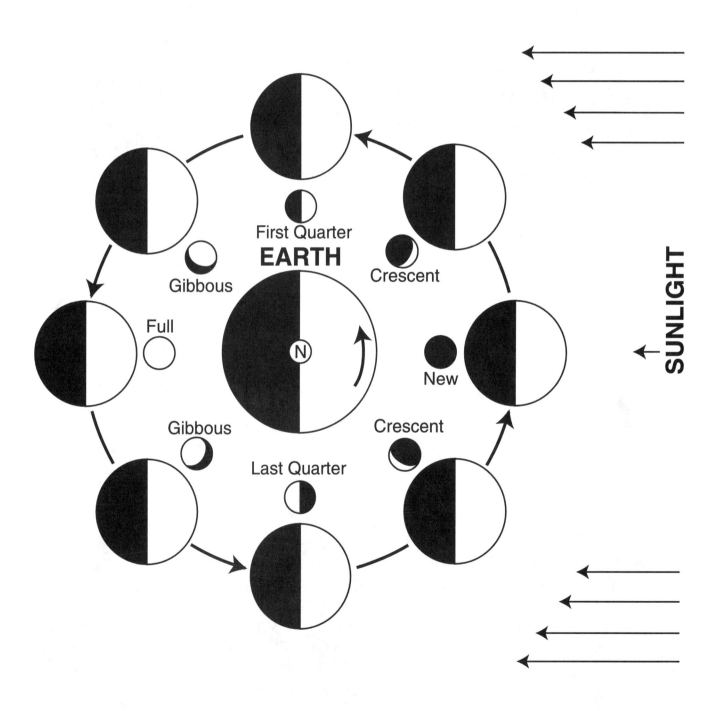

The Moon in Motion

⸻ Teacher Information ⸻

This activity serves as a culmination of the lessons about the moon phases.

Overview: *Students will make a flipbook of the moon to see how the phases change.*

Materials

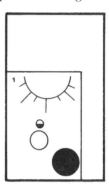

- Moon Flipbook Pages (pages 293 and 294)
- 3" x 5" (8 cm x 13 cm) file cards (16 per flipbook)
- glue
- wide clear packing tape

Lesson Preparation

- Make enough copies of the flipbook pages for each student. Cut these into sets.
- Make up a set of moon phase pictures and file cards for each student. Glue the #1 picture on the file card of each set as a model for the students. This should be placed in the lower left corner as shown.

Activity

1. Review the moon phases and how they occur. Tell the students that they are going to make a flipbook which will be like a movie of the moon's motion around Earth.

2. Distribute 16 file cards to each student. Show them the model of the first card so they will know where to glue the rest of the pictures on each card.

3. After all pictures have been glued on cards, help students lay these in a pile in numerical order, beginning with card #16.

4. Arrange each set of cards so the lowest edges are slightly offset about ¼ inch (6 mm) above the card underneath. (See drawing on page 292.) This will enable the thumb to flip rapidly through the cards when they are stacked.

5. Hold the card stack in place with a rubber band and flip through them to see if the sun can be seen clearly at the top of the cards and the moons appear to move around Earth.

6. Remove the rubber band and place a long strip of clear packing tape along the back of the cards and overlap the front card for about 1 inch (2.5 cm). This will anchor the cards in place. Run a second strip vertically around the top of the cards. Be sure to avoid locking the cards in place so they will not flip easily. If this happens, use scissors to slide through the tape at the sides until the cards move freely.

The Moon in Motion *(cont.)*

Closure

- Demonstrate to the students how to hold their books at the top in one hand and use their thumbs to flip the pages rapidly, creating the motion-picture effect. Have them do this several times and then discuss the position of sun, moon, and Earth with them as they flip the pages. They should see the moon moving around Earth. Now, have them look only at the moon phases in the lower corner of the cards as they flip the pages. The phases should rapidly change from new through all the phases and return to the new position.

- Relate this motion of the cards to what they have seen in the sky as well as when they used their moon balls in the bright light.

1. Single Card

2. Two Cards

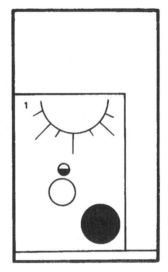

3. Stacked Cards

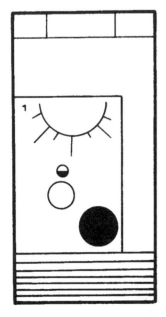

4. Flip book

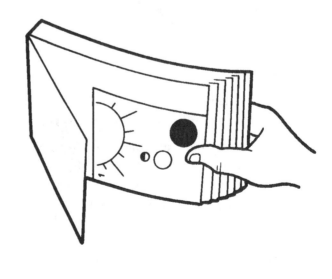

Moon Flipbook Pages

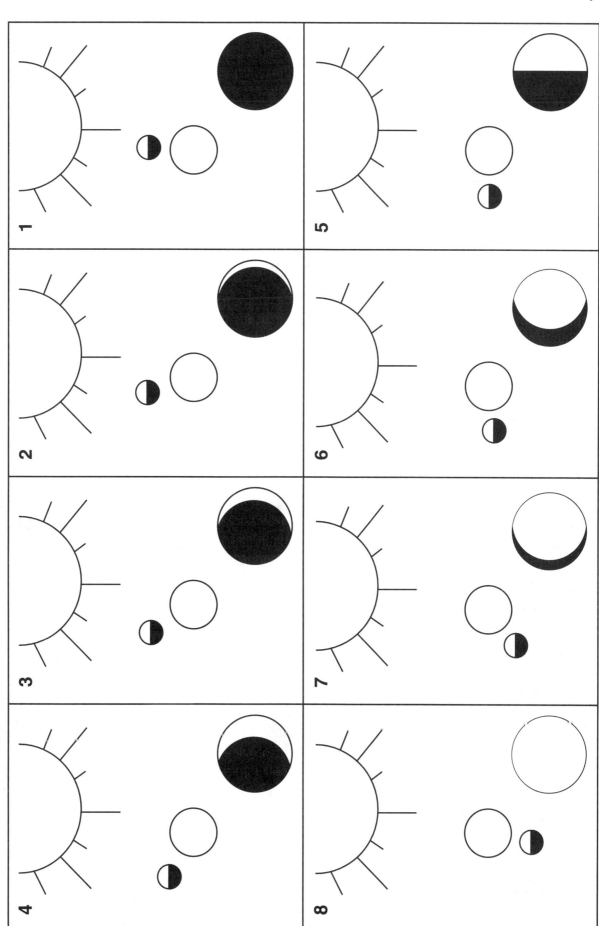

Moon Flipbook Pages *(cont.)*

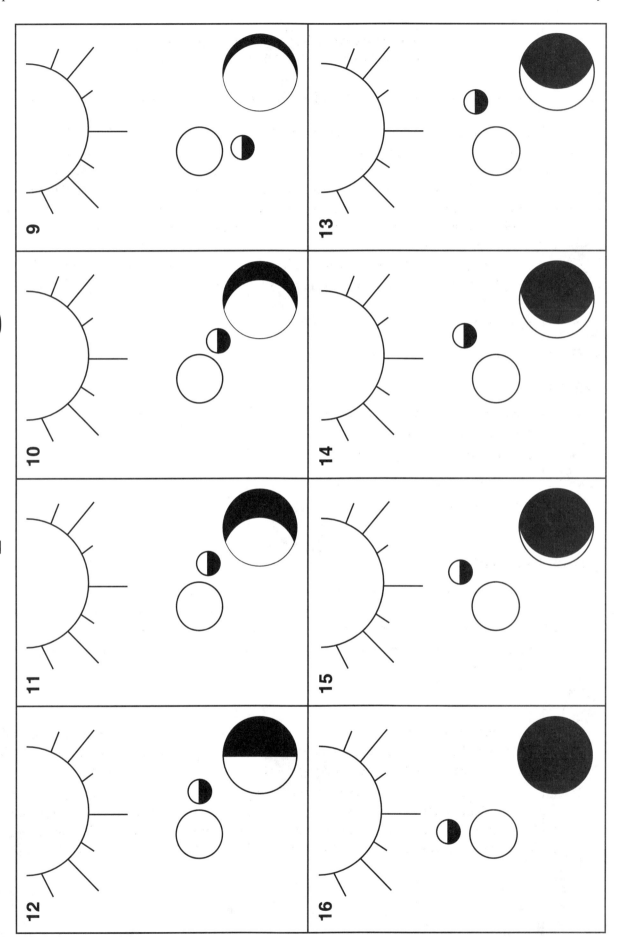

Star Patterns

— Teacher Information —

The 12 zodiac constellations appear along the path the sun seems to follow in the sky as Earth moves around it. Long ago people thought our lives were controlled by the location of planets in these constellations. Today, we know planets move in orbit around the sun and are seen against a background of zodiac constellations but have no influence on humans. The constellation shapes form a useful map of the sky which helps locate planets, comets, and other astronomical objects. A planet looks like an extra star in a constellation but gradually appears to move into the next constellation as it orbits around the sun.

The next activities will familiarize students with some constellations they will enjoy looking for. Do these lessons in winter months when the sky is dark early and many of the brightest and largest constellations (e.g., Orion) are visible.

Overview: *Students will learn about the zodiac constellations.*

Materials

- transparencies of Zodiac Constellations (pages 297–299)
- large black construction paper
- copies of The Big Bear (page 309)
- Styrofoam ball (used in moon activity)
- globe or ball to represent earth
- basketball

Lesson Preparation

- Make transparencies of the Zodiac Constellations. Project each constellation onto a piece of large black construction paper, enlarged to fill the paper. Trace each constellation with white crayon, connecting stars as shown. Write the number on the constellation charts to keep them in order.
- Enlarge copies of the picture of each constellation (e.g., bull for Taurus) and glue these in one corner of the paper.

Activity

1. Ask students if they have seen any star patterns in the sky. Tell them these patterns are called *constellations*. On the board, have students draw constellations with which they may be familiar. Tell them they are going to begin studying constellations.
2. Select 12 students and distribute the constellation pictures to them. Take the class outside to a large field. Bring the basketball, Styrofoam ball, and globe. Have students with the pictures stand in a large circle. The numbers of the pictures will be in order from right to left, as they appear in the sky as Earth moves in a counterclockwise direction around the sun.

Star Patterns *(cont.)*

Activity *(cont.)*

3. Select a student to hold the globe and another to hold the moon ball. Place them in the center of the circle. Have the rest of the students stand within the circle.

4. Give the basketball to one student. Tell the children that this ball will represent the sun. Have the sun stand between the children and the circle of constellations.

5. Explain that although we cannot feel any motion, Earth is moving. Remind students of what they learned about Earth's motion in the lesson Me and My Shadow—that Earth spins on its axis every 24 hours, giving us day and night.

   Have the child who is holding the globe begin to spin it counterclockwise on its axis to demonstrate Earth's motion. Tell the students that at the same time, the moon is slowly moving around Earth. Remind the students of their study of moon phases and point out that from Earth a viewer would see the moon changing phases.

6. Have the child holding the globe begin to walk around the sun in a counterclockwise path; the moon should continue to slowly circle the earth. Point out that from Earth, it appears as if the sun is moving across the sky, gradually moving toward the east.

7. Explain that the stars are very far from Earth, farther than the moon and sun as well as all the other planets. Show the order of the constellations and explain that these star patterns were noticed long ago by people who studied the sky. They discovered that it looked as if the sun traveled in front of these constellations, returning to about the same position a year later.

8. Have the students acting as Earth and the moon stop moving. Remove the moon so students can concentrate on Earth and the sun. Show that from Earth you would not see the constellation which was behind the sun because it is too bright. The constellations you would see would be in the opposite direction. Point to the constellations which would be visible if Earth were in the position it is in this model. Let Earth continue to follow its orbit around the sun and then stop again. Have students pick the constellations which could *not* be seen at this time. Let them tell which constellations would be visible (*those opposite the sun and Earth*).

9. Have other students try the Earth/sun walk to see how the constellations change.

Closure

Poke holes where the stars appear on the black constellation charts. Make the holes different sizes, depending upon the size of the dot for the star. Tape these pictures to the window in order, running right to left. The stars will be made visible as the sunlight shines through the holes in the chart. This will help students become familiar with the constellation shapes and thus find them easier to locate in the night sky.

Zodiac Constellations

To the Teacher: On each picture below, the month stating when the constellation is visible is the best month to see it. However, it will also be visible the month before and after. Visibility of these constellations also depends on your latitude.

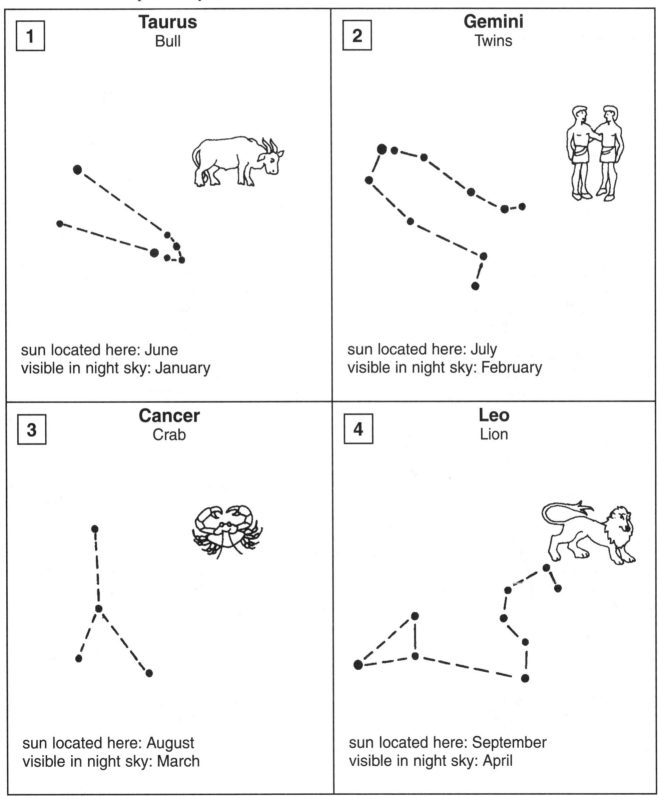

1 **Taurus**
Bull

sun located here: June
visible in night sky: January

2 **Gemini**
Twins

sun located here: July
visible in night sky: February

3 **Cancer**
Crab

sun located here: August
visible in night sky: March

4 **Leo**
Lion

sun located here: September
visible in night sky: April

Zodiac Constellations *(cont.)*

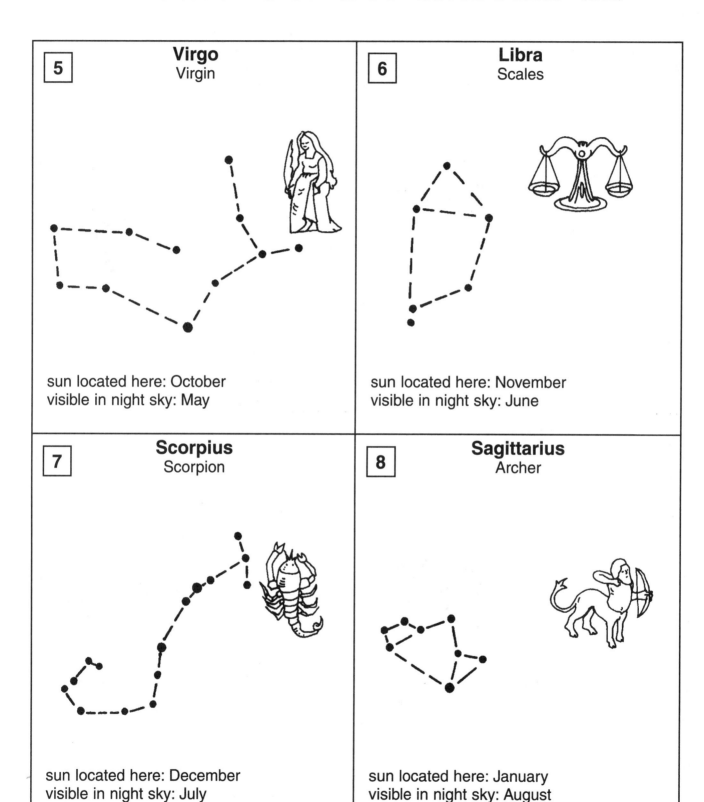

Zodiac Constellations *(cont.)*

9	**Capricornus** Goat	10	**Aquarius** Water Bearer

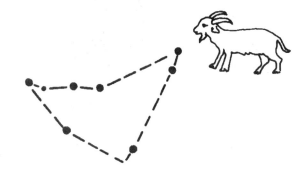

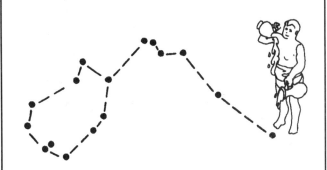

sun located here: February
visible in night sky: September

sun located here: March
visible in night sky: October

11	**Pisces** Fish (2)	12	**Aries** Ram

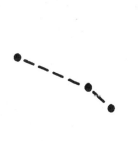

sun located here: April
visible in night sky: November

sun located here: May
visible in night sky: December

Pictures in the Sky

Overview: *Students will become familiar with constellations visible at the current season.*

Materials

- transparency and copies of seasonal constellation charts on pages 302–305 and zodiac constellations found on pages 297–299
- black butcher paper and white crayon

Lesson Preparation

- Cover a bulletin board with black butcher paper. Make a transparency of the seasonal constellation chart for the current season. Project it onto black paper and use white crayon to trace the stars and connecting lines for the constellations. Outline the Milky Way as it spreads among the stars. Trace the dotted line which is the *ecliptic*—the path the sun and planets appear to follow across the sky.
- Copy the zodiac constellations for this season; they should match those on the seasonal constellation chart. Cut them out, glue them on one page, and white out lines connecting stars. Make a transparency and student copies of these zodiac constellations.
  Note: Some zodiac constellations formed by very faint stars are not shown on these charts. For this activity, include copies of these missing constellations which are visible for this season.
- Make a copy of the current constellation chart for each student. Mount them inside a file folder to make them sturdy.
- Make copies of the parent letter on page 301.

Activity

1. Review zodiac constellations with the transparencies. Explain that long ago people looked into the sky and saw a way to connect stars to form pictures of animals, people, and familiar objects. Show students constellations visible in the current night sky and drawings of the pictures made by connecting these stars. Ask them if the stars look like their pictures (*many do not*).

2. Distribute copies of the zodiac constellations for this season without the connecting lines. Tell students that they should look at the stars and connect them to make their own pictures of animals or objects. Use one of the constellations on the transparency as an example and have students suggest a new picture. Draw lines on the transparency to create the new picture. Tell them to give their constellation a name.

3. Have students share their new constellations in groups.

4. Show students the seasonal constellation chart on the black paper to see what tonight's sky will look like. Point out the Milky Way and ask if they have ever seen this. Say that it looks like a hazy river across the sky, very faint so it can only be seen away from city lights. Tell them that long ago people believed it looked like spilled milk, thus the name.

Closure

Distribute copies of the current constellation chart and parent letter to students. Explain that they are to match the chart with the stars in the sky every night for the next week. Tell them it is important that the sky be dark and without too many clouds. Say the class will discuss what they observe at the next meeting.

Parent Letter for Sky Observations

To the Teacher: Distribute this letter with the seasonal constellation chart.

Date_____

Dear Parents:

Now that we have observed the moon and learned about its phases, we are turning our attention to the stars. Your child has received a constellation chart for the current season. The students have done a variety of activities to help them recognize the shapes of some of the most prominent constellations that can be seen at this time of the year. It is now time to try to match these pictures with the stars they see in the real sky.

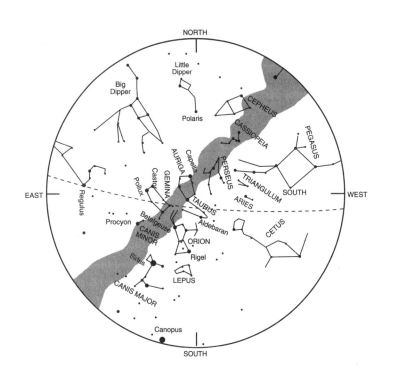

If it is clear tonight, please go outside with your child to help him or her find these star patterns. You will need to go where it is dark, away from house and street lights if possible. It will be helpful to have a dim flashlight to look at the chart while matching it to the stars. If the flashlight is too bright, cover it with your fingers and let only a little light filter through. This will help your eyes stay adjusted to the dark.

When using the chart, face south and hold the chart with north at the top. Try to locate one of the brightest constellations first. The larger the dot (star) on the chart, the brighter the star will appear.

Each day, we will be discussing what the children were able to see in the sky during the previous night.

Thank you for helping your child learn about the constellations. The other three seasonal constellations charts will be distributed to the students at the end of our study. This will enable the children and their families to continue their study of the sky throughout the year.

Cordially,

Fall Constellations

The gray patch represents the Milky Way, an area of faint light coming from the distant stars at the outer edge of the galaxy in which we live (Milky Way Galaxy). This area reminded ancient astronomers of spilled milk, so they named it the *Milky Way*.

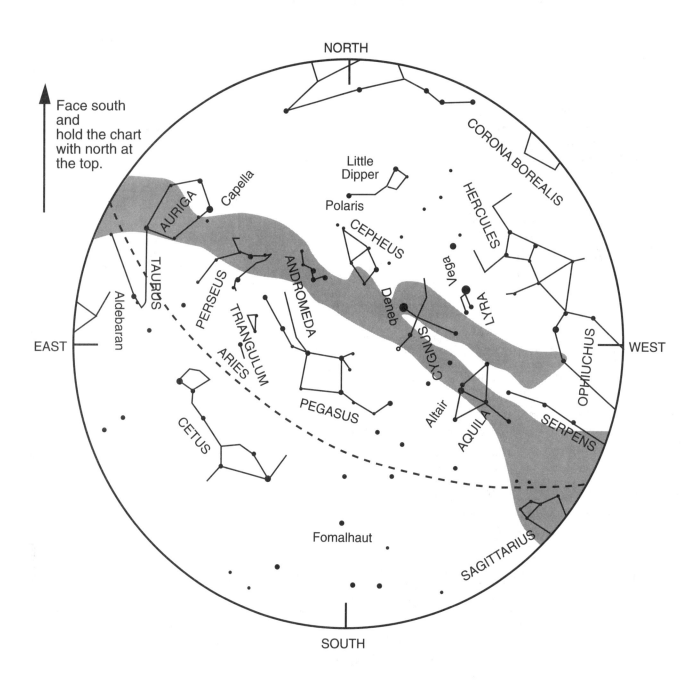

Winter Constellations

The gray patch represents the Milky Way, an area of faint light coming from the distant stars at the outer edge of the galaxy in which we live (Milky Way Galaxy). This area reminded ancient astronomers of spilled milk, so they named it the *Milky Way*.

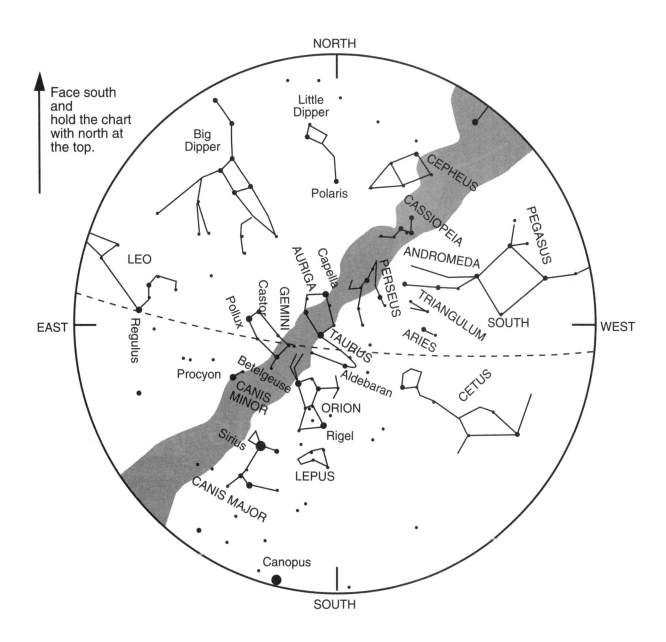

Spring Constellations

The gray patch represents the Milky Way, an area of faint light coming from the distant stars at the outer edge of the galaxy in which we live (Milky Way Galaxy). This area reminded ancient astronomers of spilled milk, so they named it the *Milky Way*.

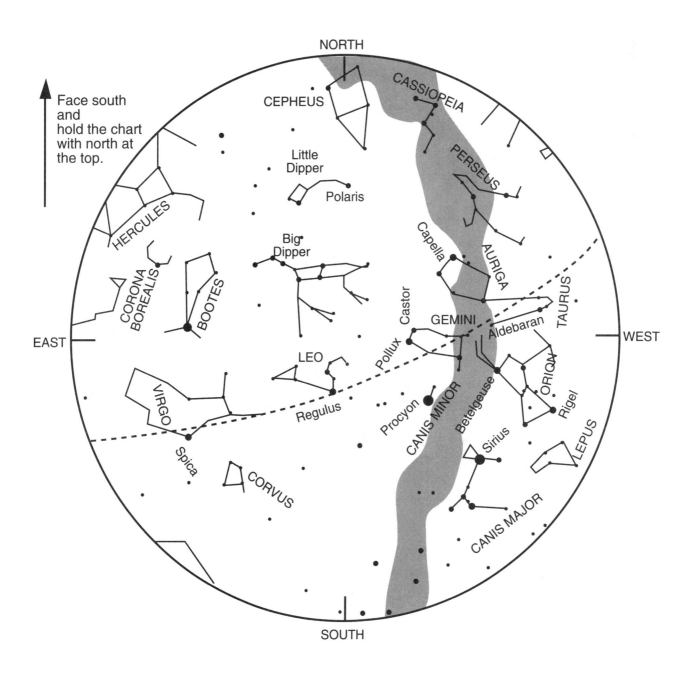

Summer Constellations

The gray patch represents the Milky Way, an area of faint light coming from the distant stars at the outer edge of the galaxy in which we live (Milky Way Galaxy). This area reminded ancient astronomers of spilled milk, so they named it the *Milky Way*.

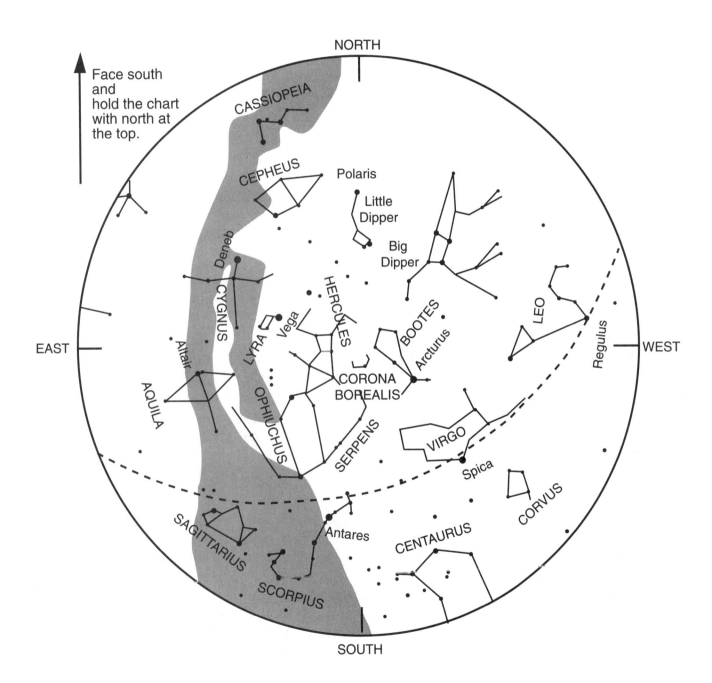

The Big Bear

Overview: *Students will see how stars are used to form constellations.*

Materials

- seasonal constellations and North Polar Constellations charts on black paper.
- transparency and copies of Dipper In the Bear activity sheet on page 308 and Ursa Major (The Big Bear) on page 309.
- scissors

- crayons
- glue
- transparency and copies of North Polar Constellations (page 307)
- black butcher paper

Lesson Preparation

- Use the transparency of the North Polar Constellations and white crayon to make a large copy on the black butcher paper.
- Connect the dots on the transparency of the activity sheet and superimpose it on the drawing of the bear on page 309.

Activity

1. Review constellations students have seen during their past viewing sessions. Point out the new chart showing North Polar Constellations. Explain that these constellations are so high in the sky that they can be seen during most of the year.

2. Point out the Big Dipper on the chart. Tell students this is an easy constellation to find. Show how the pointer stars show the way to Polaris, the star over Earth's North Pole. Polaris does not move in the sky like all the other stars which rotate clockwise around it as Earth spins on its axis. For travelers, Polaris became the most important star to follow and not get lost.

3. Distribute a copy of The Dipper in the Bear activity to each student. Explain that they are to connect the numbered dots with pencil and the letters with crayon. When finished, they can cut out this picture and glue it inside the picture of the bear.

Closure

- Show a transparency of the Dipper inside Ursa Major and point out the shape of the dipper. Tell students that some cultures saw this group of stars as a plow, a dipper, or a long-handled pot. The Indians thought this group and other stars in this area looked like a big and little bear with long tails. They knew that bears did not have long tails, so they made up a story to explain it. An Indian brave was being chased by a mother bear and her cub. He became tired of running and decided to stop and fight. He grabbed both bears by their short tails and began to swing them around his head. Their tails began to stretch longer and longer. Finally, he let go and the bears flew up into the sky and turned into stars. There they remain to this day, swinging around the star Polaris at the tip of the little bear's tail.

- Arrange a family observing night at the school so all can look at the constellations and moon. Plan this on a night when the moon is between four and eight days old so that it will not be so bright the stars cannot be seen. Arrange to bring a telescope or binoculars to look at the moon.

The North Polar Constellations

Instructions: Face north and rotate the chart so the present month is at the top. This should match your view at about 9 P.M. If you are using this before 9 P.M., rotate the chart slightly counterclockwise.

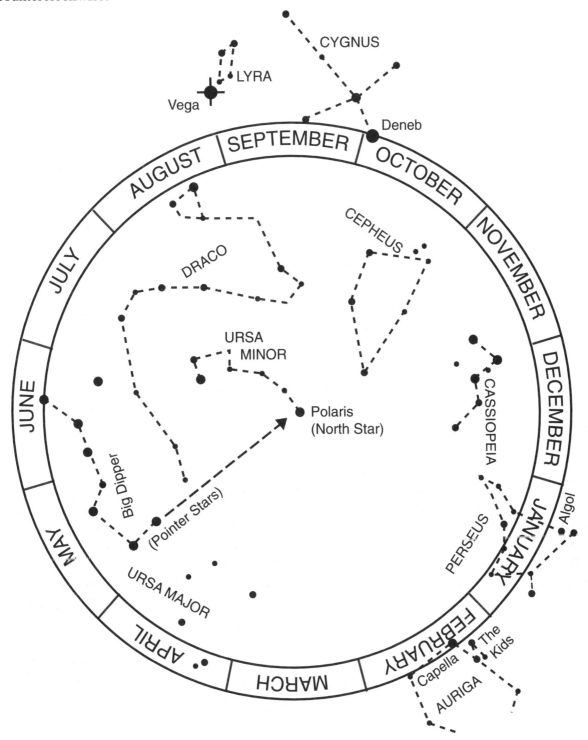

The Dipper in the Bear

To the Student: Connect the dots to find a picture of a dipper and a bear.

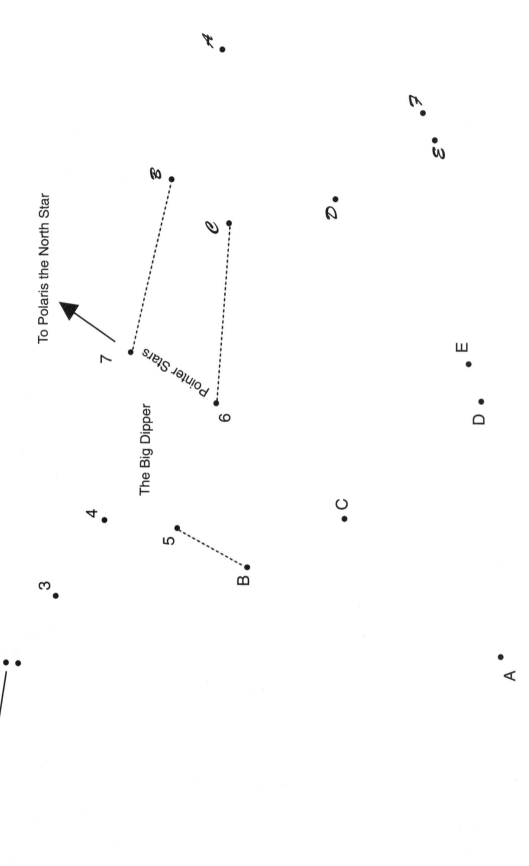

To Polaris the North Star

The Big Dipper

Pointer Stars

Ursa Major (The Big Bear)

Scale Model of the Planets

Overview: *Students will learn the sizes of the planets and compare them to Earth.*

Materials

- one piece each of red, gray, blue, white, and black construction paper approximately 6" (15 cm) square
- piece of white and yellow 4' x 1' (120 cm x 30 cm) butcher paper
- piece of blue and orange 2' x 1' (60 cm x 30 cm) butcher paper (not the same color as the other butcher paper)
- meter stick
- 15 yards (13.5 m) string
- four index cards
- compass to draw circles

Lesson Preparation

- Make paper scale models of the five smallest planets by drawing a circle according to the radius sizes and colors of paper indicated on the chart below.

Planet	Paper Color	Circle Radius
Mercury	gray	1.9 cm
Venus	white	4.8 cm
Earth	blue	5.0 cm
Mars	red	2.7 cm
Pluto	black	0.9 cm

Scale: Earth's radius of 3,837 miles (6,378 km) = 5 cm

Scale Model of the Planets *(cont.)*

Lesson Preparation *(cont.)*

- Using the same scale, make larger circles or half circles to show the four largest planets. Since the compass is not large enough to draw circles of these planets, cut strings which are the lengths of the radius, leaving extra string at each end so one end can be tied to an index card and the other can be tied into a loop. Put the name of the planet on the card with its string attached. Place the paper on the floor and have someone hold the card in the center of the paper while you put the pencil in the loop at the other end, stretch the string taut, and draw the circle. For the larger planets, hold the card in the center of the long edge of the paper and then stretch the string with the pencil to draw a half circle.

Planet	Paper Color	Circle Radius
Jupiter	white	56 cm
Saturn	yellow	47 cm
Uranus	green	20 cm
Neptune	blue	19.5 cm

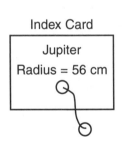

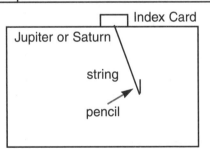

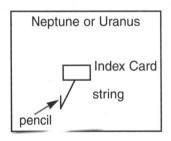

- Cut string to represent the sun's diameter—about 870,000 miles (1,392,000 km). Using the same scale as used for planets, the string will be 10.9 meters, 109 times the diameter of Earth.

Activity

1. Place planet models on the board (or floor) in order from largest to smallest. Show students the Earth model and label it. Say that the diameter of our planet is 7,973 miles (12,756 km) but that the circle is only 10 cm across. Explain that other planets have been reduced to show how big they are compared to Earth.

2. Let students pick which planets they think are Jupiter, Mars, and Pluto. Do not correct them if they are wrong.

Scale Model of the Planets *(cont.)*

Activity *(cont.)*

3. Label all planets. Begin with Jupiter and place on the board as in the diagram below. Tape in place, except for Earth.

(1) **Earth**

(2) **Venus**

(3) **Mars**

(4) **Mercury**

(5) **Pluto**

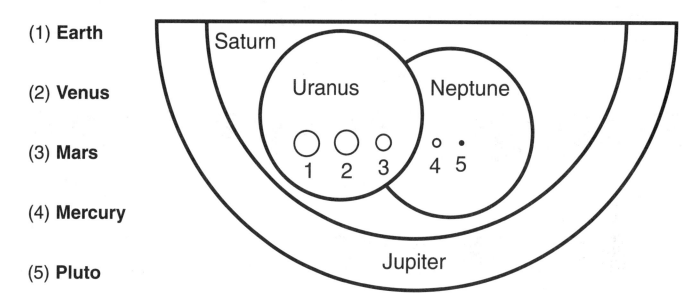

4. Fold the Earth model in half and let students estimate how many "Earths" would fit across the diameter of Jupiter. Write the extremes of their estimates on the board.

5. Begin measuring how many Earths will fit across the diameter, using the Earth circle placed at one end of the diameter and moving it along. Have students help count, stopping halfway to ask them to make another estimate. Update the estimates on the board. Continue counting the remaining number of Earths (about 11) that fit across Jupiter.

6. Compare the smaller planets to Earth. Point out that Venus is nearly the same size as Earth and Mars is about half that.

7. Show students that Uranus and Neptune are nearly the same size. Fold one in half to compare the diameters with that of Jupiter, using the same technique as used with Earth's model.

Closure

- Take students outside to compare the string which represents the sun's diameter with the planets. Have two students hold the models of the planets and begin stretching the string at one end of Jupiter's diameter, across its length, and then to the end. Be sure students know the sun is a star, not a planet. Explain that stars are different sizes and our sun is an average-size star. Some stars are so huge they would stretch beyond the orbits of Mercury, Venus, and Earth, all the way to Mars.

- Place the scale model of the planets on a bulletin board for the students to look at and become familiar with their sizes.

Scale Model of the Solar System

Overview: *Students will learn the distances between the planets.*

Materials

- at least 300' (100 m) of heavy string
- six pieces of heavy cardboard, approximately 5" x 8" (13 cm x 20 cm)
- three pieces of heavy cardboard, approximately 8" x 10" (20 cm x 26 cm)

Lesson Preparation

- Label small cardboards with the names of the first six planets shown on the chart. Label larger cardboards with the remaining planets. Place a hole in the center of the long edge of each cardboard.

- Tie one end of the string to the card and measure the length of string needed to represent the distance of each planet from the sun as shown on the chart below. Tie a washer to the end of the string to prevent it from fraying. Longer strings are needed for the last four planets. Wind the strings for these planets as you measure them, to avoid their becoming tangled.

Planet	Length of String
Mercury	0.4 meters
Venus	0.7 meters
Earth	1.0 meters
Mars	1.5 meters
Jupiter	5.2 meters
Saturn	9.5 meters
Uranus	19.2 meters
Neptune	30.1 meters
Pluto	39.4 meters

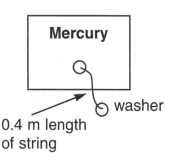

Scale: Earth's average distance of 93 million miles (149 million km) from the sun= one meter

Activity

1. Review the scale model of the planets made in the last lesson. Tell students this lesson will show them the order of the planets from the sun, as well as how far they are away from the sun and each other. Let them know that the scale for this model is very different from the one that was used with the planets. Stretch out the string for Earth and explain that it is only one meter but that our planet is actually 93 million miles (149 million km) from the sun.

2. Select a student to be the sun and stand in the front of the room. Choose four other students, each to take one of the inner planet cards (Mercury through Mars). Have the student with the Mercury string give the end of it to the "sun" and stretch the string across the front of the room. Let each of the remaining three planets follow in the order shown on the chart. Talk about how close these planets are to each other and the sun.

Scale Model of the Solar System *(cont.)*

Activity *(cont.)*

3. Ask another child to stretch out the string for Jupiter. Students will immediately see it is much farther away from the sun than the inner planets. Explain that in the space between Mars and Jupiter there are many small planets called *asteroids*. Scientists think these formed at the same time as all the other planets but never pulled together to form one planet.

4. Explain that in order to show the rest of the solar system, they will need to move outside. Have the string for the five planets wound on their cardboards.

5. Take students to a field outside which is at least 40 meters long. Select three students to be the sun and have them stand side by side, facing the end of the field.

6. Give the planet cards to nine students. Have them stretch out the four inner planets' strings, letting one "sun" hold the washers at the ends of the strings. The strings will be stretched in one line. Let the students stretch out the planets in order, waiting until one string is fully extended before beginning the next. Divide the strings among the remaining two "suns." Have students lay the strings on the ground and return to the sun's position.

7. Explain that all planets move in the same direction around the sun but not at the same speed. The closer the planet is to the sun, the faster it moves. Mercury takes only 88 days to go once around the sun. Earth takes 365 days for this trip. Pluto is the slowest, taking 248 years to get around the sun once. This means the planets do not travel around the sun in a straight line, as the strings are now laid out.

Closure

- Take a "walk" along the solar system, pointing out that the inner four planets are small, rocky, and very close together. Point out that Jupiter through Neptune are huge, mostly made of gases, and very far from the sun. Remind students that Pluto is the smallest planet and, like the inner planets, it is rocky.

- Have one student return to the sun's position and let students see how small he or she appears from the distance of Pluto. Explain that if they were on Pluto, the sun would be only a small star in the distance. Since the sun is so far away, the sky would always be dark, and the stars could be seen all the time.

- As students walk back to the sun, tell them the farther we get from the sun, the colder it gets. So planets beyond Mars are very cold. When you reach Mars, explain that its temperature is cold but that people might someday live there. They will need special space suits to keep warm and to stay at the same air pressure as that of Earth. They will also need tanks of air to breathe, just as astronauts did when they went to the moon.

- As you pass Earth, explain that it is getting very hot as they get nearer the sun. It would not be possible for people to live on Venus because of its poisonous atmosphere and great heat. When you reach Mercury, let them know that it would be so hot there that the metal lead would melt.

- Read *The Magic School Bus® Lost in the Solar System* (see Resources section).

Resources

Related Books

Allison, Linda. *Blood and Guts: A Working Guide to Your Own Insides*. Little, Brown, 1976. This book is full of great ideas to investigate the human body.

Bosak, Susan. *Science Is . . . A Sourcebook of Fascinating, Facts, Projects, and Activities*. Scholastic Canada LTC., 1992. This huge, award-winning K–8 grade teacher's guide is packed with hands-on experiments covering a wide range of science topics. Activities have been tested and use readily available materials. Available through NSTA (see Related Materials).

Bruun, Ruth Dowling and Bertel. *The Human Body: Your Body and How It Works*. Random House, 1982. Beautiful and accurate illustrations and easy-to-read text cover the topics of the regions of the body and the body systems.

Cole, Joanna. Scholastic, Inc. *The Magic School Bus® series: Inside the Earth* (1987), *Inside the Human Body* (1989), *Lost in the Solar System* (1990), *Inside a Beehive* (1996), and *Inside a Hurricane* (1995). These delightful books are both entertaining and filled with great science information that correlates with many of the activities in *Science Is Fun*.

Dickinson, Terence. *Exploring the Night Sky*. Firefly Books, 1987. This is an award-winning children's book which takes a step-by-step cosmic voyage from Earth to a distance of 300 million light years, as well as detailed investigations of the planets and information about observing constellations.

Eyewitness Visual Dictionaries. *The Visual Dictionary of the Human Body*. Dorling Kindersley Books, 1991. This book is a dictionary of all the body parts, shown in vivid photographs and illustrations.

Fabiny, Robert. *The Human Body*, 1993. Order from Carolina Science Materials (800) 334-5551. The acetate pages of this book peel back layer by layer to show muscles, skeleton, lungs, heart, and other structures.

Gallant, Roy A. *Our Universe*. National Geographic, 1994. This outstanding picture atlas includes chapters for each of the planets, illustrated with NASA photographs and excellent information, as well as deep space objects, shuttle, and future space exploration.

Imes, Rick. *The Practical Entomologist*. Simon and Schuster, 1992. This is a great resource for teachers, covering topics on insect anatomy, behavior, life cycles, and describing how to collect and house insects for observations.

Jefferies, David. *Thematic Unit: The Human Body*. Teacher Created Materials, Inc., 1993. This book covers topics such as the senses, fingerprints, bones, and nutrition.

Macaulay, David. *The Way Things Work*. Houghton Mifflin Co., 1988. This creative book is a visual guide to the world of machines. It is written in simple language and uses engaging cartoons to explain how things such as turbines, ball bearings, and levers work.

Resources *(cont.)*

Related Books *(cont.)*

Mammana, Dennis. *The Night Sky*. Running Press, 1989. This book provides interesting and easy-to-do investigations and observations of the constellations, planets, moon, and stars.

Mound, L. *Eyewitness Books: Insects*. Alfred A. Knopf, 1990. This book contains general information about the behavior, life cycle, and anatomy of insects. It also discusses the important role insects play in Earth's ecology and includes beautiful color photographs of rare and exotic species.

Morgan, Sally. *The Butterfly*. Dimensional Nature Portfolio Series, 1991. This book includes beautiful illustrations and interesting information about butterflies, enhanced by pop-up representations of a monarch.

National Science Education Standards. National Academy Press. (800) 624-6242, 1996. This project was approved by the Governing Board of the National Research Council and sets as its goal establishing science standards for all students. These standards were adopted nationwide in 1996. This book covers science standards for teaching, professional development, assessment, content and science education programs for K–12 grades.

Pathways to the Science Standards, Elementary Edition. National Science Teachers Association, 1997 (see reference below). This excellent companion to the National Science Education Standards provides teachers of K–6 with practical ideas for applying the standards in all areas of their science programs.

Resources for Teaching Elementary School Science. National Science Resource Center, National Academy Press, Washington, D.C., 1996. (800) 624-6242. This is an outstanding resource guide to hands-on, inquiry-centered elementary science curriculum materials and resources. Each reference in this guide has been carefully evaluated and is fully described, including addresses and prices.

Sneider, Cary, I. *Earth, Moon, and Stars*. Great Explorations in Math and Science (GEMS), Lawrence Hall of Science, 1986. Order from NSTA (see Related Materials section). This teacher's guide includes activities related to early concepts of astronomy, Earth's shape and gravity, moon phases and eclipses, and star maps.

Stein, Sara. *The Body Book*. Order from National Science Teachers Association, Arlington, VA (800)772-NSTA, 1992. Photos, diagrams, and lively writing detail many of the body's functions and processes.

Suzuki, David. *Looking at the Body*. Toronto, ON: Stoddard, 1987. This is a good publication that contains information and activities related to the human body.

Suzuki, David. *Looking at Senses*. Toronto, ON: Stoddard, 1986. This is a good reference that contains information and activities related to the human senses.

Walter, Marion. *The Mirror Puzzle Book*. Tarquin Publications, Norfolk, England, 1988. (available through Barnes and Noble) The book includes 144 different puzzles to try, from easy to challenging. The puzzles consist of figures to change with the mirror to try to match the master card.

Resources *(cont.)*

Related Books *(cont.)*

Woelflein, Luise. *The Ultimate Bug Book: A Unique Introduction to the World of Insects in Fabulous, Full-Color Pop-Ups.* Western, 1993. Here is a pop-up book containing extraordinary creatures that catch you by surprise. It includes some general facts and characteristics of insects.

Young, Ruth M. *Science/Literature Unit: Magic School Bus Inside a Beehive.* Teacher Created Materials Inc., 1997. The activities in this book include raising butterflies and ants, and a shadow puppet show based on the life in a beehive.

Young, Ruth M. *Science/Literature Unit: Magic School Bus® Lost in the Solar System.* Teacher Created Materials Inc., 1996. This unit is filled with activities which will help students become familiar with the planets, moon, comets, and astronomical events.

Zim, Herbert & Clarence Cottam. *Insects.* Golden Press, 1987. Here is an excellent, easy-to-use, reference about insects, including 225 species in full color and brief, informative text.

Related Materials (Call for free catalogs.)

Acorn Naturalists, 17300 East 17th St., J-236, Tustin, CA 92680. (800) 422-8886, http://www.acorn-group.com. Supplies nature books for all ages, including those about ants and butterflies.

Astronomical Society of the Pacific, 390 Ashton Avenue, San Francisco, CA 94112. (800) 335-2624. Supplies a variety of slides, poster, videos, and computer software on astronomy. Teachers are eligible for free copies of *The Universe in the Classroom*, a quarterly newsletter by ASP. Request this newsletter on school letterhead.

Carolina Biological Supply Co., 2700 York Road, Burlington, NC 27215. (800)334-5551. Supplies materials about insects including books, live specimens, and habitat equipment; also apparatus such as micropipets and dropper bottles.

Delta Education, PO Box 915, Hudson, NH 03051-0915 (800)258-1302 http://www.delta-ed.com. Supplies replacements parts for the Elementary Science Study (ESS) series, including mineral samples and streak plates.

Delta Education, Inc., PO Box 3000, Nashua, NH 03061-9913. (800) 442-5444. Web site: http://www.delta-ed.com Supplies a variety of science materials for K–8 grade levels. They offer iron filings, wide assortment of magnets, bug boxes, and stethoscopes.

ETA Science Catalog, 1997. 620 Lakeview Parkway, Vernon Hills, IL 60061-9923 (800) 445-5985 Internet: info@etauniverse.com Supplies mirrors and 96-page book *Mirrors* with 50 easy experiments with mirrors and flashlights.

Flinn Scientific, Inc., PO Box 219, Batavia, IL 60510-0219. (800) 452-1261. Supplies chemicals and biological materials. Request a free *Chemical Reference Manual* which describes individual minerals available for sale, as well as any hazards they may pose.

Resources *(cont.)*

Related Materials *(cont.)*

Genesis, Inc., PO Box 2242 Mount Vernon, WA 98273. (800) 4PELLET. Sells owl pellets individually or in bulk. Also offers the videotape *Ecology and the Barn Owl*.

Insects Lore, PO Box 1535, Shafter, CA 93263. (800) LIVE BUG, http://www.insectlore.com Supplies painted lady butterfly larva, ant farms and live ants, silkworm eggs, and books on insects, including books and videos about ants and butterflies. Call for a free catalog.

National Geographic Society, PO Box 2118, Washington, DC 20013-2118. (800) 447-0647. Supplies maps and posters such as The Heavens, The Earth's Moon, Solar System/Celestial Family, and The Universe. Back issues of *National Geographic* may be ordered. Call for catalog.

National Science Teachers Associations, 1840 Wilson Boulevard, Arlington, VA 22201. (800) 722-NSTA, www.nsta.org/scistore Supplies science books and materials for K–12 grade teachers. Also, Bare Bones Poster, a full-size skeleton model of 10-year old child to assemble, teacher background included.

Radio Shack. (800) 843-7422, http://www.radioshack.com This is a good source of strong, inexpensive magnets which are circular or rectangular with a hole in the center.

Scientifics (Edmund Scientific Co.), 101 East Glouchester Pike, Barrington, NJ 08007-1380. (800) 728-6999 or on the Internet at http://www.edsci.com Supplies colored filters and other science equipment and toys, including magnetic marbles and cow magnets.

Sky Calendar. Abrams Planetarium, Michigan State University, East Lansing, MI 48824. Supplies calendars showing a daily positions of astronomical objects for each month, as well as the constellations and planets located among them for each month.

Answer Key

Changing Letters (page 10)

Letters which are underlined can be recreated using the mirror.

<u>A</u> <u>B</u> <u>C</u> <u>D</u> <u>E</u> F G <u>H</u> <u>I</u> J <u>K</u> L <u>M</u> N <u>O</u> P <u>Q</u> R S <u>T</u> <u>U</u> <u>V</u> <u>W</u> <u>X</u> <u>Y</u> Z

A	B	C	D	E	F	G	H	I	J	K	L	M
H	H	O	O	H	H	O	I		U	I	I	I
	D		I		I	U	A		I	H	I	W
						V		V	A			V

N	O	P	Q	R	S	T	U	V	W	X	Y	Z
V		V		D	O	I	O	X	XX		I	
I		I		K				M	M		X	
		B		H				W				
		H		B								
		D		I								

Note: These are not all the possibilities. Accept any answers which students can prove.

What Color Do You See? (page 15)

- red + green = brown
- green + blue = dark green
- blue + yellow = green
- red + yellow = orange
- blue + red = lavender or purple
- yellow + green = light green

Color Chart (page 16)

See previous combinations for answers to the color chart.

- Red + Green + Yellow = amber/brown
- Green + Blue + Red = blue/brown
- Blue + Yellow + Green = green
- Red + Blue + Green + Yellow = green/brown

Note: These colors may vary, depending upon the amount of coloring added to the water.

Mixing Paints (page 18)

(A) Red + Green = brown

(B) Red + Yellow = orange

(C) Green + Blue = dark green

(D) Blue + Red = brown

(E) Blue + Yellow = dark green

(F) Yellow + Green = dark green

Answer Key *(cont.)*

Station 1: Popping Paper (page 86)

Some of the circles jump from the paper to the plastic box. Others jump back and forth, while still others remain on the paper but stand on edge. There is a popping sound made as the circles hit the plastic box. If left alone for a while, the circles lose the static charge but can be reactivated by rubbing the box again.

Station 2: Jumping Peanuts (page 87)

If the charged balloon is held about three inches (7.5 cm) above the Styrofoam peanuts, they will leap up and cling to it. When shaken gently, the peanuts continue to adhere to the balloon. They can be chased around the balloon when another charged peanut on the balloon is pushed toward them.

Station 3: Weird Water (page 88)

The stream of water will bend away from the charged balloon when it is held about one inch (2.5 cm) from it.

Station 4: Dancing Balloons (page 89)

When both hanging balloons are charged with the duster, they will repel each other. If a hand is placed between the balloons, they will be attracted to the hand but will move away (repelling) from each other when the hand is removed.

This Is My Body (page 221)

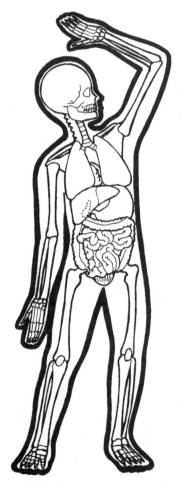